THE FRONTIERSMEN

THE FRONTIERSMEN

By the Editors of

TIME-LIFE BOOKS

with text by

Paul O'Neil

TIME-LIFE BOOKS / ALEXANDRIA, VIRGINIA

Time-Life Books Inc.
is a wholly owned subsidiary of
TIME INCORPORATED

Founder: Henry R. Luce 1898-1967

Editor-in-Chief: Henry Anatole Grunwald
Chairman of the Board: Andrew Heiskell
President: James R. Shepley
Editorial Director: Ralph Graves
Vice Chairman: Arthur Temple

TIME-LIFE BOOKS INC.

Managing Editor: Jerry Korn
Executive Editor: David Maness
Assistant Managing Editors: Dale M. Brown (planning),
George Constable, George G. Daniels (acting),
Martin Mann, John Paul Porter
Art Director: Tom Suzuki
Chief of Research: David L. Harrison
Director of Photography: Robert G. Mason
Senior Text Editor: Diana Hirsh
Assistant Art Director: Arnold C. Holeywell
Assistant Chief of Research: Carolyn L. Sackett
Assistant Director of Photography: Dolores A. Littles

Chairman: Joan D. Manley
President: John D. McSweeney
Executive Vice Presidents: Carl G. Jaeger,
John Steven Maxwell, David J. Walsh
Vice Presidents: Nicholas Benton
(public relations), John L. Canova (sales),
Nicholas J. C. Ingleton (Asia), James L. Mercer
(Europe/South Pacific), Herbert Sorkin (production),
Paul R. Stewart (promotion), Peter G. Barnes
Personnel Director: Beatrice T. Dobie
Consumer Affairs Director: Carol Flaumenhaft
Comptroller: George Artandi

THE OLD WEST

EDITORIAL STAFF FOR "THE FRONTIERSMEN"
Editor: Thomas H. Flaherty
Text Editors: Anne Horan, Gerald Simons
Designer: Edward Frank
Staff Writers: Stuart Gannes, Gregory Jaynes,
David Johnson, John Manners, Michael Roberts
Chief Researcher: Martha T. Goolrick
Researchers: Peggy Bushong, Rhea Finkelstein,
Jean Getlein, Lois Gilman, Donna M. Lucey,
Jack Weiser
Editorial Assistant: Diane Bohrer

EDITORIAL PRODUCTION
Production Editor: Douglas B. Graham
Operations Manager: Gennaro C. Esposito,
Gordon E. Buck (assistant)
Assistant Production Editor: Feliciano Madrid
Quality Control: Robert L. Young (director),
James J. Cox (assistant), Michael G. Wight (associate)
Art Coordinator: Anne B. Landry
Copy Staff: Susan B. Galloway (chief),
Patricia Graber, Barbara F. Quarmby, Celia Beattie
Picture Department: Alex George

THE AUTHOR: Paul O'Neil began his career in the Far West as a Seattle newspaperman. In 1944 he migrated eastward to New York, where for three decades he distinguished himself as a staff writer for *Time, Sports Illustrated* and *Life*. A full-time freelancer since 1973, O'Neil has also contributed the volumes on *The Rivermen* and *The End and the Myth* to the Old West series.

THE COVER: His broken rifle lying useless on the ledge beside him, a desperate frontiersman has only a knife to save himself from a black bear in this oil painting entitled "A Fight for Life," by the 19th Century artist Otto Sommer. The early Americans who infiltrated the passes of the Appalachian Mountains to explore and then to settle the wilderness west to the Mississippi risked violent death not only from wild beasts but from Indians, foreign armies—and sometimes each other. Thomas Hughes, the solitary homesteader armed with long rifle, tomahawk and scalping knife in the frontispiece, was ambushed and killed by Indians in western Virginia in 1778.

CORRESPONDENTS: Elisabeth Kraemer (Bonn); Margot Hapgood, Dorothy Bacon, Lesley Coleman (London); Susan Jonas, Lucy T. Voulgaris (New York); Maria Vincenza Aloisi, Josephine du Brusle (Paris); Ann Natanson (Rome). Valuable assistance was also provided by: Joyce Leviton (Atlanta); Sue Wymelenberg, Richard Kaffenberger (Boston); Giovanna Breu (Chicago); Andrea Naversen (Cleveland); Julie Greenwalt (Detroit); Robert Kroon (Geneva); Fred Travis (Nashville); Patricia Chandler (New Orleans); Carolyn T. Chubet, Miriam Hsia (New York); Mimi Murphy (Rome).

TIME
LIFE
BOOKS
®

For information about any Time-Life book, please write:
Reader Information
Time-Life Books
541 North Fairbanks Court
Chicago, Illinois 60611

CONTENTS

1 | A trade-off in terror

"The rough, hardy air of the stranger bespoke him to be of distant regions, to have been reared among dangers, and to be familiar with fatigues." The stranger was from the Kentucky frontier, and the Philadelphian regarding him with wonder in 1800 added, "I thought I could see in that man one of the progenitors of an unconquerable race."

The rifle, the ax and arrogant self-confidence were the weapons that tamed America's first frontier. The men who plunged into the forests of Kentucky, Tennessee and Ohio did so not only in defiance of the Indians who roamed the vast hunting grounds but also over the objections of the nervous politicians who hoped to keep peace by discouraging settlement there.

The backwoodsmen were a law unto themselves. A man had no use for Eastern society or any of its restrictions when he could hack out a clearing, stack up a log shelter and settle in, cocksure that his rifle would supply him with food and clothes.

When game got scarce or the neighbors too close, lone families moved even deeper into the wilderness. Miles from the nearest settlements, these families were targets for Indian raiders, who slipped out of the forest as silently as shadows, cracked the stillness with their chilling war whoops and attacked with savage purpose. For the frontiersman who found his cabin in flames and his family mutilated, horror quickly hardened into a desire for vengeance. Backwoods morality teamed God and right against the "redman." Every Indian was fair game in the all-out warfare that ravaged the early frontier.

James Smith, a road builder ambushed in the Pennsylvania wilderness in 1755, struggles with his captors while a third Indian scalps his partner. Smith was taken prisoner but escaped five years later.

Drunken Indians in 1720 prepare to burn John Harris — whose trading site became Harrisburg, Pennsylvania — because he had refused to

sell them more rum. Harris' slave Hercules fetched friendly Indians who rushed in to save him as the pyre was about to be ignited.

A parish of Christian Indians are hacked to death at Gnadenhutten, Pennsylvania, in 1782. A missionary wrote of one frontiersman who

felled 14 Indians with a cooper's mallet, then told a comrade, "My arm fails me. Go on in the same way. I think I have done pretty well."

Two weeks after butchering six peaceful Conestoga Indians in 1763, a mob from Paxtang, Pennsylvania returns to slaughter 14 others sheltered in the Lancaster County jail. Ben Franklin wrote, "Guilt will lie on the whole Land, till Justice is done," but no one was punished for the crime.

The fever to strike westward to a hard new life

The mountain men, cowpunchers and gold seekers of the Far West did not spring into being, full blown, at Fort Benton, Deadwood and Cheyenne; their restlessness, hardihood and impatience with authority were legacies from still earlier frontiersmen—backwoods riflemen who pushed into the mountains of Pennsylvania, Virginia, the Carolinas, Tennessee and Kentucky before the Revolution and helped settle the country beyond the Appalachians after the war was won. Very few of these woodsmen imagined the American future they were making possible, but a later breed of celebrated mountaineers and plainsmen—of cattlemen, to pick a dramatic example, like a giant named Charles Goodnight—acted as their heirs in that enormous, dusty, mountain-rimmed and myth-bordered realm beyond the Mississippi River.

Goodnight fought Comanches as a Texas Ranger, became a friend of the famed half-breed chief Quanah Parker (after helping feed his starving tribesmen when the buffalo disappeared), and more unusual yet, recognized opportunity when he saw it. He presided, in his middle years, over one of the mightiest of the early cattle kingdoms—1,335,000 acres of Texas prairie that nurtured more than 100,000 longhorns. He had a shrewd eye as well for life, man and the mustang horse—an animal, he noted, that had "simmered itself down to one color—bay with black mane and tail. Nature," he added, "always does that; takes the strongest there is and makes the uniform."

He was talking, in a sense, about himself, for he was the end product of four generations of men and women who had advanced the frontier and thus represented the beginnings as well as the culmination of that most American of impulses—the fever to possess the continent. His great-grandfather Michael—a German who, like many other Germans, fled Europe for the New World—came to Pennsylvania in 1752 and took his family south and west through Virginia and Kentucky. He paid a dreadful, if common, price for his temerity—death and scalping at the hands of Indians. Goodnight's grandfather Peter was a captain in the Kentucky militia. His father, Charles, a restless frontiersman, moved the family west to southern Illinois on the bank of the Mississippi. When his father died and his mother remarried, the stepfather pushed on across the river and continued westward until the family finally wound up settling in Texas, 100 miles south of a trading post called Dallas.

The family followed a classic route into the far plains; but Western expansion, it is now often forgotten, began with the Scotch-Irish, the English and the Germans of Goodnight's great-grandfather's generation—hunter-settlers of the Appalachian woodlands who were so altered by their new environment and who became so singularly American as to seem like a new race of man to the world of their day.

Two forces shaped them and the attitudes they handed on to pilgrims of the Platte and the Rio Grande: the trackless wilderness they invaded and the woodland Indians who gave them cruel instruction in survival and war.

The Scotch-Irish farmers of Draper's Meadows, Virginia, whose cabins clustered amid cornfields in a hollow of the Appalachians, had become accustomed to the sight of passing tribal bands during seven peaceful years in their remote settlement. Their clearings lay in the great north-south trench west of the Blue Ridge

A frontier family rests by the road to Pittsburgh. One traveler complained that ruts "were worn so deep that an army of pigmies might march into the bosom of the country under the cover they would afford."

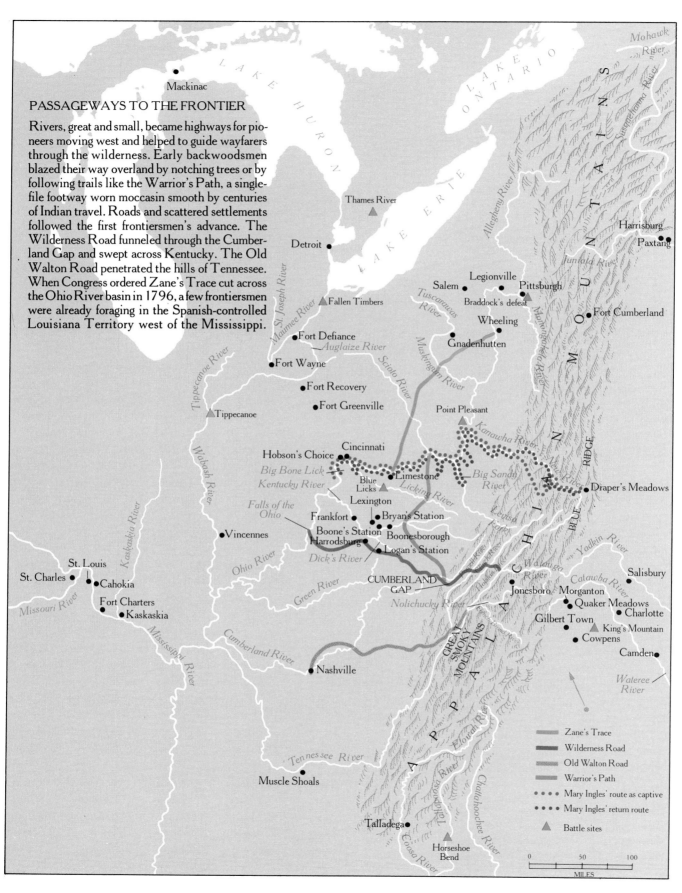

PASSAGEWAYS TO THE FRONTIER

Rivers, great and small, became highways for pioneers moving west and helped to guide wayfarers through the wilderness. Early backwoodsmen blazed their way overland by notching trees or by following trails like the Warrior's Path, a single-file footway worn moccasin smooth by centuries of Indian travel. Roads and scattered settlements followed the first frontiersmen's advance. The Wilderness Road funneled through the Cumberland Gap and swept across Kentucky. The Old Walton Road penetrated the hills of Tennessee. When Congress ordered Zane's Trace cut across the Ohio River basin in 1796, a few frontiersmen were already foraging in the Spanish-controlled Louisiana Territory west of the Mississippi.

Mackinac

LAKE HURON

LAKE ONTARIO

Mohawk River

LAKE ERIE

Thames River

Detroit

Harrisburg

Paxtang

Susquehanna River

Salem
Legionville
Pittsburgh
Braddock's defeat

Fort Cumberland

Allegheny River

Tuscarawas River

Wheeling

Gnadenhutten

Muskingum River

Monongahela River

Juniata River

APPALACHIAN MOUNTAINS

St. Joseph River

Fallen Timbers

Maumee River

Fort Defiance
Auglaize River

Fort Wayne

Scioto River

Tippecanoe River

Fort Recovery

Fort Greenville

Point Pleasant

Kanawha River

New River

BLUE RIDGE

Hobson's Choice
Cincinnati

Big Bone Lick

Big Sandy River

Draper's Meadows

Tippecanoe

Wabash River

Kentucky River

Blue Licks

Limestone

Licking River

Lexington

Falls of the Ohio

Frankfort

Bryan's Station

Boone's Station
Harrodsburg

Boonesborough

Logan's Station

Levisa Fork

Vincennes

Dick's River

CUMBERLAND GAP

Watauga River

Jonesboro
Morganton

Salisbury

Catawba River

Vadkin River

Quaker Meadows
Charlotte

St. Louis
St. Charles
Cahokia

Green River

Ohio River

Nolichucky River

Gilbert Town

Cowpens

King's Mountain

Fort Charters
Kaskaskia

Missouri River

GREAT SMOKY MOUNTAINS

Camden

Cumberland River

Mississippi River

Nashville

Holston River

Wateree River

APPALACHIAN

Tennessee River

Elk River

Coosa River

Muscle Shoals

Chattahoochee River

Talladega

Coosa River

Horseshoe Bend

Zane's Trace
Wilderness Road
Old Walton Road
Warrior's Path
Mary Ingles' route as captive
Mary Ingles' return route
Battle sites

0   50   100
MILES

Mountains—a natural highway from Pennsylvania to Georgia for Indians as well as settlers moving ever deeper into virgin forestland. The New River, which bordered their isolated enclave, flowed north and west into what today is West Virginia. It perforated the wall of the Appalachians through deep gorges in doing so and opened a route from Ohio for Shawnees and other tribes of Algonquins bent on raids against Catawbas of the South.

But on the morning of July 8, 1755, the Shawnees did not pass by. This time they came through the mountains as newly committed allies of France to ravage the English frontier. Draper's Meadows had not the slightest inkling of danger. William Ingles and John Draper, its husky young founders, were in distant corners of their fields as the painted, half-naked braves materialized among the log dwellings. Colonel James Patton, a militia officer who was sitting inside one of the cabins, managed the settlement's only moments of resistance. Patton was 63 years old, but he was six feet four inches tall and habitually carried a broadsword. This weapon was lying on a table before him as two Indians burst into the room. He seized it and hacked them to death before he was killed by a third marauder who fired a shot through the open door.

Others of the war party raced among the remaining cabins and jerked open their doors. They trapped and shot two more men, killed Draper's mother and stopped his wife, Bettie, in her tracks with a bullet, which broke one of her arms after she picked up her baby and tried to escape. An Indian seized the infant by his ankles and smashed his head against a log house. The whooping intruders rifled the cabins and set them on fire, and then having rounded up the settlers' horses, hoisted the wounded woman onto the back of one of them. William Ingles' wife, Mary, was nine months pregnant, but she was hoisted up on a horse, too, with her four-year-old son, Thomas, and his two-year-old brother, George. All were carried away as the Shawnees left the blazing cabins behind.

This savage and tragic little incident initiated a far more important chapter in American history than any of the participants could have suspected. Early frontier families like the Ingleses and Drapers were flanked, north and south, by foreign enemies as they pushed into the West—by the French and later the British in

Canada, and by the Spanish and French in Florida and Louisiana. All three used Indians as auxiliaries in their schemes of empire, and backwoods settlements were subject to raids so constantly for 50 years after the incident at Draper's Meadows that the threat of forest war became as much a part of border life as hunting and planting corn.

The Indians tortured frontiersmen and slit the bellies of their pregnant wives; the frontiersmen ambushed, murdered and scalped the Indians and their women in return. Simultaneously, since they were largely ignored by those in power, pioneers on the Western frontier developed a stubborn resentment of Eastern politics, Eastern taxes and the elitist attitudes of those who ruled in towns and plantations on the coastal shelf. They became a breed unto themselves: stern, violent and clannish, but brave, upright and wildly independent. Danger made them stoic, suspicious and rudely realistic, and attuned them to concepts of righteous revenge straight from the Old Testament. These qualities played an integral part in shaping the United States, in pushing the frontier across the Eastern mountains, from where it never ceased moving, and in altering politics forever by sending Andrew Jackson to Washington later on.

Other aspects of the American West evolved, too, as these rough woodsmen fought their way into Kentucky, Tennessee, Ohio and Illinois and pressed on toward the Mississippi River. The wilderness was not only a hunting ground for Indian fighters and deerslayers but for a race of speculators that was to perpetuate itself on the moving frontier for 200 years. It sometimes seemed as if virtually every man of power in the American colonies was involved in grandiose land ventures in the Mohawk and Kanawha valleys, in Kentucky, in Virginia, in Ohio — schemes that were continuously complicated by unclear claims of title, overlapping boundaries, failed or faulty treaties with the Indians, and the insistence of backwoods squatters that the land belonged to the man who built a cabin on it. The outlaw, the renegade, the eye-gouger and the braggart evolved just as rapidly, for the frontier attracted debtors, felons and ne'er-do-wells. And they in turn spawned Western vigilantism. Gangs of "regulators" banded together in the Carolina hills, rode down rapists, cattle thieves and others suspected of wrongdoing,

Artistic legacy of a pioneer naturalist

More than a century before John James Audubon won fame as early America's greatest wildlife artist, a tall, taciturn English botanist had quietly captured the living marvels of the frontier. He was Mark Catesby, who arrived in the Carolinas on May 3, 1722, having been commissioned by the Royal Society to describe not only wilderness plants, but also the mammals of the bush and the birds of the wind.

Catesby worked westward from Charles Town, painstakingly building his record with notes, sketches and water colors. Beginning with the bald eagle, he identified 113 birds, giving enduring names to the "Blew Jay," the "Redheaded Woodpecker" and the "Blew Bird." Forty-six fishes and dozens of insects, reptiles and mammals were scrutinized. He drew — and ate — alligator, unhappily noting that he could "never relish it with pleasure." Encountering an Alleghenian spotted skunk, Catesby suffered a staggering dose of "fetid effluviums."

Understandably, he made errors, as in the hearsay-based note on the Carolina parakeet: "Their guts are certain and speedy poison to cats." But overall, his three-year study was remarkably careful, embracing everything from the lowly cockroach to the majestic buffalo, a beast that settlement would exterminate east of the Mississippi by 1819.

In 1726, Catesby returned home to spend the next 19 years writing and illustrating a natural history that would stand until Audubon's time as the best single treatment of North America's flora and fauna. As for Catesby, who had impoverished himself on the project, the reward was scientific respect, no remuneration. He died in 1749, at 66, leaving little more than the 220 magnificent plates whose completion had consumed a major part of his life.

THE AMERICAN BISON

THE PIGEON OF PASSAGE

THE COACHWHIP SNAKE

THE ROUND-CRESTED DUCK

THE WOODCOCK OF AMERICA

and whipped or hanged them without recourse to the niceties of formal law.

Backwoods life was a hard, often agonizing experience for even the strongest of men and women. The settlers of Draper's Meadows learned this earlier than most. Yet the travail they endured at the hands of the Shawnees was only typical of a thousand episodes of death and abduction that were to break up families and instill an implacable hatred of Indians in early pioneers. William Ingles and John Draper were forced to choose between suicide and a wretched prudence when they heard the distant sounds of whooping and gunfire at the Meadows settlement. Each concealed himself helplessly until his wife and children were taken away. This kind of bitter realism was condoned in the backwoods country, but each harbored a profound need for revenge, and both became well-known wilderness militiamen in the years that followed.

The Indian raiders of Draper's Meadows did not hurry as they started their stolen horses on the long journey back to the Ohio country. They came upon two outlying cabins within half an hour and stopped at both. They killed and decapitated an old man named Philip Barger at the first, and—having put his head in a sack—handed it, grinning mightily, to a woman they hauled forth on reaching the second dwelling. But glee now altered their demeanor; the woman was left unharmed to savor their humor, and the captives were herded along without rancor as the war party turned northwest through the New River gorges into the wilderness of western Virginia.

Mary Ingles gave birth to her baby during the third night of the party's retreat, but rode on with her captors the next day with the infant clutched to her. John Draper's wife, Bettie, suffered the pain of her shattered arm with equal stoicism. But they preserved themselves only to be parceled out as prizes of war when they were led into the principal town of the Shawnees at the juncture of the Ohio and Scioto rivers. Bettie Draper was forced to run the gantlet and then began a life of slavery and concubinage. The little boys were carried off by different bands—George to Detroit, Thomas to a village in Ohio.

Mary Ingles was luckier. She found that the Shawnees had come into possession of a bolt of brightly checked cloth, set herself to converting it to shirts, and

achieved instant fame when each recipient ran through the village waving his treasure on the end of a stick. Her reputation for industry got her included, with an old Dutch woman who had been captured in Pennsylvania, in a salt-making party bound for Kentucky's Big Bone Lick. She was able not only to escape after arrival at these saline springs but also to lead the other woman back through the Appalachians—a feat of resolution and stamina and a conquest of untracked wilderness unique in the annals of the West.

Big Bone Lick was located so far from human habitation—90 miles from the Shawnee town and 260 miles on a direct line from Draper's Meadows—that the two women were left unguarded when they were not at work boiling brine into salt amid the skeletal remains of prehistoric animals that gave the place its name. Mary Ingles was 23 years old and an athletic woman, proud of being able to mount a horse in one bound. But she did not have any of the necessities for travel except a stolen tomahawk and a blanket. And having already lost two sons, she knew she must leave her baby behind to be casually killed if she was ever to rejoin her husband, which she perceived as her overriding duty. She wept beside the infant's bark cradle for a few minutes when the Dutch woman finally agreed to join her, but wasted not another moment in setting a headlong pace for the bank of the Ohio River.

Her plan was simplicity itself: she proposed to walk east along the Ohio to the mouth of the Kanawha River and to ascend this stream until it became the familiar New River, which would lead her, with luck, to her home. No pursuers came after the two women; the Shawnees assumed, after firing a few signal shots, that their captives had wandered off to pick grapes and had gotten themselves killed by animals. The Ohio obliged the women by appearing through the trees on their second day of flight. But stream after stream poured into it along their route. Since they could not swim the deep, swift waters, they were forced to travel upstream for miles to find shallows they could wade, and then walk back down the opposite banks before heading once more for the distant Kanawha. They had no nourishment but nuts, roots, berries and wild grapes, they had no means of making fire, and they had no shelter but what they could find in hollow trees or in heaps of dried leaves. Their moccasins disintegrated.

They wrapped their feet in strips torn from their clothing and hurried on.

Fortune smiled thrice on them. They found an abandoned cabin and beside it a corn patch, where they gorged themselves on the hard kernels of the dried ears and slept, for once, under a roof. They were awakened at dawn by the sound of metal on metal and were alarmed because they were now just across the Ohio from the Shawnee town. But they discovered, on peeping out, that fate had presented them with an old, belled horse. And they evaded an Indian hunting party after they set out (the bell stuffed with leaves) with one riding and one leading their newfound companion. But they were soon afoot again. They tried to lead the horse across a stream on a log jam and had to leave the beast to die when it fell astraddle some timber with all four legs thrust inextricably into the water.

Both women were weak with hunger when they came, at last, to the Kanawha, and both chewed on pieces of a rotting deer's head they found lying in the shallows. Their plight was exacerbated by cold and rain—it was now mid-November—and their labors were increased as the river's gorges closed in upon them. They clambered endlessly over huge, slippery boulders and forced themselves into the river to pass the bases of high cliffs. The Dutch woman made a frenzied proposal one evening: one should kill and eat the other. She pulled her benefactor to the ground and grappled feebly for her throat. Mary Ingles wrenched herself away and ran upstream to hide. She went on alone the next morning, buoyed by a breakfast of two raw turnips she had found in the ground outside an abandoned camp and by landmarks she felt were no more than 30 miles from the ruins of her old home.

But one last barrier lay before her: Anvil Rock, described by John Hale, a great-grandson who later documented her ordeal, as a "gigantic cliff, hundreds of feet high, the base in the water, the crown overhanging." He wrote: "She had crawled around or over the huge cliffs just below the mouth of Stony Creek. She had by some means gotten beyond that grand wall of cliff jutting into the river for two miles to Doe Creek.

"Night was approaching: snow had fallen, and it was bitterly cold. At last her progress seemed utterly barred. She had nothing to eat. In despair, she threw herself down on the bare ground and rocks and there lay, more dead than alive, until next morning. With the dawning of the day she thought of the only possible remaining way of passing this gigantic barrier: this was to climb around and over the top of it, but in attempting to rise she found her limbs were so stiff and swollen from the wet, cold and exposure that she could scarcely stand. Slowly she wound her devious, tedious and painful way, almost tempted to let go and tumble down to sudden relief and everlasting rest. Climbing and resting, resting and climbing, she at last reached the summit and the day was far spent. As long as she lived she referred to this as the most terrible day of her eventful life."

But safety, food and rest were close at hand—and more than 700 miles of walking almost done. A settler named Adam Harmon heard her "hallooing" in his corn patch and with his two sons, carried her to his warm cabin. She was reunited with her husband a few days later. The Dutch woman—whose name has escaped history—came upon a hunter's camp and was rescued as well.

Mary Ingles never again heard of her baby or the younger of the captured boys. The older, Thomas, was traded back from the Indians at 16—a wild, furtive creature who regarded his parents as strangers. John Draper did not see his wife, Bettie, for six more years and found, on buying her freedom, that she was no longer the woman with whom he had slept and eaten before the Shawnees carried her away. Such were the realities that shaped a hard, new people in a wilderness unimagined by Europeans.

The whole American subcontinent west to the Mississippi—except settled areas on the Atlantic Coast—was one vast forest at the beginning of the 18th Century, its enormity further dramatized by occasional areas of marsh or prairie. It was punctuated by large, tangled stretches of laurel and rhododendron along the high ridges of the Appalachians and was interrupted by clearings burned out by Indians to drive game toward waiting hunters. Huge spruce, hemlocks and firs covered the heights of northern New England and the highest peaks down to Tennessee. Oaks and chestnuts flourished from New Jersey and Pennsylvania to northern Virginia, while pines and oaks dominated the Southern forests. In places the forest rose out of under-

Kentucky-bound pioneers make their way
along the Wilderness Road blazed by Daniel Boone through the Cumberland Gap
in 1775. The mountain pass was named
by Thomas Walker *(above),* a Virginia
gentleman-farmer turned land speculator,
who explored the Appalachians in 1750.

brush that made a man invisible at 20 feet. Few song-birds lived in its darkest depths; the silence, Alexis de Tocqueville noted, was like that at sea.

Indians were not the forest's only dangerous inhabitants. Buffalo, deer and squirrels existed in it in great numbers, but so did bear, wildcats, panthers, venomous snakes and wolves so bold that they ignored gunfire. The forest could swallow the unwary. Its broadest paths or traces (the word trail had not yet evolved) had been trampled out by buffalo, but these were often capricious as to direction, and the routes of Indian travel were dim to the untrained eye. The hunter and explorer moved through the woodland by guess and by God, fording and refording rivers, and blazing trees as points of reference to be used in extricating themselves from its depths. The forest presented backwoodsmen with endless difficulty and exasperation when they pressed beyond its established clearings with their wives, children, cattle and swine, and surrounded them with constant menace once they had settled on virgin land. Indians could slide from it and vanish into it like ghosts, but the frontiersman's cabin was easily distinguishable and immovable in its midst.

This vast wilderness lay virtually unplumbed during the first century of English colonization on the Atlantic Coast. Such an obvious trans-Appalachian gateway as the Cumberland Gap—an ancient Indian passage through which settlers would later flow into Kentucky — was scarcely known to whites until Dr. Thomas Walker, a Virginia speculator, explored and named it in 1750. This was only five years before Mary Ingles saw the all-but-impassable gorges of the New River to the east.

The invasion of the West was triggered in the Old World—by the poverty of Germans in the Rhinish Palatinate and by bad harvests and rebellion at high rents (as well as at the suppression of Presbyterianism) among Lowland Scots and Englishmen who had been settled for a hundred years in Northern Ireland's Ulster plantation. Both colonial land speculators and the British Crown were delighted to assist these Protestants in their hopes for better lives across the sea—and to use them to fill empty spaces in America being eyed by Catholic France and Spain. The British Army, in fact, housed the overflow of some 14,000 German emigrants in tents in London public squares during the winter of 1709 to 1710 to assure their passage to the New World in the spring.

Immigrants crossed the Atlantic by the thousands every year in the decades before the Revolution. More than 400,000 of them had arrived in America by 1770. This tide spread into Pennsylvania and moved into the forest when better land was gone. It then turned north into New England and south down the Appalachian trench until it reached the foothills and wooded valleys of the Carolinas, and finally moved west and north again into the wilderness beyond the Eastern mountains.

The Scotch-Irish led this woodland invasion. Most German immigrants had an instinct for permanence. They squared up timbers to build solid houses and stayed where they found good land. But the Ulster Scots were a more restless lot. They simply notched the ends of logs to make their cabins and were often content to kill trees by girdling them, but leave them standing, and to farm the sunlit spaces between them until the soil was exhausted or they felt the itch to move on. All manner of men were attracted to the deep frontier—Englishmen, Huguenots, Scandinavians and Highland Scots drifted into the forest as time wore on, and so did the more footloose Germans and their sons. But the Scotch-Irish were chief among the peoples from whom the leathery backwoodsmen evolved, and they formed the cutting edge of Western expansion for most of the century.

Germans and Swiss, however, became the frontier's first armorers. It is hard to say exactly when the Pennsylvania rifle (later called the Kentucky rifle) appeared on the frontier. But by 1720 there were Swiss gunsmiths in Lancaster, Pennsylvania, who understood the art of cutting spiral grooves into the bore of a gun—a craft that had been practiced in Central Europe for 200 years while the rest of the continent used smoothbores. These artisans seem to have begun modifying the firearms of Old World mountain hunters and marksmen almost immediately to fit the needs of rovers of the American forests. What evolved was a long-barreled (roughly 43 inches) flintlock rifle with a narrow "wrist" in its hardwood stock and with reduced calibers to conserve powder and lead.

The heavy weapon was often fired after being braced against a tree, since the eccentricities of the

flintlock—which ignited powder inside the gun by
first igniting powder in an external flashpan—forced a
marksman to hold steady on his target for several frac-
tions of a second after he had pulled the trigger. It was,
nevertheless, the most advanced firearm in the world
and was wonderfully accurate.

This deadly and ingenious arm became a paramount
tool—with the ax—of frontier existence and helped
shape both the character and the aims of the first
Westerner. It provided much of his food and clothing.
It gave a hunter enormous mobility; a man with a few
pounds of salt, some cornmeal, a long rifle, a scalping
knife and an awl for stitching moccasins could sustain
himself for months in the wilderness. The rifle was his
primary insurance against tribal raiding and—as he
gradually learned the bitter lessons of Indian warfare—
a weapon that made him vastly superior to regular
troops in woodland skirmishes.

European soldiers of the 18th Century were trained
to attack in massed charges with the bayonet. They
fired in volleys when they were allowed to fire at all,
since the odds were long against hitting anything with
a single shot from their inaccurate weapons. But a
backwoodsman was deadly at 200 yards and had a
nasty habit of picking off officers at that range. The
world's armies were forced to emulate him in the end.
But not too soon. Regular troops of America's Continental Army were issued a variety of muskets during
the Revolution, while the French stuck with their
Charleville musket and the British with their Brown
Bess through the Napoleonic Wars — leaving the backwoods sharpshooter to be regarded as a marvel until
the day of muzzle-loaders was done.

More marvelous yet was the rapidity with which
scores of thousands of Old World immigrants and their
children adapted themselves to the sort of life in which
the need for such a weapon was commonplace and the
finality with which they abandoned the habits, even
the memories, of the lives they had left behind. They
emerged — almost like *Lepidoptera* breaking out of
nymphal casings — as the first settlers who looked west
into America rather than east to Europe for the meaning and goals of existence. Most of them, of course,
didn't have much choice. They had to hack a living
out of the forest or die. This was equally true of
settlers in western Pennsylvania, in the mountain

country of western Virginia, in the valleys of the
Clinch, the Nolichucky, the Holston and other tributaries of the Tennessee River, and in the wilds of
Kentucky. The attitudes forced upon them by this
constant struggle with nature were remarkably similar
everywhere on the moving frontier, as were their means
of coping with the awful difficulties involved.

Very few people in modern days have been so dependent on their own labor and ingenuity. The dirt- or
puncheon-floored log cabin was built entirely without
nails, usually in one or two days with the help of
neighbors and relatives. Furniture — a rough table, a
plank bed or so, some three-legged stools and a few
wall pegs for clothing — was knocked together on the
spot. Utensils were also hastily made. Some of the
more affluent might boast a couple of pewter dishes
and metal spoons, but the frontier family ordinarily ate
and drank from horn spoons, wooden bowls, trenchers

and noggins, and halves of gourds or hard-shelled squashes. Sifting was accomplished with a piece of parchment-thin deerskin stretched over a wooden hoop and perforated with a hot wire. The yard adjacent to the cabin invariably boasted a hollowed hickory block in which corn was pounded with a crude pestle and a sunken wooden tanning vat in which deer hides were worked into usable leather.

Still, no family was completely detached from the outer world. Hunting knives, hoes, iron skillets or cooking pots, awls, metal needles, salt, firearms, powder, lead and bullet molds were beyond their powers of manufacture. These items were mostly obtained with the backwoodsman's rifle: money was practically nonexistent and such treasures were largely acquired by barter in deer hides. From this practice evolved the term "a buck," since a buckskin brought a dollar's worth of goods for many years.

All frontier dwellers adapted themselves to diets peculiar to the wilderness. The Scots had refused to countenance pork during their century in Ulster, but pigs were easy to raise and their flesh particularly well suited to salting and smoking, so bacon and ham were prized on the frontier. Deer, buffalo, bear, woodchuck and squirrel were common sources of meat as well; corn was the common grain, and milk the common drink of those possessing cattle (coffee and tea were considered "slops"). But backwoodsmen ate turkey breasts for bread when short of corn and poured bear's oil on their mush if no milk was at hand.

Their homemade clothes reflected this same adaptability to the exigencies of forest life. The hunting shirt — a loose wraparound frock that reached halfway down the thighs — clothed the upper body. It was made of coarse linen loomed from flax grown in the forest clearings or if a little wool was obtainable, too, made of warmer linsey-woolsey. Only in cases of dire necessity was it fashioned from buckskin, which got wet and clammy in the rain and seemed to magnify winter cold. The woodsman used his shirt as a kind of carryall as well as a garment. He could stuff a chunk of cornbread or a bundle of tow for gun cleaning inside it next to his skin, and the belt — which tied always in back — not only served to lash it to his body but to suspend his scalping knife, tomahawk, bullet pouch and powder horn. Most men protected their legs with a

pair of breeches and leather leggings below the knees — though young buckoes often aped the Indians and costumed themselves in a breechcloth and high leather stockings, which left their upper thighs and most of their buttocks naked.

Moccasins were the footwear of all. They rose into flaps that were tied above the ankle with leather straps, or "whangs," to keep out pebbles or snow. They were comfortable in cold weather, since they were customarily stuffed with an insulation of deer hair or dried leaves, but like buckskin hunting shirts they soaked up water and were "just a decent way of going barefooted" in rain. Though women wore moccasins as well as men, they usually went barefooted in summer and while doing household chores. The woman who possessed more clothes than a linen sunbonnet, a simple linsey-woolsey dress, a petticoat, a handkerchief and a bedgown — which was also worn as a kind of party dress on social occasions — was the envy of her sisters on the frontier.

These uneducated, mostly illiterate backwoods people had no knowledge of their era's medical arts, which was probably a blessing in most instances. They responded to injuries and illnesses with a whole curious pharmacopoeia of old wives' remedies. Poultices of slippery elm bark or flaxseed were applied to bullet wounds; scrapings from a pewter spoon were given with sugar to those patients harboring worms; garlic or roasted onions were administered to children with "bold hives" or croup. Snake bites were sometimes incised with a sharp knife and the resultant wound packed with gunpowder, which was mercifully not ignited. The occasional black cat found on the frontier was usually earless and stub-tailed, these appendages having been clipped away, bit by bit, to provide blood for treating the skin inflammation of erysipelas, or St. Anthony's fire. The prognosis in all cases was the same: the strong (and the lucky) often survived, the weak (and the very young) often died.

But all was not danger, toil and hardship, though danger, toil and hardship were the common denominators of existence. Rifle matches provided a common sport, and storytelling was an almost universal source of entertainment on winter nights. The favorite tale was "Jack and the Giant." There were many variations of this romantic story; one of the favorites in-

The trusty weapon that made every man a marksman

A blade joined to an antler provides a serviceable knife. This was used to trim the greased patches in which rifle bullets were wrapped and then rammed down the bore.

"If you're for a buck, or a little bear's meat, Judge, you'll have to take the long rifle, or you'll waste more powder than you'll fill stomachs." So spoke James Fenimore Cooper's fictional character Natty Bumppo in 1823, thus introducing to literature, by one of its many names, the distinctive weapon that replenished the frontiersman's larder while protecting him from marauders.

"The Long Rifle," "The Pennsylvania Rifle," "The Kentucky Rifle," "The Stump Rifle," "The Hog Rifle," all meant one and the same design: a muzzle-loading wonder with a barrel forged of soft iron, a stock hewn from maple and a flintlock firing mechanism shaped on an anvil. In expert hands, it could plug a coin at 50 yards and kill a man at 200. Even at 400 yards, General George Washington once noted, a rifleman could hit an 8-by-10-inch sheet of paper three

shots out of five. By comparison, a man with a musket could send a ball only 150 yards — and could not be sure of scoring after the first 50.

The secret of the rifle's stunning accuracy, and the musket's lack of it, was inside the barrel. The musket's bore was smooth; the ball was simply expelled, free to spin or wobble. But the bore of a rifle had spiral grooves that gave the ball a precise spin. Once discharged, it drilled through the air along the barrel's sight line.

The rifle's great range was due to another innovation. The musket employed a tightly fitted ball that was pounded down the barrel with an iron rod. But it could not be made snug enough to prevent much of the gunpowder's explosive force from escaping around it. A rifle ball was a few hundredths of an inch smaller than the bore, but was securely "seated" by means of a greased cloth or leather

patch. The combination took no longer to load than a musket ball, yet it assured the rifleman that when he fired he got the most out of his charge.

"The Kentucky Rifle," wrote one contemporary, "is a specialty in which rivalry by any other nation is out of the question." The guns were so treasured that they were still in wide use in 1850, decades after the percussion principle had made the flintlock obsolete. And no wonder, for gunsmiths crafted each with exquisite care, and personally tested it. As a Virginia artisan named John Whitesides told his helper, Milton Warren, "Well, Milt, she's finished, but she ain't wuth a damn if she won't shoot straight. Let's try her." And if, as sometimes happened, the barrel was flawed, said Warren, "We just threw it away, made some remarks to the mountains, took a drink of spring water and welded another barrel."

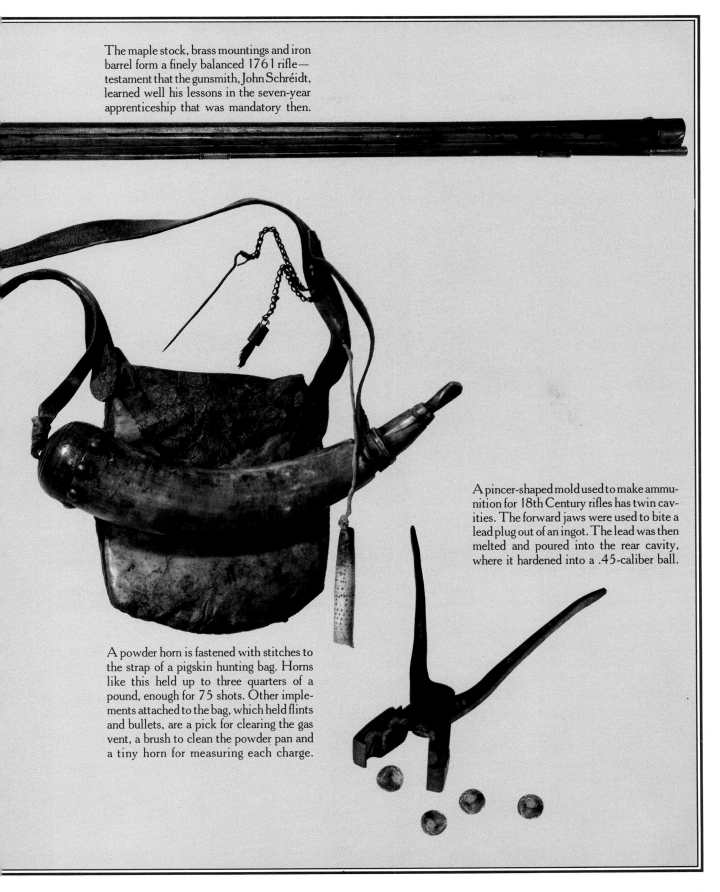

The maple stock, brass mountings and iron barrel form a finely balanced 1761 rifle—testament that the gunsmith, John Schréidt, learned well his lessons in the seven-year apprenticeship that was mandatory then.

A pincer-shaped mold used to make ammunition for 18th Century rifles has twin cavities. The forward jaws were used to bite a lead plug out of an ingot. The lead was then melted and poured into the rear cavity, where it hardened into a .45-caliber ball.

A powder horn is fastened with stitches to the strap of a pigskin hunting bag. Horns like this held up to three quarters of a pound, enough for 75 shots. Other implements attached to the bag, which held flints and bullets, are a pick for clearing the gas vent, a brush to clean the powder pan and a tiny horn for measuring each charge.

A pioneer housewife pauses in her cabin chores in this 1796 sketch with its stylized hemlock trees. With only an ax for a tool, a settler could singlehandedly raise a 12-by-15-foot house in two backbreaking weeks.

volved a virgin captured by the giant, who was rescued by Jack and restored to her own true love.

House raisings and weddings prompted a jollity that could test the stamina of the most enduring. Nothing short of war roused backwoods communities to the sort of concerted activity that attended weddings. The groom and his family and friends initiated the ceremonial by mounting horses in the morning and setting off for the cabin of the bride and her clan. The journey might be made eventful by pranksters who would tie wild grapevines across the travelers' path and hide in the brush to salute them with rifle fire. Leaders of the procession, meanwhile, initiated excitement on their own. Two young men, appointed to "run for the bottle," raced through the woods for a flask of corn whis-

key that awaited the winner at the bride's dwelling, then dashed madly back, whooping like fiends, to hand it to the groom, who drank a dram and passed it on to be shared by all who followed.

The procession and the wedding ceremony itself were merely a prelude to the food, drink, laughter, crude jokes, fiddle music and dancing that were the heart of social effort in the backwoods. Women of the bride's family felt duty bound to provide a feast of venison, bear meat and pork by the heaping wooden platter. The bride's father was expected to supply whiskey by the gallon, which was drunk, at least early in the afternoon, with a certain ritual formality. "Where is Black Betty?" the thirsty would cry. "I want to kiss her sweet lips." And on being handed the bottle: "Health to the groom, not forgetting myself."

Some time before midnight the bride's young ladies "stole her off" and got her up a ladder to a loft. The groom's friends then took him up to join her and saw to it—with vast hilarity—that he was installed at her side. The newlyweds were seldom allowed to be alone for very long. Friends felt impelled to take Black Betty up the ladder, too, or hoist up food and make certain it was eaten, and were likely to keep pestering the happy couple until dawn.

The uproar below, meanwhile, went on. Those who curled up in a corner to rest were hauled to their feet and pushed onto the floor while the fiddler broke into a song titled "Hang On Till To-morrow Morning!" And the night outside the cabin sometimes rang with the sound of struggle or of noisy woodland chases, since people excluded from such festivities were often moved to cut the manes and tails off the horses of the invited guests and seldom failed, if detected, to attract a stream of indignant drunks from the frolic inside. The revelry rarely ceased until the next afternoon and occasionally lasted (at weddings remembered as distinctly as battles) for three full days and nights.

Most backwoodsmen held harsh and simple views in basic matters of morality and behavior but were elastic in interpreting the nicer aspects of both. The Presbyterian ministers of the Scotch-Irish were horny-handed fellows who farmed and hunted on weekdays, and used the vernacular of their neighbors when they rose to preach on Sundays. But few settlements could boast a man of the gospel. South Carolina's colonial Governor James Glen was startled when visiting the Piedmont in 1753 to discover a man of 50 who had never seen a church, a minister, a ship or a "great Gun." And he was even more startled at the man's neighbors, who did not "bestow the least education" on their numerous children: "they take so much Care in raising a litter of Piggs, their children are equally naked and full as Nasty." The governor soon retreated to the comforts of tidewater.

A stubborn Anglican clergyman named Charles Woodmason left more revealing, though equally jaundiced, impressions of behavior in the back country. Woodmason was a remarkably dedicated if astonishingly stubborn man. He left London for Charleston, South Carolina, in 1752, succeeded in its trade and society, and was pursuing a career as a magistrate when he was suddenly struck—after 13 comfortable years—with the idea of carrying the light of Episcopalianism to the benighted wretches of the backwoods. He returned to England forthwith, was duly ordained, and wasted not a moment in recrossing the Atlantic, purchasing a horse and riding off to the valleys of the Wateree and Catawba rivers and beyond as an itinerant preacher. He pursued this thankless undertaking for six years, keeping an indignant and eloquent diary of his efforts to convert the Scotch-Irish, the Quakers and the Huguenots, and members of "an hundred other sects" who shared an intense, burning suspicion of the Church of England.

Although Woodmason earned little gratitude for his labors, he had no difficulty attracting crowds. His sermons were considered prime entertainment, and he preached, at times, before audiences numbering in the hundreds. But they were audiences, as he put it, that listened "with Itching Ears only, not with any Disposition of Heart or Sentiment of Mind—and seem so pleased with their native Ignorance, as to be offended by any Attempts to rouse them out of it." Woodmason did his best. "Bring no dogs with you," he beseeched. "Do not whisper, talk, gaze about, show light Airs, and do not practice that unseemly rude, indecent Custom of Chewing and of Spitting which is very ridiculous and absurd in public, especially in Women and in God's House." He did not succeed: "The Bands of Society hang Loose and Ungirt about Us here with ev'ry one left to Do as seemeth Him Meet. At Flatt Creek they went to Revelling, Drinking, Singing, Dancing and Whoring after the service and most of the Company were drunk before I quitted the spot. They were as rude in their Manners as the Common Savages and hardly a degree removed from them."

He was more disturbed at Granny Quarter Creek in January 1768 by the "lowest Pack of Wretches my Eyes ever saw. As wild as the very Deer. How would the Polite People of London stare to see the Females (many very pretty) come to Service in Shifts and a short Petticoat only, barefooted and barelegged." Later he lamented that "the Young Women have a most uncommon Practise which I cannot break them off. They draw their shift as tight as possible to the Body and pin it close, to shew the roundness of their Breasts, and slender Waists (for they are generally finely shaped) and draw their Petticoat close to their Hips to shew the fineness of their Limbs—so that they might as well be in Puri Naturalibus. Indeed, Nakedness is not censurable or indecent here, and they expose themselves often Quite Naked—Rubbing themselves and their Hair with Bears Oil and tying it up behind in a Bunch like the Indians."

Woodmason failed to understand, for all his sharpness of observation, that the people of the frontier had adopted manners and standards of their own, while rejecting as outlandish and unrealistic the standards and manners of towns and plantations to the east. Stealing was a great crime among them, and there were few settlements where it was not agreed that "a thief must be whipped." A man found in possession of another's goods was hauled before a self-appointed jury and given "forty stripes but one"—unless he evaded punishment by "painting his face," running off to become a renegade with the Indians. Minor theft was punished by tongue lashing; Virginia militiamen who caught a comrade stealing bread from their campfire shouted, "Who stole a cake out of the ashes?" on confronting him thereafter. The settler who refused to do his share of communal toil risked being nicknamed Lawrence—an epithet voiced with the same wry contempt as were names like Percy or Mortimer in later eras of Western expansion. And the man charged with lying was honor bound to fight and in many cases to risk being gouged and bitten by his accuser.

Backwoodsmen used the same rude concepts of propriety in their equally rude self-government. The most notable example occurred in the early 1770s when a pair of frontier heroes—James Robertson and John Sevier helped organize several hundred families along the tributaries of the Tennessee River into the Watauga Association. The Wataugans were among the first Americans to hold themselves independent of British colonial rule. But it was not so much a matter of rebellion as of expediency. The settlers were so far from the Coast and the seat of colonial government that they decided to draw up their own written articles of agreement, based on the familiar statutes of Virginia. The arms-bearing men elected a council with judicial as well as legislative powers. They ruled a wilderness

drained by the Watauga, the Nolichucky, the Holston and the Doe rivers until North Carolina incorporated the area as a county in 1777.

The frontier constituency was as memorable for its pair of prime organizers—both then in their 20s—as for its demonstration of the settlers' aptitude for self-rule. Robertson and Sevier were very different men. Robertson was a somber, taciturn, wiry hunter with striking pale-blue eyes below shaggy dark hair. In 1771 he guided his family and a procession of friends through the ranges north of the Great Smokies to virgin land along the Watauga and was a rock of courage and good sense to them thereafter. Sevier was his flashing opposite and, in fact, an anomaly among all on the frontier: a handsome, well-informed, pleasure-loving descendant of Huguenots who corresponded with men like Franklin and Madison and wore hunting shirts as though they were velvet. If Robertson lent his neighbors judgment and shrewdness, Sevier lent them flamboyance: he had a daring and impetuosity that won over the crudest backwoodsmen and made him an Indian fighter they would follow without question. Both men left deep impressions on the expanding frontier: Robertson as a promoter of settlement in Tennessee, Sevier as an organizer of risky speculations and quests for power after the Revolution and, eventually, as first governor of the state of Tennessee.

This pair and three other members of the ruling council managed to run their little dominion as a nation of free men. Robertson helped negotiate a treaty of peace with the Cherokees that lasted until 1776, when the tribes went on the warpath. During its years of tenure, the Wataugan council kept order generally, enlisting a militia and settling disputes over property and land rights. It issued marriage licenses, recorded deeds and wills, and settled questions of debt. It did not depart from the rude and peremptory attitudes of the rest of the frontier, however, in dealing with threats to domestic tranquility. Old records note that one horse thief was seized on Monday, tried on Wednesday and hanged on Friday of the same week.

But if the Wataugan settlers reflected a great many impulses and aspirations of the new West, their formal association, with its written rules and legislative body, embraced a kind of political structuring that was unusual in the average backwoods community. There

The great black bear: fearsome lord of the forest

Of all the beasts in the teeming frontier forests, the most formidable by far was the great black bear. Panthers, wolves and poisonous reptiles were accorded proper respect by the Indians and settlers. But a full-grown black bear, standing six feet tall and weighing up to 500 pounds, was a fearsome creature to contend with.

The Indians staged elaborate hunts in which a line of warriors, sometimes as many as 500, beat through the forest to drive bears to open ground where other hunters would launch a storm of spears and arrows. White hunters had an advantage with their long rifles and steel traps, and killed large numbers of bears for meat and fur. Davy Crockett built a legend in Tennessee by tallying 47 bears in the course of a single month.

But it was a risky business. Wounded animals were known to run hunters down and mangle them hideously. And woe, as well, to the unfortunate soul who found himself in close proximity to a she-bear guarding her cubs.

Indeed, it was just such an ursine encounter in Kentucky that provided one of the great legends of the early frontier. During the summer of 1787, a youth named Francis Downey was out with a friend searching for a stray horse when they were suddenly set upon by three Indians. Downey's companion killed one of the warriors with his rifle. But then the Kentuckians had to run for their lives, each pursued by an Indian.

Downey's friend made good his escape by turning on his assailant and wounding him with his knife. Young Downey, however, seemed to be doomed. The pursuing Indian, tomahawk in hand, was rapidly gaining when he darted around a tree and stumbled into some underbrush.

Then, according to a chronicler of the day, "It so happened—was it Providence?—that a large she-bear had made her bed underneath the roots, where the ferocious beast was then suckling her cubs.

"As the astonished savage arose to his feet, the furious bear sprang upon him, and with a terrible hug, grasped him in her powerful arms, the Indian giving an unearthly yell from the great pain." While the Indian desperately battled with the enraged bear, Downey raced pell-mell for home and safety.

Returning to the spot the next day, the settlers found the she-bear lying dead. But there was no sign of the Indian, and they never knew whether he had somehow survived or had been borne away dead, by other Indians.

Saved by a she-bear's attack on his Indian pursuer, Francis Downey escapes in this 19th Century depiction of the 1787 incident.

James Robertson, first leader of the Watauga valley settlements in Tennessee in 1771, made friends with local Cherokees, who stayed neutral when neighboring Shawnees went on the warpath in 1774.

John Sevier, who assumed leadership of the Watauga settlements in 1779, put his faith in guns, not palaver. In 1780, he led crop-destroying raids that managed to drive the Cherokees from the Clinch River valley.

was but one cohesive social force in most frontier settlements, the threat of Indian attack; but one communal building, the blockhouse; and but one seat of civic cooperation, the local militia company. No man felt that he was bound by authority, and each was convinced of his right, as Preacher Woodmason expressed it, "to Do as seemeth Him Meet." Yet no man could ignore the needs of his fellow citizens if he expected to "keep his hair." The existence of forest villages hinged on the way the inhabitants reacted to this conflict in philosophical values.

Every community of prudent frontier people built a blockhouse as soon as possible after moving to new land. These log structures were practically impregnable to raiders, since Indian bands—even when armed by the French or British—never encumbered themselves with artillery during forays in the forest. Loopholes cut in blockhouse timbers allowed defenders to meet attackers with concerted fire. A second story—which projected beyond the walls of the first—provided over-

hanging gun stations, from which the beleaguered could shoot down on any attacker who tried to shelter himself close to the walls below the lower rifle ports. Larger settlements used such blockhouses as citadels at the corners of forts, which boasted central clearings walled by heavy timber stockades and were locked with massive wooden gates.

Reaching the shelter of such forts from outlying cabins, however, was often a nerve-racking procedure indeed. "I well remember," wrote Joseph Doddridge in reminiscences of his frontier childhood, "how the family were sometimes waked up in the dead of night, by an express with a report that the Indians were at hand. The express came softly to the door, or back window, and by a gentle tapping waked the family. The whole family were instantly in motion. My father seized his gun and other implements of war. My stepmother waked up and dressed the children as well as she could, and being myself the oldest of the children, I had to take my share of the burdens to be carried to the fort. There was no possibility of getting a horse in the night to aid us in removing to the fort. We caught up what articles of clothing and provision we could get hold of in the dark, for we durst not light a candle or even the stir fire. All this was deon with the utmost dispatch and the silence of death. The greatest care was taken not to awaken the youngest child. To the rest it was enough to say 'Indian' and not a whimper was heard afterwards."

Once jammed together within their fort's confines, the defenders and their families were subject to conditions that would try the tempers of the most forbearing. Such sanctuaries were very seldom built near water, for the ground along streams was sometimes muddy and usually subject to flooding. In an astonishing number of cases, moreover, their creators failed—out of simple fecklessness or the demands of their own little farms—to provide the forts with wells. Life in any blockhouse under siege was apt to be an exercise in misery, but misery was magnified when thirst had to be endured as well as the bang of rifles, the choking smoke of gunpowder, the cries of children, the stench of unwashed bodies, and the debilitation of sleeplessness and strain. Backwoods people often fell prey to boredom once they were inside the forts. Indians soon learned that the more restless whites would go back to their cabins if they were left to their own devices for a day or so. Raiders tried the morale and tempers of settlers more severely by lurking out of sight to murder these optimists than by all-out attack. Men safe in the fort were forced to sally forth as messengers to the unwary at every new alarm and the whole process of withdrawal was reinstituted.

Every backwoods settlement had its local militia. They were informal organizations indeed. Officers were elected or "hit upon," since backwoodsmen would follow men they knew and trusted, but they would not accept discipline for the sake of discipline nor, often, orders with which they disagreed. Musters, when attempted, were usually excuses for jollity and drinking. The unkempt and slouching levies of the frontier were sometimes known as cornstalk soldiers for their habit of mocking drill—when such exercises were assayed—by shouldering tasseled stems of maize instead of their rifles and posturing outrageously with them. They seldom served in the field for long; they fought a skirmish and then hurried back to their clearings like Highland Scots of an earlier age. But every able-bodied male was a militiaman for all that and was bound to fight Indians on pain of being "hated out" of the community when danger made his duty clear.

Sufficiently stirred and properly led, the roughly clad frontiersmen were fearsome fighters, with their stoic disregard of hardship, their tradition of violence, their long rifles and their skills in the forest. They took greater losses than the Indians because they fought for land and their families; the Indians, by contrast, fought for glory and personal reputation, as well as to preserve their tribal hunting grounds, and thought it madness to die when outnumbered. Yet by the time of the Revolution, the backwoodsmen had become the Indians' approximate equal in forest combat. They had learned to use the Indian's tree-to-tree tactics against him, had learned to avoid panic when engaged in little ambushes and single combats that constituted much of forest war—and they had learned to scalp the foe as savagely as the foe scalped them.

On October 10, 1774, a thousand militiamen from Virginia fought all day against a like number of warriors under the famous Shawnee chieftain Cornstalk during the Battle of Point Pleasant and achieved a bloody standoff under conditions in which Regulars probably would have faced certain massacre. In the summer of 1776 frontier scouts silently trailed masses of Cherokees, when that tribe rose in force, and gave the warning when the marauders closed in on settlements along the Watauga, the Clinch and the Holston rivers. Militiamen under James Robertson repulsed one big band at the Watauga fort; another group of 170 went out openly hunting Indians and at a forest area known as Long Island Flats, cut to pieces a large war party that was ill-advised enough to charge en masse. As the years wore on, bold little groups of militiamen under John Sevier descended on Cherokee towns, destroying crops and burning lodges, and forced the Indians into an uneasy truce that endured through most of the Revolutionary War years.

On one momentous occasion, moreover, backwoods riflemen took the measure of British-led American Tories—and reinforced their own opinions of uniforms, drill, stiff-necked officers and all the other processes and accouterments of military authoritarianism they held in such contempt. The Revolution triggered bitter civil war in the Southern colonies. Loyalist American Tories fought, raided, hanged, and burned the barns and houses of rebel American Whigs, who raided, hanged and burned with vengeance in return. The Tories were dominant, however, by 1780, in part because of the energy and organizational talent of Major Patrick Ferguson, a daring Scottish Regular who trained and led American Loyalists in the Carolinas. Ferguson finally erred when he threatened to cross the mountains to pillage and burn along the headwaters of the Tennessee.

Isaac Shelby, who became the first governor of Kentucky after the Revolution, was at this time a leader of backwoods militia for the Watauga settlements and was first to hear of these threats from Whig refugees who had come west for sanctuary. He hastened to John Sevier's log house on the Nolichucky, and the two of them took instant action — even to the point of seizing money from a local land office against their personal guarantees — to organize a force of mounted riflemen capable of crossing the ridges to the east and of striking Ferguson before he could come west to their own valleys and clearings. They quickly recruited Colonel Charles McDowell, who had retreated into their hills with 160 North Carolina Whigs; Colonel William Campbell, a redheaded giant of a man who commanded some 400 militiamen along mountain headwaters in Virginia; and a succession of lesser local leaders capable of rallying backwoodsmen to their cause.

More than a thousand men — each with a long rifle, a tomahawk, a scalping knife and a sprig of evergreen thrust into his hat or coonskin cap — rode east with them from an appointed gathering place, the Sycamore Shoals of the Watauga, on September 26. They moved along the Doe River, went up a pass and into early snow between the Roan and Yellow mountains, passed the mouth of Grassy Creek, crossed the Blue Ridge at Gillespie's Gap after three days, and then descended into the wooded coves and softening skylines of the Catawba watershed. Here, at Quaker Meadows, they were joined by 350 North Carolina Whigs under Colonel Benjamin Cleveland, a fierce Indian fighter. This raised their numbers to 1,400 men. But Tory spies now tracked them, their quarry's

position remained vague, and regional differences threatened to split them into quarreling mobs.

Backwoods leaders were notoriously jealous and touchy men. Shelby, however, managed a magnanimous gesture: he proposed that William Campbell, who led the largest contingent of riflemen, be granted overall command. Cleveland, McDowell and Sevier as magnanimously agreed. Whig spies now began reporting Ferguson's movements; he became aware of "a swarm of backwoodsmen" and turned east from Gilbert Town toward Charlotte and the protection of Regulars under Lord Charles Cornwallis. The small mountain army — both horses and men — was so tired, having marched incessantly on little but grass and green corn, as to be incapable of hot pursuit in full force. They pushed on to Cowpens, where they were joined by 400 more men from the Carolinas. And there — on the night of October 6 — all spirits rose.

The frontiersmen found, slaughtered, roasted and feasted on a Tory farmer's cattle, and their officers heard that Ferguson was camped to the east with his wagons and stores on a narrow, stony, flat-topped ridge of King's Mountain. Leaving the weakest behind, the backwoodsmen and their Carolinian and Virginian auxiliaries — more than 900 men including several score without horses who swore to keep the pace — set out in rainy darkness after eating their meal. They did not halt until the next day, when their outriders captured a pair of Tories who told them exactly how the ridge lay between two streams and the dispositions of the enemy along its 600 yards of flattened spine. The captives also betrayed Ferguson by revealing that he wore a light varicolored hunting shirt that would make him distinguishable to all.

The frontiersmen reached the western flank of the heights about noon. They tied their horses to trees and set out on foot, each band under its local leaders, to form a line around the base of the ridge. When this was done, they demonstrated their deadly mastery of the long rifle under conditions in which their individuality could be most effective.

Ferguson had about 900 men in his camp — 200 others were out foraging — as Campbell and his fellow officers sent the backwoods riflemen climbing toward them. Some in the Loyalist bivouac were simple cutthroats and barn burners who had joined up in hope of loot. But Ferguson had 100 American volunteers, Loyalist Regulars recruited in the colonies who had been thoroughly trained in the use of the bayonet, plus hundreds of Tory militiamen who made do with knives fastened to their guns. Being on the heights he felt he was in a position of great advantage—as indeed he would have been against regular troops. He ordered drums beaten, mounted his horse and prepared to use this advantage as the first pickets sounded the alarm. He believed in cold steel, and he and his officers led bayonet charges, swords flashing, as the backwoodsmen scrambled upward, making the woods ring with their war whoops.

The little brigades of men in hunting shirts were repulsed and repulsed again by these massed charges. They were discomfited by the musket volleying from above—until they discovered that the Tories were overshooting, as they aimed downhill, almost to a man. Ferguson seemed to be everywhere, riding recklessly over the rough, slaty ground, swinging a sword in his left hand (his right arm having been crippled three years before) and blowing a piercing silver whistle to direct his troops. The frontiersmen had been instructed to scatter, then rally and strike back. "Give them Indian play," was the order, and the men were exhorted to "each be his own officer." They gave way only to take cover on the steep slopes behind rocks and trees and to snipe with deadly effect at their attackers, who labored back to the positions that they had vacated at the summit. And with Sevier, Shelby, Cleveland and Campbell riding among them to urge them back into battle, they scrambled higher at every chance.

Ferguson lost two horses while plunging downhill into the very midst of the backwoodsmen and broke his sword while hacking at some he had ridden down. But even his most violent exertions could not hold back ill-fortune. His Tories began dropping from exhaustion as well as from rifle balls. And when he charged Campbell's men on one side of the ridge, he found Shelby's howling cohorts racing up the other.

"The mountain," said a witness later, "was covered with smoke and flame and seemed to thunder." Sevier's men, nearing the summit, shot Ferguson off his horse and killed him. Resistance continued. Carolina Whigs and Carolina Tories, close enough to recognize each other, shouted curses and taunts amid the firing.

Sevier's men surged over one side of the summit as Campbell and Shelby, circling around, led more men over the other. The Tories—one third now dead or wounded—began running toward their tents and baggage wagons, raising handkerchiefs on guns and ramrods. Shelby rode among them, calling on them to lay down their arms. Campbell—his horse dead—ran among his angry backwoodsmen shouting until they reluctantly stopped killing the beaten enemy. The battle was over, having lasted but an hour.

There were ugly episodes of aftermath. The backwoodsmen believed in an eye for an eye. Having smitten with "the sword of the Lord and of Gideon," in the words of a frontier preacher who harangued them when they started east, they lost any semblance of the loose military coherence by which they had been unified in battle. They shot a number of prisoners, hanged some captured officers and scattered to loot the farms of Tory landowners. Then they vanished over the ridges as swiftly as they had emerged, having been distracted only temporarily from those hills to the west that gave purpose to their lives.

King's Mountain was a great victory because it shook the British hold on the South. But it was also—and perhaps more important—a revelation of things to come: it reflected the dynamism of those new Westerners being dammed up against the Appalachian massif, bespoke the fervent refusal of restraint that would soon send them flowing in even greater numbers over the mountain barrier and made plain, above all, their fitness to enter the vast, empty spaces that lay beyond.

The whole half century of forest settlement and forest war was an indication, in many ways, of what lay ahead. The frontier along the Appalachian trench had been an enormous and isolated training ground where the settlers had been shaped to follow the Cumberland Gap into Kentucky, Braddock's and Forbes's roads to the upper Ohio, and obscure valley passes into Tennessee. Many battles and hardships awaited them. The savage Shawnee, Miami and Illinois tribes were still thralls of the British, and the Indians of the Southern nations were still allies of the Spanish, who awaited American intrusion with hostility and fear in Louisiana and on the Gulf Coast. But the backwoods people had been forged in a fearsome furnace and believed in their souls that the continent was theirs.

American sharpshooters, fighting Indian-style from behind trees and rocks, pour deadly fire into the loyalist ranks in a climactic Revolutionary War battle at King's Mountain, South Carolina. In one hour on October 7, 1780, the frontiersmen killed or wounded 300 of the enemy.

2 | The "noble and generous" Boone

With Daniel Boone at their head, six families left North Carolina for Kentucky in September 1773. Boone, 39, had twice before roamed the wilderness on hunting expeditions, and now he intended to settle there with his kin. His wife, Rebecca, rode at his side. Their son James, 16, trailed a distance behind, traveling with some youngsters.

For two weeks the journey went well. Then, near Cumberland Gap, James and his friends were ambushed by Shawnees. The Boone boy was horribly tortured and was screaming for death when death at last came. The father heard the terrible word from a survivor and rode back to bury his son.

It was a prophetic beginning to Boone's role in the vanguard of settlement. Time and again he faced awesome tests of courage. But he endured to emerge as the overshadowing hero— "a noble and generous soul," a friend said, "despising everything mean."

After a 38-day ride, Daniel Boone and companions survey verdant Kentucky on Boone's first trek west from North Carolina in 1769.

39

As a Shawnee drags them ashore, Jemima Boone strains at the oars and her friends scream for help. Jemima's father tracked the girls for three days, killed two of the kidnappers and freed the children, providing one more Boone adventure to be painted a century later by the artist Victor Nehlig.

41

Rifle fire splits the air as Boone tries to protect his son Israel from a Wyandot at the Battle of Blue Licks in 1782. Five minutes after the ambush began, 60 Kentuckians, including Boone's son, lay dead.

With a youngster in tow, Boone is shown
leading civilization west. "Sometimes I
feel like a leaf on a stream," Boone wrote
later in life. "It may whirl about and turn
and twist, but it is always carried forward."

The legendary life of the ultimate woodsman

Europeans of the 19th Century Romantic movement equated Daniel Boone with the "noble savage," and Lord Byron, who included him in *Don Juan* and helped make him one of the most celebrated Americans of his day, called him "happiest amongst mortals." There was a measure of truth in both these views, although distant admirers contrived them in fabricating philosophical theses that would have sounded odd on the American frontier. Few backwoodsmen, certainly, could "think Indian" as could Boone. And he *was* a happy man. Life brought him more than a man's share of tribulation — two sons killed by Indians in wilderness ambushes, dreams of vast estates shattered by lawyers, debts, a burden under which he labored during many of his declining years. But he had only to vanish into the forest with Old Tick-Licker, his favorite hunting rifle, to be restored to an environment with which he was marvelously and instantly in harmony.

Boone was a man of affairs and the possessor of an active and judicious mind. He had a shrewd eye for opportunity — and a wildly original way with correspondence in pursuit of it. "Sir," he once wrote the royal governor of Virginia, "as Sum purson Must Carry out the armantstion [ammunition] to Red Stone I Would undertake it on Condistions I have the apintment to vitel [victual] the Company at Kanhowway... your Excelency most obedent omble Sarvent, Dal Boone." He was a politician of sorts. He was a surveyor. He was an officer of militia. He was a speculator in land, a blacksmith, a tavern keeper and a collector of ginseng root for shipment to China, where it was

highly valued as a remedy for almost everything from mental fatigue to old age.

But these undertakings were always secondary to his life in the forest. No matter what else he was, Boone was forever the staunch yeoman of the wilds who proudly carved, "D. Boon cilled a bar on this tree." There was something of genius about his woodsmanship — his sensitivity to variations of light, shade, sound and flow of air, and to the wild men and wild animals who moved so softly in the wilderness. The most notable of his achievements all turned, in one way or another, upon this facet of his nature.

Boone was one of the earliest of the "long hunters" who crossed the Appalachians in the 1760s to roam for months — and, in his case on one expedition, for two years — through the game-rich wilds of Kentucky. He was a captain of the permanent settlers who began laboring westward over the mountains with families, cattle and goods, to occupy the Bluegrass country in 1775. It was Boone, thanks to financing by a flamboyant North Carolina promoter, Judge Richard Henderson, who hacked the first rude road over the Cumberland Gap to found Boonesborough, that enduring bastion of the American frontier.

He was not, of course, the only leader of this first exodus from Eastern watersheds; James Harrod, a hot-tempered Pennsylvanian, and Benjamin Logan, later a Virginia legislator, founded little settlements of their own a few miles west of Boone's enclave on the Kentucky River. Neither was he the only defender of Western outposts during the Revolution: Harrod, Logan and Virginia's frontier soldier, George Rogers Clark, all played dramatic roles in border warfare with the Algonquin Indians and the Appalachian confederacies. But Boone had a style and method all his own. He not only frustrated the most determined of these tribal attacks, at Boonesborough in 1778 — very prob-

---

Only the white mane suggests his age as Daniel Boone peers with piercing blue eyes from a portrait based on one painted in 1818, two years before Boone died at 86.

45

ably saving Kentucky for the white man — but did so on his own, through an exercise of cunning and derring-do that made him unique among frontier scouts and made him the earliest of Western heroes.

Boone was drawn to the wilderness even as a Quaker boy in the quiet corner of Pennsylvania where he spent his childhood. Boone's parents were peaceable and industrious people from Devon. His father, Squire Boone, set up as a weaver and blacksmith after settling near Reading, was admitted to the local Meeting, dressed in gray and encouraged his 11 children in learning — most of the Boone clan being well educated for their day and station and Daniel considered remarkable as its only bad speller. Daniel was "different"; his father wisely did not try to change him. The Boones kept cattle on a distant tract and the boy, after he was 10, was sent to watch them, to live in the woods and learn things not in books.

Daniel studied animals. Pennsylvania Indians were peaceful; he studied them, too, and learned to hunt with a spear. He was given a rifle at 13. After that he learned to work metal in his father's blacksmith shop — rifles were often in need of repairs. And shortly, Daniel found wider forests to roam.

The Friends of Exeter Meeting were looking askance at the romantic affiliations of the older Boone children. Daniel's sister Sarah not only "married out" — took a "worldling" as her husband — but did so, as two female Quaker investigators discovered, after first getting pregnant by the man. Squire Boone placated the critics by assuming the responsibility. According to the minutes of the meeting, "He confesseth himself in a Fault and hopeth to be more Careful." But then Daniel's brother Israel married out too. Squire Boone was "disowned" by the Friends of Exeter Meeting until such time as he would come to "a Godly Sorrow in himself." He refused, stiffened his neck against criticism, sold land, animals, house and tools and, in May 1750, took his family south to the Yadkin River on North Carolina's western frontier.

This was wild country. A hunter like Daniel — he was then 15 — could shoot a dozen deer before noon, and a youth with his innate instinct for profit could carry hides east by pack horse for sale in the little market town of Salisbury. He entered at once upon his life's most enduring vocation. He encountered a hostile Indian for the first time two years later, when a Catawba named Saucy Jack, enraged at Boone's superior marksmanship, threatened to tomahawk him.

Boone saw many more hostiles when he signed on with the big British expedition by which Major General Edward Braddock hoped to take France's Fort Duquesne at the forks of the Ohio River. Boone, serving as a wagoner, did the sensible thing when Braddock's bewildered redcoats were ambushed by 800 French and Indians at Turtle Creek: he cut his team loose of its wagon, rode to safety and waited to give help to the British survivors on their retreat to Fort Cumberland on the Potomac.

Less than a year after his return in the summer of 1755, Boone married a tall, dark-haired girl named Rebecca Bryan, whose brother was already married to one of the Boone sisters, Mary. He took Rebecca to Virginia for safety from Indian raiders and began hauling tobacco to market for a living. But not for long. The young couple were back on the Yadkin in 1759. Old records show that Daniel Boone, planter, bought 640 acres there from his father for £50 — and Rebecca's husband was off west into the mountains almost as soon as he had built her a cabin and put in a crop of corn. This was to be the pattern of their lives. Boone farmed a bit in the spring and summer and then disappeared — to hunt in the autumn and to trap beaver in the winter through the "vast solitudes," as Theodore Roosevelt described the early Appalachian wilderness more than a century later, "whose utter loneliness can with difficulty be understood by those who have not themselves dwelt and hunted in primeval mountain forests."

Rebecca emerges from history only in little flashes of remembered folklore and as a figment of the 19th Century biographers who labored to make Boone a creature of their own philosophical concepts: "Rebecca Bryan, whose brow had now been fanned by the breezes of seventeen summers, was 'very fair to look upon' with complexion rather dark, her whole demeanor expressive of her childlike artlessness. . . ." The Virginian epic-poet Daniel Bryan made her rather more dramatic: " 'My Boone!' She cried, / And press'd him to her groaning breast; 'My Boone! / How can you leave your Home, your Wife and Babes! /

Simon Kenton was a consummate woodsman, second only to Daniel Boone, and had he been less heroic on April 24, 1777, he could have inherited first place. On that day, Boone was shot in the ankle as he and the 21-year-old Kenton battled a band of Shawnees outside Boonesborough. After killing two warriors as they tried to slay Boone, Kenton hefted his 170-pound mentor and dashed to the safety of the fort. *Harper's Monthly* illustrated his bravery in 1864 *(right),* more than 40 years after Kenton sat for the portrait above. Kenton's reward for the deed was Boone's accolade: "Indeed you are a fine fellow!"

How shall I rest in peace when dangers watch / To take away my dear Companion's life?' . . . "

Rebecca, in fact, was a tough and practical young woman who developed an awesome capacity for getting along by herself through her long life. She shot seven deer from a tree one day while Boone was away from their home on the Yadkin River. She hoed their garden, chopped wood, bore 10 children and helped run a tavern he opened on the Ohio River later in life. She had a will of her own. She jibed at Boone when he was courting her for slopping blood on his hunting shirt while cleaning deer and refused, utterly, to take up land in Florida after they were married. But she followed him to rawer frontiers without complaint and went into the Missouri woods to cook for him and help him boil maple sugar when both were old.

Young Boone was only one of many adventurers who went through the mountain gaps into Tennessee and the jumbled uplands of eastern Kentucky. Nathaniel Gist, son of George Washington's old guide, Christopher, was one such rover of the wilds; so was a large, strong Dutchman named Mike Stoner, and so, a little later, was Simon Kenton, a Virginian who was Boone's own match as a reader of Indian "sign."

Boone's explorations were more than simple adventure. He hunted incessantly in order to support Rebecca and a growing family; and he often got £100 or more when emerging with his peltry at Salisbury. He became as well known to men of influence there as to woodsmen with whom he shared campfires—and particularly to Judge Henderson, who seems to have financed him in some of his expeditions even before they joined forces to found Boonesborough.

The longest, most ambitious and most telling of these excursions was inspired, in 1769, by one John Finley who, like Boone, had been a teamster with Braddock. Finley came to the Boone's Yadkin cabin with a peddler's pack on his back. He had chanced floating down the Ohio with trade goods two years before, had delighted the Indians he met with ribbons and trinkets, had traveled with them, and knew where a speculator in land might get rich as Croesus. In the course of his journey with the Indians, they had taken him to the fertile uplands of Kentucky's Bluegrass country. He wanted to return, but he had no wish to risk his hair among the Indians on the Ohio again. It

struck him that a man like Boone would know ways through the mountains. He talked of game to Boone; game in endless, trampling herds, deer crowding the springs. Boone agreed to take him west. Boone, too, had the fever for new land. And the costs of maintaining a farm and feeding a growing family had plunged him into debt. Game meant money.

No hunter bent on profit simply wandered into the woods with a rifle. Boone assembled riding horses and pack animals, kettles, traps, salt, lead, gunpowder, spare guns, blankets, a bit of rum, and rations for the early going, before he left the Yadkin with Finley on

the first of May. Nor did they go alone. John Stuart, Boone's youngest sister Hannah's husband, came to hunt as well, and three "camp-keepers"—Joseph Holden, James Mooney and William Cooley—rode along to cook, prepare hides and kill game too, if need be. Daniel's 24-year-old brother, Squire Boone the younger, agreed to follow them west in early winter with fresh horses and supplies. They did not hurry. Boone liked to look at the country, to carve his initials or instructive legends on trees ("Come on boys here's good water"), to camp in comfort when he could and at times—with an audience assembled in the fire-

light—to read aloud from a copy of *Gulliver's Travels* he kept in his belongings.

By June, having crossed the Cumberland Gap, they established a base on a tributary of the Kentucky River they called Station Camp Creek. Boone hurried west alone, climbed a high hill and looked out, at last, on the rich, level, game-filled land they had come to find; buffalo by the hundreds sent clouds of limestone billowing up from the traces.

Finley led him deeper into it a few days later. It was, indeed, the land speculator's paradise the peddler had described—8,000 square miles of untouched

49

woodland and rolling, grassy glade. It was a hunter's paradise as well: the six men divided into teams of two, and for seven months of steady shooting harvested deer without incident. By the end of it they had piled a small fortune in hides in their central camp. But the sense of peace and well-being the country inspired in them was illusory. One day in December, while Boone and Stuart were hunting along a buffalo trail, a band of mounted Shawnees burst from a canebrake, seized the two hunters, found the main camp, loaded up all of the hides and stores, stole their horses and led the two captives north toward the Ohio.

The Indians, delighted with their haul, turned the pair loose after two days of riding, and their chief—known to whites as Captain Will—gave them powder, lead, a small rifle and a piece of advice. "Go home," he commanded, adding that "yellow-jackets" would sting them if they ever returned. Boone and Stuart tracked the thieves instead, boldly stole back half a dozen horses after the Indians camped and kept them going across country all night as insurance against pursuit. But as soon as they stopped to water the animals the next morning, there came Captain Will and his warriors, yelling in triumph and grinning from ear to ear. Captain Will tied a bell around Boone's neck and ordered him to hop clangingly up and down. "Steal hoss, ha?" he cried. He led the two north once more. But this time the captives ran into a canebrake at night, and got safely back to their looted base on foot.

Finley and the camp-keepers headed glumly for home. Boone and Stuart stayed stubbornly on. Brother Squire came in soon with fresh horses, guns, supplies and a fellow hunter named Alexander Neeley. But fresh disaster waited in Boone's wild paradise. Stuart crossed the Kentucky River on a hunt and did not return. Boone tracked him to the ashes of a campfire and a tree bearing his initials. There the trail disappeared. Stuart was never seen again. This was too much for Neeley, who headed, moving carefully, for home. But the Boones had business in "Kaintuck'" and still felt impelled to transact it. Daniel was fascinated by the new country—Indians and all—and ached to see more of it.

The brothers took extraordinary precautions against further disturbance by marauders. They made a camp in deep woods far from the Warrior's Path, walked in a nearby stream and swung above ground on wild grape vines when they could. But they hunted steadily for all that. By May 1770, they calculated that there were enough hides to pay their debts. Squire loaded the pack string and rode east. Daniel, alone, "without bread, salt, sugar, horse or dog," began a singlehanded investigation of western Kentucky in which he learned the land as thoroughly as the Indians—and brought to a kind of apogee the intuitive, primitive arts of survival in a hostile wilderness.

Boone had been incautious in locating the initial hunting party's base camp. But now, with no more baggage than rifle, ammunition and blanket, he wandered as slyly and freely as a wolf. He left his fire burning after he cooked his meat at night and moved on in the dusk to sleep in canebrakes or in the limestone caves he found in his travels. He coursed the Kentucky and Licking river valleys and followed the Ohio west to its falls. Indians spotted—and trapped—him just once, when he risked exploring a precipice above Dick's River, a tributary of the Kentucky. He gripped his rifle and leaped off—to land in the foliage of a big maple tree below. The Indians did not follow and no other Indians saw him, though Boone watched them from cover and with impunity.

Squire rejoined him in July and the pair drifted slowly south and east to safer country, hunting as they traveled. He found an old Indian left by his tribe to die in the forest, and brought him a deer to eat. Autumn came but Boone could still not bring himself to leave the wilds. It was March by the time the brothers loaded up their last big haul of hides and pelts and moved into the approaches of the Cumberland Gap. And, once more, they lost everything they owned. A half-dozen Indians came politely into their firelight in Powell's Valley, ate their meat, jumped them with tomahawks held high, went off with horses, rifles and furs—then laid an ambush, which the brothers sensed as they followed in the dark and avoided in time.

Boone finally returned home in June 1771, after two years of dangerous and exacting toil. The journey left him burning with the conviction that the Bluegrass country would make him his fortune. And the hope of a "great speck" (as he described any risky adventure that promised profit) led him west again in the autumn of 1773—this time with Rebecca, his eight sons and

After paying off debts and provisioning his family, Squire Boone rides to rejoin brother Daniel with "a new recruit of horses and ammunition" for a 1770 deer-hunting expedition in the Kentucky wilderness.

daughters and five other families from the Yadkin River—to make a permanent home in Kentucky. But this party of 40 people got no farther with their driven cattle than the Powell River at the eastern approaches of the Cumberland Gap. Boone sent his eldest son James down their back trail in early October to fetch extra flour and some farm tools from Captain William Russell's station, which they had left but a few days before; as James and Russell's son, Henry, headed west again with these additional supplies and equipment, Indians ambushed, tortured and killed them

both. The war party scattered the shaken travelers' livestock. All retreated for safety to Snoddy's Fort on the Clinch River and disbanded there to make their separate ways back home.

Boone went on believing that Kentucky was to be his Utopia, nevertheless, and now renewed attempts to gain backing from the same Judge Henderson of North Carolina, in whom he had earlier confided his belief in the future of the Bluegrass country. Henderson responded with both fascination and cupidity to Boone's description of the new paradise, where elms that could shade a hundred men rose out of a rich sward of grasses and clover, where deer, elk and buffalo roamed in vast herds and wild turkeys fed in flocks of thousands. There were legal difficulties: the laws of both Virginia and North Carolina prohibited private land purchases from Indians, and England by a royal proclamation in 1763 forbade settlement west of the Appalachians. Henderson decided to bet, however, that he had come upon a loophole in this maze of restrictions: a section of English law condoning private dealings with reigning Indian princes and kings. The law actually referred to potentates on the Asian subcontinent.

But Henderson chose to interpret it differently. He sent Boone traveling through Cherokee towns as a herald of his intentions. The judge then met with the more rapacious of the tribal chieftains at the Sycamore Shoals of the Watauga River and talked them into selling him 20 million acres south of the Kentucky River for £10,000 worth of blankets, shirts, mirrors, tools and other trade goods.

Boone set out in early March of 1775 with 30 armed and mounted axmen — and a Yadkin neighbor, Colonel Richard Callaway, who would eventually assume a kind of administrative dominance of the new settlement. In 14 days they hacked a pack-horse trace over the Cumberland Gap and thence west along the ancient Warrior's Path. Henderson came over the mountains behind them with a first contingent of settlers, and "git Down," as one of them wrote, "to Boons foart about 12 oclock wheare we Stop."

Boone's "foart" was nothing save a few rudimentary shacks along the Kentucky River. But the judge assembled a meeting of "delegates" under an elm tree to establish a government of "Transylvania" — the "corner-stone," as he explained, "of an edifice whose superstructure is now in the womb of futurity."

Transylvania, alas, survived less than a year. The Revolutionary legislature of Virginia condemned land purchases from Indians without express authorization, which it refused to grant. The new Continental Congress as well turned a deaf ear to Henderson's pleas for sanction. And finally, the settlers — whom Henderson came to consider "a set of scoundrels who scarcely believe in God or fear a devil" — rebelled at his plan for collecting rents of two shillings per 100 acres in perpetuity. But if the "Government of Transylvania" dis-

solved, the settlements themselves — Boonesborough, Harrodsburg and Logan's Station — were embraced by Virginia and persisted. New ones were begun. And now tribe after tribe of Indians suddenly grew alarmed by this white occupation of country that all — including the Cherokees who had "sold" it — regarded as a common game preserve.

England's military commander and lieutenant governor at Detroit, one Henry Hamilton, encouraged this restiveness by supplying arms and supplies to Ottawas, Miamis, Shawnees and Delawares, and rewarded those who returned from Kentucky with scalps by giving the triumphant warrior as great a weight of goods as could be held in his arms. Thus, his chilling nickname: the "Hair Buyer." At Hamilton's instigation, every log compound below the Ohio River was subject to incessant raiding by 1777 — always described as the "Year of the Bloody Sevens" by those who lived to marvel at the danger, hardship and alarums they endured before it was over.

Settlers from small, exposed and isolated enclaves abandoned them early and either joined Boone or retreated east to safety beyond the mountains. Boonesborough, Harrodsburg and Logan's Station all weathered the attacks that were visited upon them. Daniel's brother Squire Boone had "the best little Indian fight ever" when caught outside the Boonesborough stockade by a brave who hit him on the head with a tomahawk and kept trying to kill him even after Boone, dripping blood, rammed a short sword completely through his assailant's body. "Both parties," said Squire with some admiration of his dead adversary, "stood and fought so well." But the raiders killed cattle, ruined the little apple trees that had been carried over the mountains, destroyed cornfields, burned outlying cabins, murdered men caught hunting or working in clearings — and kept coming back . . . and back.

By January 1778, Boonesborough was not only short of supplies but out of salt as well — and salt was critical to life on the frontier since it was essential in the curing of hides and meat and a basic article of barter (one bushel was worth a cow and a half). Boone responded by leading a party of 30 men and a string of pack horses laden with great iron kettles to the Blue Licks, a series of saline springs near the Licking River in north-

central Kentucky. He launched himself, in so doing, on the most complex and crucial of adventures, one in which he became, successively, a captive, an adopted member and a fugitive of the Shawnees, a herald of the heaviest assault ever launched on a Kentucky stockade, a defender of Boonesborough and finally, for all his pains, defendant in a court-martial in which he stood accused of treasonous collaboration with Indians and of "being in favour of the British."

Saltmaking was a dangerous business in the best of times. Every hunter of animals — and men — knew his quarry would sooner or later be drawn to a big lick. In the case of men, the quarry would be stationary for weeks at a time, since more than 800 gallons of brine had to boil away to produce one bushel of salt. Boone had been at the Blue Licks for a month when he came to grief in early February. Four Shawnees tracked him in the snow after he shot a buffalo to feed the salt party. Following a chase in which bullets began whistling uncomfortably close, he took refuge behind a tree and placed his rifle before it in a sign of surrender. His

captors were delighted at having gotten the better of the famous Wide Mouth; they laughed uproariously and shook hands all around.

But Boone began to be alarmed — about the fate of Boonesborough as well as the fate of the salt party and Daniel Boone — as they led him amicably to their camp in a creek bottom a few miles away. An enormous bonfire blazed amid the trees. Around it sat more than 100 warriors armed and painted for war. Blackfish, a famous chief, sat with them. Worse yet, Boone recognized a group of British agents — among them James and George Girty, renegade brothers of Simon Girty, a "white Indian" accursed by all on the border for his cruelty to those of his own race.

Boone by now was 43 years old. He was a muscular five feet nine or ten inches in height, with blue eyes, a fresh, fair complexion, the broad mouth by which Indians identified him, and light brown hair worn "plaited and clubbed up" behind his head. His hard and dangerous years in the wilderness had augmented an iron constitution and a capacity for physical endur-

Daring deeds in "the Year of the Bloody Sevens"

As pursuing Indians gape in awe, Samuel McColloch leaps his horse off a cliff at Wheeling Creek. Incredibly, both survived.

The year 1777 was the most harrowing in the memory of the early frontiersmen. Those who endured it would remember it bitterly as "the Year of the Bloody Sevens."

The Revolution was under way in deadly earnest, and British strategists found eager allies in the warrior tribes west of the Appalachians. Plying the Indians with rum and arming them with muskets, hatchets and scalping knives, British agents fanned the smoldering resentment the tribes felt toward settlers pushing into the wilderness. The British objective was twofold: to stem the westward flow of Americans, and to distract the Continental Army from its main business on the Eastern seaboard.

For the settlers, the terrors of 1777 began with an attack on Boonesborough in March, when Daniel Boone himself was wounded, and reached a peak in September, when Fort Henry at Wheeling Creek in western Virginia was attacked twice within three weeks. No settlement inside the 600-mile arc of the Ohio River from Fort Pitt to the Mississippi was safe from marauding Indians.

Sometimes the Indians attacked in bands of fewer than 20; sometimes they swept down in fearsome troops of 200 or 300, screaming, shooting and launching flaming arrows of cane and hickory over the stockade walls.

Any male settler caught outside the safety of the log forts was murdered and scalped; women and children were carried off as prizes of war. And before galloping away, the Indians would raze the homesteads abandoned by the settlers crowded inside the stockade. "Thus a great proportion of the inhabitants were left without a bed to lay on, a morsel of bread or milk to feed their families, or even many of them without a garment to

Elizabeth Zane, a member of Wheeling's founding family, braves the fire of besieging Indians to fetch a keg of precious gunpowder.

clothe themselves," wrote a defender of one Kentucky fort.

The terrible year spawned legendary tales of courage and sacrifice. According to one such story, while some 400 Indians were besieging Wheeling on September 2, Major Samuel McColloch — "the pride of the settlements, and a terror to the savages," in the words of one early storyteller — found himself trapped by Indians on the edge of a 200-foot cliff overhanging Wheeling Creek. There was only one course: McColloch spurred his horse straight over the precipice. "A plunge, a crash — crackling timber and tumbling rocks were all that the wondering savages could see or hear," ran one account. "But, lo! ere a single savage had recovered from his amazement, what should they see but the invulnerable major on his steed, galloping across the peninsula."

Elizabeth Zane, the young sister of Fort Henry's founder Colonel Ebenezer Zane, is the heroine of another famous legend. All through the twin sieges the women stood valiantly by their men. They melted down their pewter plates and spoons to make bullets, loaded guns and braved the enemy fire. At one point, when gunpowder ran low, Elizabeth Zane remembered that a supply of the stuff was stashed in her brother's home. "You have not one man to spare," said the gallant lass to the menfolk — and off she sped, while the Indians watched, stunned, exclaiming "a squaw, a squaw!"

Wheeling lost 41 of its able-bodied men before the Indians finally gave up and faded back into the forest. Across the frontier hundreds of settlers were killed before winter ended the attacks. The survivors doggedly rebuilt their cabins and plowed their fields anew when spring arrived.

ance few men of any age could match. They had also cemented an aspect of character much rarer on the frontier: a kind of serenity that seemed proof against the most outrageous misfortune. Boone seems, as a result, to have puzzled compatriots who lacked his sixth sense in the forest. He was not a reckless man but he sometimes acted with a boldness others found foolhardy — only to confound them at other times, particularly in dealings with Indians, by all the manifestations of good-humored resignation. In fact, he was a realist who was very seldom swayed by emotion.

Boone had no illusions about Indians. He had been a perceptive observer of their traits, customs and responses since boyhood. He regarded them with an interest and tolerance few backwoodsmen shared. This capacity to see them as individuals persisted even after his son James was tortured to death near the Wilderness Road. Never an Indian hater, he shot them out of necessity at times but did not boast about having done so. He never took a scalp and, like the Indians themselves, did not relish impossible last stands that could cost him his.

Boone tried his best to look delighted, thus, when led past back-patting Indians to meet Blackfish — though back patting was sometimes a sardonic prelude to torture. And he spoke with friendly regret when the chief announced that he had come to destroy Boonesborough. The town, said Wide Mouth, was simply too strongly fortified for so few warriors. Boone went on to predict, however, that it would fall peacefully if overawed by a larger force in the spring — when its women and children could travel comfortably to Ohio to live as one with the Shawnees. Blackfish let him know that Indian scouts had seen many young men at Blue Licks. His own men, said Boone, proudly. Let Blackfish promise that they would not be harmed and Boone would engineer a peaceful surrender.

This bargain was not consummated without difficulty. The more bloodthirsty Indians howled for the right to kill the salt party once Boone had induced it to lay down its arms; and the British agents insisted, correctly, that Boonesborough was ripe for the taking. But a solemn council was convened and wholesale murder was averted — by a vote of 61 to 59 — after Boone had delivered an impassioned speech. The war party refused, however, to delay a triumphal return with

so astonishing a haul of dangerous "Long Knives."

The white prisoners were hard used on being driven to Little Chillicothe, a Shawnee town on the Little Miami River. All were tied, sitting up in the snow, to trees at night, and one man was forced to march naked with "a load of Bare meat" on his back. But all survived. Seventeen of the 28 men the Indians had captured were honored by membership in the tribe; the rest were sold to the British. Boone was adopted, as a son, by the great Blackfish himself.

Boone, renamed Sheltowee, or Big Turtle, was a great prize and Blackfish took him off to Detroit at the first opportunity to exhibit him to the British garrison there. He was received with punctilio by the notorious Henry Hamilton. The "Hair Buyer" personally and privately considered the more barbarous practices of his Indian allies lamentable — even though he felt duty bound to encourage them as a matter of military necessity. He himself treated white prisoners with civility if they fell into his hands. Hamilton addressed Boone as "captain" and listened as credulously as had the Shawnees to his hints that Kentuckians might come over to the British side in the spring. Hamilton went so far, in fact, as to offer Blackfish £100 for the distinguished prisoner, and gave Boone some new clothes (which Blackfish grabbed for himself) when the chief indignantly refused. Boone was not unduly disturbed. He had no pressing engagements, looked on with interest as Blackfish visited Mingos and Delawares to recruit warriors for the forthcoming expedition against Boonesborough, and was content enough with life among the Shawnees when they returned to Ohio.

Blackfish treated Boone as an admirable and entertaining fellow. He seemed embarrassed when Boone, who had been sent out to chop trees, complained that this was no work for a warrior and excused him from such menial toil. He drew maps on the ground to explain the lay of the country, urged Boone to go hunting (although he permitted him very little powder and ball) and was happy to see his "son" take part in rifle-shooting matches with tribal marksmen.

Boone, remembering his run-in with Saucy Jack some years back, made a point of missing a good deal in these contests, and noted "the greatest expressions of joy when they exceeded me." And he played a clever trick on his captors calculated to ease a certain innate suspicion some of the Indians seemed to entertain. He emptied the bullets from all the loaded guns he could find, announced that he was about to run away, headed for the nearest trees and dared his new brothers to shoot him before he escaped. The Indians finally leaped for their arms. Boone wheeled as they began firing and made a great show of catching rifle balls in his leather apron. He walked back, grinning mightily, made an even greater show of returning bullets to his startled audience and cried: "Here! Boone ain't going away!" Time and ego lulled the Indians further; it was hard for the Shawnees to believe that anyone in his right mind would *not* be one of them if he had the chance. They brought him guns to repair. He had an unstocked rifle, some powder and a few bullets when the imminence of Blackfish's new invasion of Kentucky led him to decide, in mid-June, that he had been a Shawnee long enough.

Sheltowee (Boone) lingered in camp with a few Indian women when men of a hunting party ran into the woods after a flock of wild turkeys. As soon as he heard them banging away in the distance, he picked up his rifle, climbed aboard a horse — with the women all howling in protest — and simply rode off into the trees. He kicked the animal into a run as soon as he was out of view, kept it moving down stream beds to mask his trail during the night and ran it until it collapsed the next morning. He then ran on afoot until he came to the Ohio and floated across it on a log. He thereafter paused to lash a crude stock to the rifle, to shoot a buffalo, to roast its hump and to soak his aching feet in an "ooze" made of oak bark, but he did not stop again until he was back in Boonesborough, having covered 160 miles in just four days and nights.

He had arrived, it was instantly obvious, just in time. The village fort was a shambles after months of neglect. Boone sent messengers asking for reinforcements from Harrodsburg and Logan's Station, and set his fellow settlers to the prodigious tasks of raising a new stockade and of building two new blockhouses, which — with the two built earlier — provided enfilading fire from all four corners of the enclosure.

June passed. No Indians arrived. July wore on. Finally, in mid-month, William Hancock, a member of the salt party, staggered into Boonesborough — having taken nine days after his escape to cover ground Boone had covered in four — to say that 400 warriors would start for Kentucky in less than two weeks.

Boone was immediately moved to lead more than a dozen hardy men across the Ohio in the hope of stealing horses and beaver skins from the Indians as they prepared to attack him. Boone's party found no booty (beyond three horses stolen during a sharp woodland skirmish) but dogged the cumbersome Indian column advancing on Boonesborough, counted 444 warriors and 12 French Canadians serving as British agents, and got back in time to sound an alarm with 24 hours to spare. The settlers "forted up" on September 5, and spent the night molding bullets, storing food, filling containers with water and loading their rifles.

But Blackfish, as things turned out, was hurt rather than hostile. He felt that Sheltowee — for all his running off when Shawnee backs were turned — was duty bound to surrender the village and get its population started for Detroit. He sent a captured black man named Pompey up to the stockade with a white flag to say that he had letters from Governor Hamilton and wanted to talk to Captain Boone. The captain forthwith walked out to meet him. The settlers, watching from loopholes, felt that Boone was "gone" but the chief shook his hand and said:

"Well, Boone, how d'y?"

"How d'y, Blackfish?"

"Well, Boone, what made you run away from me?"

Sheltowee was sure Blackfish would understand: he had simply wanted to see his family. Why then, asked the chief, had he not told his father — who would have let him go? Boone ducked that question for one of his own: why had not the Shawnee fought better when surprised by Boone a few weeks back? Blackfish clapped his hands to imitate rifle shots and to suggest that his warriors had been outgunned. But to business: he handed over a letter from Hamilton asking Boone to help prevent a massacre. Boone threw up his hands. He was no longer in command. Virginia had sent a bigger captain. He walked to the fort, opened the gate a bit and exhibited Major William Bailey Smith, the nominal commander, who was impressively attired in a red coat and ostrich trimmed "macaroni" hat.

There were no more than 30 men and 20 boys capable of firing a rifle inside the Boonesborough stockade. But Hamilton, having been deceived by a cap-

The white architect of tribal savagery

If the frontiersmen feared and cursed their Indian adversaries, they reserved their most venomous hatred for one of their own. His name was Simon Girty, and he was an anomaly of Western history: a white leader of Indians, a renegade who became the architect of vicious acts of cruelty against settlers. As one particularly disdainful utterance had it: "No other country or age ever produced so brutal, depraved and wicked a wretch."

That was an exaggeration, of course. But Girty was bad enough. He was born in 1741 near Harrisburg, Pennsylvania, then the edge of wilderness, and experienced a ghastly childhood. One night when he was 10, his father and a more or less "tame" Indian went on a binge in the Girty cabin; the drunken men quarreled, and Simon watched in horror as the Indian sank a tomahawk into his father's head. Five years later, a raiding band of Delawares took the family captive; again the boy watched in terror, this time as his stepfather was tortured and scalped. Simon's mother and three brothers were held by the Delawares, but he was given to the Senecas, who kept him three years.

Girty was 18 in 1759 when the Senecas returned him to civilization, a warped creature with a grim past and a malignant future. He worked around Fort Pitt until 1777 as an interpreter between Indians and traders. He signed on for a time recruiting for the Continental Army but, in 1778, disappointed that he was not made a captain, he lit out for Detroit to offer his services to the British. Two of Simon's brothers, George and James, soon joined him, and together they worked for 20 years to enflame the frontier.

Simon was the most adept at it. Dressing like an Indian, he went among Mingos, Shawnees and Wyandots, preaching death and destruction while distributing guns and ammunition. "Brothers!" he cried in one speech. "The Long Knives have overrun your country and usurped your hunting grounds. They have destroyed the cane, trodden down the clover, killed the deer and the buffalo.

"Brothers! Unless you rise in the majesty of your might and exterminate their whole race, you may bid adieu to the hunting grounds of your fathers."

Scores of war parties followed Girty in raids from Detroit down as far as Kentucky. He reputedly encouraged the torture of captives, and was supposed to have looked on with glee. When the American Colonel William Crawford was burned alive in 1782 *(page 72)*, he was said to have begged Girty to kill him, but Girty reportedly turned his back with the comment: "I have no gun."

When the colonists offered an $800 reward for his head, Girty responded with stepped-up ferocity. Outside Dunlap's Station in 1791, Girty, leading a force of 300 Indians, said to a white prisoner: "Tell them in the fort to give up and we won't harm their lives or belongings; but if they don't, by God, we'll kill you." The fort did not yield. Girty kept his word. "They stripped him naked," said a witness inside the blockade, "pinioning his outstretched hands and feet to the earth, kindling a fire on his abdomen. His screams of agony were ringing in our ears during the remainder of the night, becoming gradually weaker and weaker till toward daylight, when they ceased."

The white renegade never was captured. With the British withdrawal from Detroit in 1796, Girty fled to Canada, and there he stayed perpetually drunk until he died in 1816. For years his acts of cruelty were told and retold in the West. And no such round of stories ever omitted a favorite Kentucky expression: "I have a good-for-nothing dog, and his name is Simon Girty."

Simon Girty is portrayed armed to the teeth.

tured Kentuckian, had warned Blackfish at the outset that all three Kentucky forts had been reinforced by big contingents of Virginia militia. The Shawnee chief wanted to go on talking. The people in the fort, and particularly Colonel Richard Callaway — a settlement leader who looked upon Boone's general "foolhardiness" with a jaundiced eye — preferred death over captivity. But none were against buying time and both Callaway and Smith agreed to accompany Boone to another council outside the log palisade.

Blackfish and his fellow chiefs were all hospitality. They spread a panther skin for the whites, ordered lesser warriors to shade them with branches and gave them smoked buffalo tongues to take back to the fort. "I come to take you away easy," said Blackfish. The negotiations went on for three days, with Blackfish trying as hard to gull the whites as they were trying to gull him. The chief raised a Union Jack, produced an interpreter and a cloth-covered table, offered a formal peace treaty and lured eight of Boonesborough's moving spirits outside to sign it. He produced a peace pipe. Then he ordered handshaking: two Indians advanced on each white, seized an arm apiece and tried dragging the lot of them over an embankment above the river.

The Battle of Boonesborough began at that second. Boone knocked Blackfish down; his companions began struggling, and they broke away, one by one, as riflemen in the fort opened up. The whites ran frantically for the stockade gate. Indians hidden in the underbrush began banging away at them. Boone's brother Squire was knocked flat by a bullet, but rose after a moment and gained the fort. The gate was shut and barred — leaving one hapless negotiator outside behind a stump, which, happily, sheltered him until he rejoined his companions after nightfall. The frustrated warriors whooped from cover and were answered by the howls of children and the bawling of cattle inside the stockade. Boone dug the bullet from his brother's shoulder with his knife; Squire went shakily to bed, with an ax at hand just in case. The fort's riflemen settled down beside their loopholes and Blackfish settled down, out yonder, to starve them into submission.

Indians were seldom prepared, temperamentally or technically, to besiege a frontier fortress. But they had seldom tried to do so in such large numbers, either, or with the weight of ammunition and supplies that Ham-

ilton had provided Blackfish. The warriors at Boonesborough, it was soon evident, had come to stay. Their noisy fusillading soon ceased. But snipers fired sporadically, day after day, at the fort's loopholes. Others climbed trees or high ground across the river and shot into the stockade from above — wounding an occasional settler, and also Old Spot, a cow that had learned to sense Indians when at pasture and had often warned the settlement by her resulting peculiar behavior.

On the seventh night, Indians darted out of the dark to heave burning brands against the stockade, and to launch flaming arrows at roofed structures. The settlers fired wildly at these incendiaries and Indian gunners fired as wildly at men who appeared atop the blockhouses to knock the arrows off with brooms.

A settler named William Patton, who had been off in the woods when the Indians came and who had hidden there until this night assault, hurried to Logan's Station to warn it that Boonesborough had fallen. "The Indians made in the night a Dreadfull attack on the fort," wrote Daniel Trabue, who was at Logan's when Patton arrived. "They run up a large number of them with large fire brands or torches and made the Dreadfullest screams and hollowing that could be imagind Mr Patton thought the Fort was taken and he actuly Did hear the Indians killing people & he heard the women and children & men also screaming when the indians was killing them."

In fact, the Indians' daring venture was badly timed. An earlier drizzle, as the defenders found to their relief, had made the wooden stockade too damp to burn. It was not their only satisfaction. Squire Boone, a man who healed quickly, built a wooden cannon, reinforced it with a wagon wheel's iron tread, loaded it with rifle balls and made "the Indins skamper perdidiously" when he fired it at a group approaching the stockade in the morning mist. Another settler risked loading his rifle with an enormous powder charge, took aim at an Indian who had been climbing a tree across the river and waggling his naked buttocks at the defenders, and blew him off his limb like a turkey. But these were minor matters. Scores of Indians were toiling, day after day, to build a tunnel from the riverbank to the nearest wall of the stockade.

Boonesborough — now in its second week of siege — was on its last legs as it confronted this ominous phenomenon. Food was running short and hoarded water was all but gone. Wounds, sleeplessness, strain and personal animosities were fast eroding the little garrison's responsiveness to danger. The defenders did what they could: dug a countertunnel at right angles to the one they could hear the enemy digging and hoped the Indians would break through into it to be encountered one by one. Many anticipated a more hideous fate. Blackfish had powder to burn and his warriors had begun yelling: "Digging hole! Blow you to hell tonight!" But night brought thunder and torrential rain and morning a sight they could hardly believe: a silent and empty landscape. They sent out scouts. Every loophole on the stockade was ringed with a lacework of lead (they dug out 125 pounds of it, later, to make bullets of their own). The tunnel, however, had collapsed in the downpour, and the drenched and disgruntled Indians had vanished to a man.

Resistance at Boonesborough was crucial to the Revolution in the West. Henry Hamilton had hoped to wipe out the Kentucky settlements as a first step in taking Fort Pitt—key to all the frontier because of its position at the fork of the Ohio River. This would enable him to push American influence east of the Appalachians for good, and to restore the upper Mississippi and all its drainage to England's tribal allies and to the embrace of English trade. Boone's early manipulation of the Shawnees, his fortuitous escape from captivity, and his purchase of time before the battle had all been central to salvation. An attack begun three days earlier—before the fort was repaired—along with a tunnel driven through before the rain, might well have meant the end of Boonesborough, and the end of Logan's and Harrod's enclaves as well.

Boone's adventures of 1778 crowned the achievements that were to make him the earliest of Western heroes, and constituted, in many ways, the apex of a dramatic life. Others, however, found them outrageous. Richard Callaway and Benjamin Logan accused him of having surrendered the salt party to the Shawnees and having collaborated with the British. He was completely exonerated by a court-martial called by the Virginia militia at Logan's Station; the evidence supported him so totally, in fact, that he was promoted from captain to major of militia. But he was

taken aback by the malice of men he had believed to be his friends. Indeed, Boone had rescued Callaway's daughter, Betsey, from Indian kidnappers just two years before. And Callaway's son, Flanders, was married to Boone's daughter, Jemima. In disgust, Boone left Boonesborough and founded another settlement—Boone's Station—north of the Kentucky River.

He was soon engaged in self-recrimination more bitter by far than anything others said about him at his trial. Boone rode to Virginia early in 1780 with $20,000 of his own money—raised by selling land he owned in Kentucky—and $30,000 belonging to friends to buy from the state land office at Richmond warrants that were necessary in establishing title to unclaimed acreage. All were intent on beating Eastern speculators to broad areas of the Bluegrass. But Boone lost it all when a thief got into his room at a tavern in James City, Virginia, and vanished with his saddle bags as he slept. Many friends supported him: Thomas Hart, a heavy loser, wrote: "I feel for poor Boone, a Noble and generous soul and freely grant him discharge for Whatever Sums of mine he possest at the time." But he was tarred by the scandal nevertheless. And his military career ended in tragedy: his son, Israel, was needlessly killed on August 19, 1782, when a force of backwoods militia ignored Boone's warnings, plunged into an Indian ambush at the Battle of Blue Licks—the last considerable combat of the Revolution—and were mowed down before they could wade back across the Licking River to safety.

This bloody melee was the aftermath of a raid into Kentucky by a force of more than 400 Ohio Indians under the notorious Simon Girty. The renegade white man's target was Bryan's Station, north of Boonesborough. The settlement boasted a huge stockade and Girty, hoping to catch its defenders in the open, concealed his warriors at night and waited for an opportunity. He prompted one of the most chilling little dramas in frontier history by doing so. The defenders somehow sensed that they were about to be besieged, deduced the hidden enemy's strategy, and gambled the lives of their wives and daughters by sending them out with pails at dawn to bring precious water from a nearby stream. The Indians let them pass—probably thinking to preserve the element of surprise—which was a great mistake, since the station's 44 riflemen

barred its gate once the women were back and defended it against every attempt to breach its walls.

Girty retreated, thereupon, toward the Licking River—leaving a plain trail, even to blazing trees, in the hope of luring the militia companies that had begun converging on him from all the settlements to the south. Boone was with the first force to pursue—fewer than 200 mounted men under Lieutenant Colonel John Todd. Boone was troubled; he assumed that they were being led on, since Indians simply split up if they intended to avoid an enemy, and calculated that at least 500 warriors waited somewhere ahead. The hills across the Licking River seemed empty when they arrived. But Boone noted two brushy ravines—in which the Indians were, in fact, hiding—and strongly suggested that they wait for Benjamin Logan who was coming up behind them with 400 more men. A Major Hugh McGary of Lincoln County had made the same suggestion earlier on. Todd had scoffed at McGary, and now, burning at what he took to be an insult, he turned from Boone and faced his milling horsemen.

"By Godly," he yelled, "what have we come here for? All who are not damned cowards follow me!"

He rode into the stream, brandishing his rifle, and the whooping backwoodsmen began to follow. Boone and Todd managed to bring a little order into the haphazard attack; to get most of the men off their vulnerable horses and organized into three companies before leading them across the stream into the woods. All was silence as these little columns climbed the first hill. But Indians then boiled toward them out of the ravines, while others ran downhill to cut them off at the water's edge. The Kentuckians began fleeing for their lives. Boone's son fell dying, blood spurting from his mouth, near the river. Boone tried carrying him, dropped him to fight an Indian attacker, and left him to hurry other men into the river and back across. Only five minutes had passed. The triumphant warriors — busy scalping the wounded and dead — did not pursue.

Boone found Israel's body five days later when he returned to the scene with Logan's force. He recognized it, the weather being hot, only by its clothing. "We proceeded to Bury the Dead," he wrote, "which were 43 on the ground, and Many more we Expect Lay about that we Did not See." Boone never shook off a sense of guilt for having failed to halt the attack at Blue Licks before it began and could not speak of Israel's death without weeping.

Still, the great woodsman, now almost 50 years old, was about to become one of the most famous men in the world; and, in addition — as thousands of settlers poured into Kentucky — a member of the state legislature, horse trader, tavern keeper, surveyor, and one of the richest, if also one of the most naïve, of the state's speculators in land.

Boone was ushered into the pantheon of American heroes by the most unlikely of intermediaries: a Pennsylvania schoolteacher named John Filson, who traveled to Kentucky in 1782. Filson dabbled in acreage, interviewed old settlers, among them Boone, and retired after two years to Wilmington, Delaware, to produce a promotional work — *The Discovery, Settlement and present State of Kentucke* — which seems to have been calculated to send Easterners hurrying across the Appalachians in search of bargains in real

estate. Of course, a few of those prospective bargains were in the possession of the author, who had conveniently bought up large tracts of Kentucky wilderness before setting pen to paper.

The book included a map watermarked with the legend "Work & Be Rich," and suggested that Kentucky was a new Eden: "flowing with milk and honey, a land of wheat and barley, and all kinds of fruits." But the writer also included a long chapter about Boone — since most Americans were aware of the state's reputation as the "Dark and Bloody Ground" — and portrayed him as a man who not only had overcome its perils but also had improved his soul in the process. Filson asked his leading man to sign a foreword with James Harrod and one Levi Todd in which all recommended the book as a "great utility to the publick."

This turned out to have been a shrewd move indeed, for the subsection entitled, "The Adventures of Col. Daniel Boon" was received with fascination by thousands. The "Adventures" were done in the first person, with Boone purporting to be telling his own story in his own words. The hero, as interpreted by Filson, spoke in insufferably highfalutin language: "My footsteps have often been marked with blood. Many dark and sleepless nights have I been companion for owls and pinched by the Winter's cold. But now peace crowns the sylvan shade." The account was shot through with error, and such unpleasant subjects as the torturing of Boone's son by the Indians were ignored so as not to overshadow the real subject of Filson's Boone narrative: the "peace and safety, sweets of liberty, and Bounties of Providence" to be had — for a price — in "Kentucke." Regardless of the errors, its effect was stupendous.

The "Adventures" — which described Boone's exploration of Kentucky, his captivity among the Shawnees, the siege of Boonesborough and many other episodes in the forest — were soon extracted from the rest of Filson's work. They were published and republished in America and England, and were translated into many European languages. Filson made his adventurer a superman of the wilderness, a bold if gentle soul who had embraced nature, bested savages at their own cruel pursuits, and had achieved a nobility, in so doing, that was denied men whose virtues had been abraded by the temptations of great cities. Boone became a

The womenfolk of Bryan's Station, Kentucky replenish their water supply under the noses of a Shawnee war party in 1782. By acting as if absolutely nothing were amiss, the ladies so mesmerized the Indians that they were able to bring back water enough to last throughout the attack.

figure of myth in his own lifetime—and a model for all the heroes of literature and drama who later celebrated the winning of the West.

Fame brought him the means of possessing enormous areas of virgin countryside at last. Easterners could imagine no sounder way of taking a flyer in Kentucky land than by calling upon the great woodsman himself to locate, survey and stake out a suitable tract as their proxy. The great woodsman struck a hard bargain: he asked that half the land be deeded over to him in return for his services. But Eastern investors, and indeed, many newcomers to the West, felt that Boone was well worth his fee. He knew Kentucky as did few men. He was a competent surveyor. He was honest. And there was a certain cachet about hir-

ing the hero that the more prosaic found irresistible.

Boone moved to Limestone on the south bank of the Ohio and set out, as a man of affairs, to savor the privileges and embrace the opportunities due a founder of the new Eden. He not only operated his tavern at Limestone but dealt in all manner of commodities: skins, furs, horses, an occasional slave and, to use his spelling, much "Flower," "Backer" and "Whiska." He lent money. He collected and shipped ginseng root, or "sang" as he called it, by the ton. The "Land Bissness," however, was his passion. By 1788, he owned at least 50,000 acres. But he had sowed the seeds of his own ruination in dealing for them.

Many early surveys in Kentucky were inexact, and vast areas of land were "shingled" with conflicting

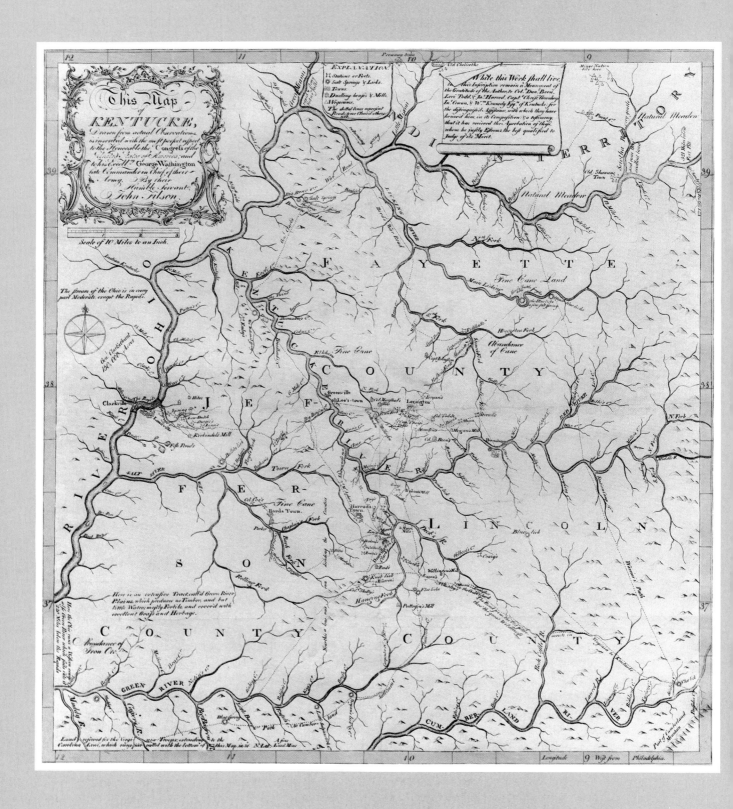

John Filson (*above*) published in 1784 an account of Daniel Boone's adventures that turned the modest woodsman into literature's first Western hero and earned Filson recognition as Kentucky's first historian. But Filson was better known to his frontier contemporaries as a land speculator and surveyor whose early map of "Kentucke" (*left*), advertising the region's fertile, lightly timbered "fine cane land" and "moderate" rivers, was accurate enough to guide the army of settlers it was designed to attract.

claims. Boone, who tended to go on feeling that he was still moving through an untrammeled wilderness, at times claimed land for his customers and himself that had already been staked out by others. He detested New Englanders—preferring not to live "within 100 miles of a d----d Yankee"—and the kind of legalistic thinking Easterners brought to the West. He had a lamentable tendency—after locating and surveying land—to put off establishing clear, legal title to it while he went hunting; it never occurred to him that others might use the delay to establish title themselves. His mail in the 1790s grew increasingly bitter:

"The thousand acres warrant that I put in your hands cost me dear," wrote one Charles Yancey in 1796, "but I have neither warrant nor land. A number of locations you charged me for are not surveyed or returned and may be lost to us forever. I am informed by Wm. Lipscomb, that he can find no deeds to him either in Fayette or Lincoln Counties, that many settlers are on those lands and that it may finally be lost."

Boone discovered, to his horror, that Kentuckians had begun to regard him as a fraud who made "chimney corner" surveys (stayed at home and guessed at the boundaries of land he offered). He heard rumors that he was to be assassinated. He was deluged by lawsuits. He sold land to pay his multiplying debts. But much was not his, he discovered, to sell.

Boone was not alone in his travail. Hundreds and hundreds of other early settlers—people who had believed, in their innocence, that hacking out a clearing was enough—were also deprived of land as courts and lawyers established themselves in Kentucky. These other unfortunates were not forced to endure calumny as well. But neither did many of them possess the resources by which stronger mortals shrug off disaster.

As of old, Boone frequently disappeared into the forest to hunt. A backwoodsman was startled, in the mid-1790s, to come upon Boone—now turned 60—living with his wife Rebecca, two daughters and their husbands in open-sided lean-tos near the Big Sandy River. They had one butcher knife, had contrived forks from pieces of cane and were eating from wooden troughs. Boone was ecstatic. He had, he said, just shot "the master bear of the Western country" and was happy to say that he expected a good price for its skin and several others he had drying near his campfire. ◉

Taking the measure of the new land

Hard on the heels of the adventurous "long hunters" who first opened up the wilds of Kentucky came parties of men with a more prosaic mission. These were the surveyors, who penetrated the rolling Bluegrass country during the late 1700s to map and parcel out land claims for thousands of westward-moving settlers.

To acquire land in Kentucky a settler — or speculator — first had to secure a warrant from Virginia, which governed the area as a territory. Veterans were entitled to anywhere from 200 to 5,000 free acres, depending on their rank; all others had to pay, generally one to eight dollars an acre. The warrants did not specify the boundaries of the holder's new land. That was left to a surveyor, who went into the wilderness and marked these off.

A Kentucky surveyor generally traveled with two "chainmen" to measure distances, a "landmarker" to slash blazes on trees, and a "spy" to hunt for food and keep a sharp eye out for Indians. The surveyor, or "pilot," took compass bearings from easily recognizable landmarks and jotted down distances in 16½-foot units called poles. He then converted pole measurements into acres on a ratio of 40 square poles to one acre. Back at the local county seat, with measurements for scores of clients in his field notes, a surveyor would register each claim and make plats, or maps, of the land showing each new owner's property lines.

The Virginia warrant system put a premium on knowing the lay of the land, and it was natural for men like Daniel Boone, who had wandered the length and breadth of Kentucky, to turn suveyor in hopes of great profit. But it was a risky business. Slow-moving survey parties were constantly in danger of Indian ambush. Many of Boone's close friends, including his biographer, John Filson, were killed while on survey

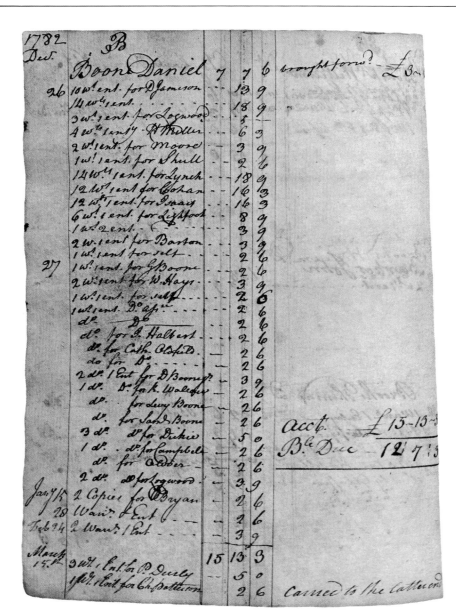

The Virginia land office records list Daniel Boone's survey entries from December 1782 to March 1783. The account, 15 pounds, 13 shillings and 3 pence, included charges for registering warrants and titles, which Boone passed on to the landowners.

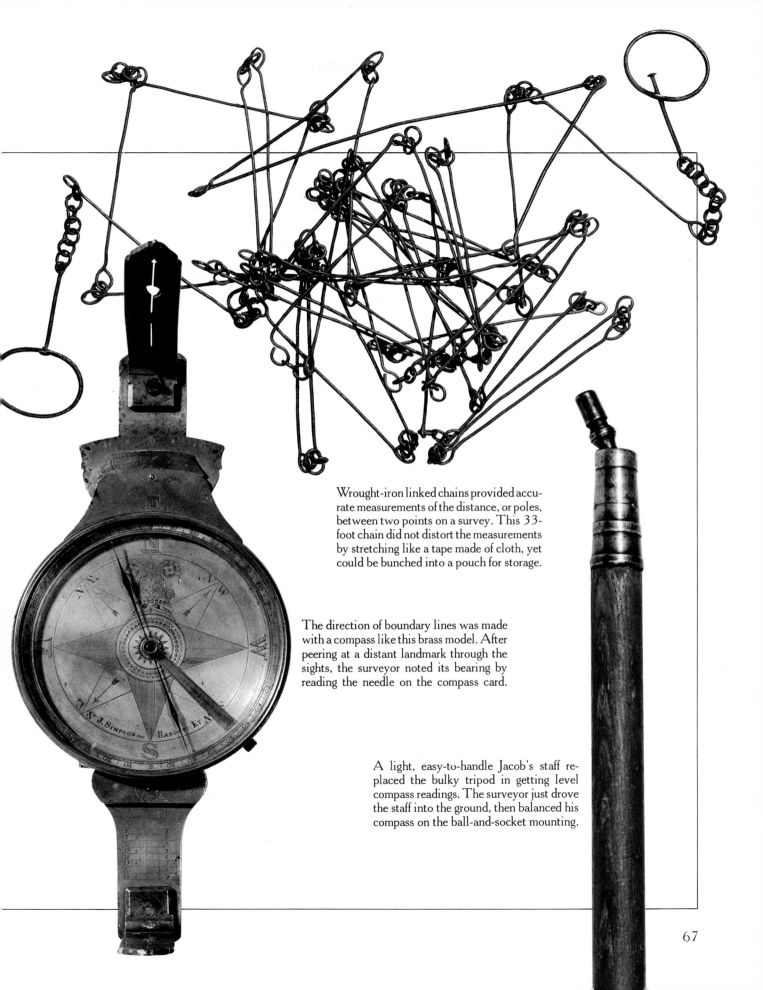

Wrought-iron linked chains provided accurate measurements of the distance, or poles, between two points on a survey. This 33-foot chain did not distort the measurements by stretching like a tape made of cloth, yet could be bunched into a pouch for storage.

The direction of boundary lines was made with a compass like this brass model. After peering at a distant landmark through the sights, the surveyor noted its bearing by reading the needle on the compass card.

A light, easy-to-handle Jacob's staff replaced the bulky tripod in getting level compass readings. The surveyor just drove the staff into the ground, then balanced his compass on the ball-and-socket mounting.

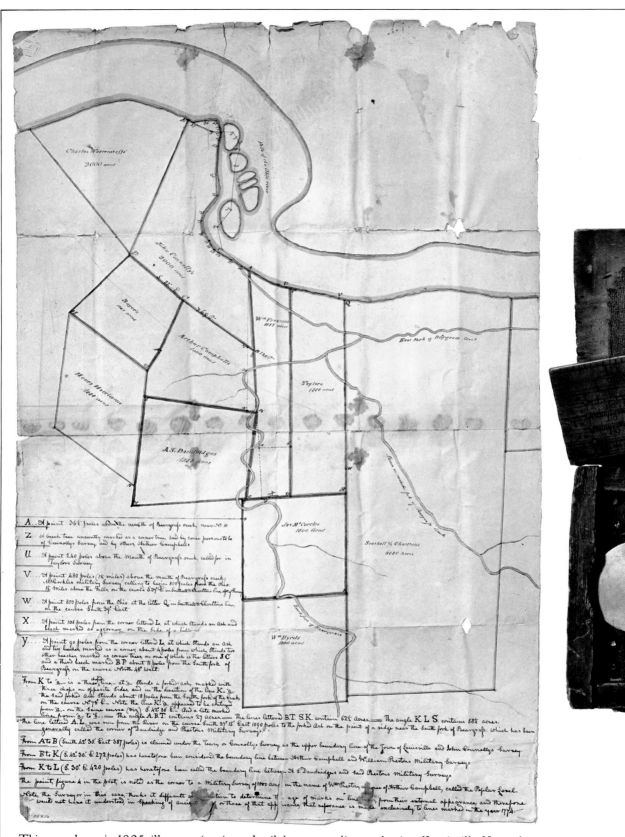

This map, drawn in 1825, illustrates in minute detail the property lines at the site of Louisville, Kentucky.

journeys into Kentucky. A 19th Century historian proposed conferring "immortality" on surveyors who "ran equal risk of life from danger as soldiers with less prospect of eclat, yet produced more lasting benefit to this country."

The perils of the forest hardly daunted the likes of Daniel Boone. But disputes at the land office drove him and many others to distraction—and eventual bankruptcy. A surveyor was supposed to have an encyclopedic knowledge of which pieces of land had been claimed and which were still available. In many cases, however, Boone found himself claiming land that had already been spoken for. To compound the trouble, overlapping, or "shingled," surveys were unavoidable on the frontier, where crude instruments made even the most meticulous measurements mere approximations.

The Kentucky land squabbles dragged on for decades, and court fights over the old warrants made rich men of quite a few lawyers. There seems to have been one side benefit: the disputes provided an example to Congress in 1785 when it was considering how to handle the virgin lands north of the Ohio River. Instead of adopting the Virginia warrant-and-surveyor system, the lawmakers stipulated that the entire area must be carefully surveyed first —and only then could homesteaders claim specific, preregistered property.

A surveyor's map-making instruments include a wooden ruler, a protractor for measuring angles, and a folding brass "sector"—a forerunner of the modern slide rule—for doing trigonometric calculations.

The public outcry by Boone's creditors died as it became obvious that he was intent on paying every debt. The state, in fact, named a county for him in 1798—a year in which sheriffs sold 10,000 acres of his holdings for taxes. It was too much. He turned his affairs over to a nephew, Colonel John Grant, ordered payment of every honest claim (a process that left him without an acre in the end), and refused to concern himself with his land interests any longer. But game was thin. He was only marking time.

His son Daniel Morgan Boone had visited authorities in Spanish Missouri on his behalf and had returned with flattering news: the government of the Most Catholic King of Spain would be delighted to receive so famous an American and would not only grant him much land but would make generous grants to any relatives and servants he might choose to bring with him.

Boone—now 64—went west again in 1799 with his wife, his sons Daniel and Nathan, Nathan's wife, his brother Squire and family, and his daughter Jemima and her husband Flanders Callaway. The Spaniards paraded their garrison in his honor in St. Louis, and by winter the various Boones were settled on tracts of land totaling some thousands of acres above St. Charles on the lower Missouri River.

The old woodsman had made exactly the right decision. He not only reigned as a kind of backwoods patriarch through the last two decades of his life, but—with a yawning wilderness once more on his doorstep—he became again the long hunter of his youth and roamed the forest almost until the day of his death. The Spaniards made him the syndic—a kind of military governor—of the district of Femme Osage and as such he settled estates, kept the peace, witnessed notes and punished crime. He seldom inconvenienced culprits by sentencing them to the *calabozo* in St. Charles; instead, he tied most of them to a sapling after trying them under a "Justice Tree" near his cabin, laid on the lash, and sent them on their way after marking them "whipped and cleared" on his records. Travelers made a practice of stopping to observe him and most regarded him with something very close to awe.

Creditors from Kentucky still harassed him. Three of them arrived on his doorstep after hearing that Congress had approved his ownership of the "thousand arpents" Spain had given him before the Louisiana Purchase. He sold it all to pay them off. But his sons and relatives had land—and the whole, empty continent lay off to the west. He trapped every winter. Rheumatism, the bane of old woodsmen, bothered him increasingly but he continued to make long journeys into the wilderness. Officers at Fort Osage, near present-day Kansas City, were astounded when he plodded into their compound at the age of 82. "He goes a hunting twice a year to the remotest wilderness," one of them reported. "He left us for the River Platt, some distance above." He talked of going to the Rockies, and there were old Missourians, after his death, who believed he had explored the Yellowstone River.

Age eventually began to leave its marks on him. His trapping expeditions grew shorter. His eyesight began to fail. He had a cherrywood coffin built to his own specifications, kept it under his bed and after Rebecca's death in 1813 began spending time by the firesides of his children and grandchildren. He busied himself with scraping powder horns. For the fall hunt, he would say. Having once read *Gulliver's Travels* to his companions of the forest, he now urged others to read aloud from Filson's "Adventures of Col. Daniel Boon." He was delighted to hear himself being credited with the work's appallingly ornate prose and would say, wagging his head: "Every word true! Not a lie in it!" The last of his debts were paid and he felt "relieved from a burden that has long oppressed me. No one will say, 'Boone was a dishonest man.' I am perfectly willing to die."

The old fellow fell ill while visiting his daughter Jemima in the autumn of 1820—he was now 85—and was put to bed. But he shortly announced that he felt better, got up, dressed, mounted his horse Old Roan, and rode off to see his son Nathan. He soon took a turn for the worse, however, and was put back under covers again—for good. He "passed off gently" three days later, was placed in the custom-built coffin that he had kept waiting and was buried on a knoll overlooking the Missouri River. He stayed there for 25 years. The people of Kentucky, having driven him out, then came for him at last. They dug up his bones, took them back to Frankfort, gave him a military funeral and buried him beside his Rebecca in the earth he had come over the Gap to find so many years before.

Boone and a warrior grapple in a classic stance, while his wife cradles her child like a backwoods Madonna in this lithograph of an imaginary frontier struggle. By 1874, the year this picture appeared, Boone's legend had assumed mythical stature.

3 | A ritual of death by fire

In the summer of 1782, General George Washington told his army that "no person, should at this Time, suffer himself to fall alive into the Hands of the Indians." The suggestion was prompted by news of the horrifying fate that had befallen Colonel William Crawford, captured by Delaware Indians thirsting for revenge after the massacre of a number of their people.

As the scene at right (reconstructed years later) shows, Crawford wound up tethered to a stake inside a ring of fire, pelted with embers and jabbed with red-hot poles by tormentors who had already torn off his ears and scorched every part of his body with gunpowder fired at point-blank range. A second captive, Dr. John Knight *(lower right corner),* was also marked for death—with charcoal-blackened face—but escaped to recount the awful tale.

Crawford could at least be thankful that the Delawares despised him. The more the woodland Indians respected an enemy, the more mercilessly they tortured him. A great warrior put to the stake would die only after enduring agonies more terrible than Crawford's, suffering it all with apparent relish, even asking for more.

Death by torture was a ritual contest in which the victim's manhood was the prize. He could keep it—win the game—by proving, as one scholar wrote, that "his courage was equal to any trial, and above the power of death itself." Adversaries took these roles so seriously that Indians who shaved their heads left one tuft of hair for the scalping convenience of a victorious foe.

Small wonder that the whites who encountered these fierce frontier tribal groups considered them unspeakably barbarous and viewed their philosophies as utterly beyond comprehension.

Delaware tribesmen burn a Revolutionary officer—Colonel William Crawford—in Ohio

in 1782. To the Indians an execution was a festive event, and the fire was arranged so as to keep the victim alive as long as possible.

Artful and disciplined warriors of the woods

I have often heard British officers call the Indians undisciplined savages," wrote James Smith, a Pennsylvania border soldier who spent five years, in the 1750s, as the captive of a warlike tribe in Ohio. "But this is a capital mistake; they have all the essentials of discipline—they are under good command, punctual in obeying orders: (there is no such thing as corporal punishment used) they can act in concert by each man observing the motion or movement of his right hand companion. They can perform various necessary manoeuvres, either slowly, or as fast as they can run: form a circle or a semi-circle; also a hollow square. When they go into battle, they are not loaded or incumbered with many clothes, they commonly fight naked, save only the breech-clout, leggins and mockasons. They are commonly well equipped, and exceedingly active and expert in the use of arms.

"Their officers plan, order and conduct matters until they are brought into action, they will cheerfully unite in putting all directions into immediate execution. General orders are commonly given in the time of battle, either to advance or retreat, and this is done by a shout or yell and then each man is to fight as if he were to gain the battle himself. Indians do not regard the number of white men against them. If they can only get them in a huddle, they will fight them ten to one."

Smith observed that the Indians "are very artful in spying" and that even the ever-present dogs around frontier settlements rarely posed a problem. The Indians told him that their scouts simply waited until the wind blew so the dogs could not smell them, then slipped up to the windows and peeped in to count the people by the fireside. "When an army is on the way against them," continued Smith, "they take every method possible to discover their numbers, their mode of marching, encampments, etc. They send out their most active runners as spies, who will, when the wind is high, that the centinels cannot hear them crawling, slip past and view the camp. If they find the enemy encamp on a small piece of ground, and in close order, it greatly encourages them to make an attack; because if they can suddenly rush in around them, and get behind trees, they have frequently killed twenty to one."

In General Edward Braddock's awful defeat in 1755, recounted Smith, the ratio of British-to-Indian dead rose to an almost incredible 100 to 1. When the shattered army finally regrouped, the British listed 700 men missing, but from the best information Smith could get, only seven Indians had been killed.

"Could it be supposed," wrote Smith, "that undisciplined savages could defeat Braddock, etc., etc. Let us now take a view of the blood and treasure that was spent in opposing comparatively a few Indian Warriors, in addition to the amazing destruction and slaughter that the frontiers sustained in being laid waist from Round-Oak to Susquehanna and about thirty miles broad. I apprehend we are far behind them in their manoeuvres, or in being able to surprise, or prevent a surprise."

The Indians were ordinarily quick to retreat whenever the battle turned against them—"they will not stand cutting like the Highlanders or other British troops," Smith commented—but this was because of the tactics they favored rather than the slightest cowardice. Indeed, if trapped with no alternative except surrender, the Indians would often fight valiantly to the death. "When Col. Armstrong surrounded the Cattanyantown, Capt. Jacobs a Delaware chief with some warriors took possession of a house and was called on

An Iroquois warrior brandishes his war club, fashioned with a menacing knob at the end, in this 1787 engraving. The decorations festooning his rifle muzzle are scalps.

75

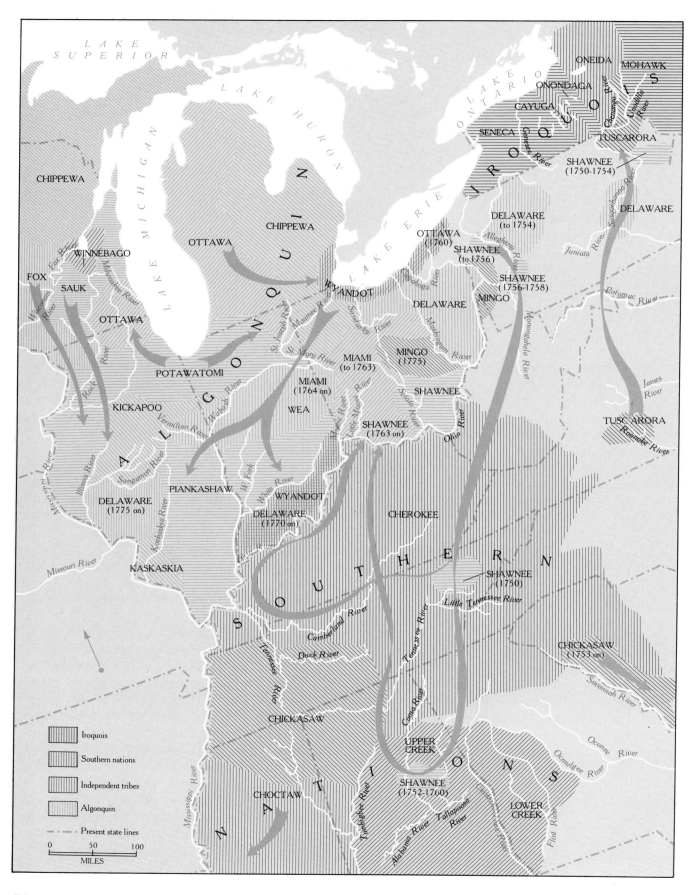

LAKE SUPERIOR

LAKE HURON

LAKE ONTARIO

LAKE MICHIGAN

LAKE ERIE

CHIPPEWA

ONEIDA

MOHAWK

ONONDAGA

CAYUGA

SENECA

Genesee River

I R O Q U O I S

Chemung River

Unadilla River

TUSCARORA

SHAWNEE
(1750-1754)

DELAWARE

CHIPPEWA

OTTAWA

A L G O N Q U I N

WYANDOT

OTTAWA
(1760)

DELAWARE
(to 1754)

Allegheny River

Susquehanna River

DELAWARE

WINNEBAGO

Fox River

Milwaukee River

SHAWNEE
(to 1756)

SHAWNEE
(1756-1758)

Juniata River

FOX

SAUK

Wisconsin River

OTTAWA

St. Joseph River

St. Mary River

Sandusky Rd.

MIAMI
(to 1763)

MINGO
(1775)

DELAWARE

MINGO

Potomac River

Muskingum River

Monongahela River

POTAWATOMI

Rock River

MIAMI
(1764 on)

WEA

Wabash River

Miami River

Little Miami River

SHAWNEE

Scioto River

James River

KICKAPOO

Vermillion River

Sangamon River

Illinois River

W. Fork

White River

SHAWNEE
(1763 on)

Ohio River

TUSCARORA

Roanoke River

Mississippi River

PIANKASHAW

WYANDOT

DELAWARE
(1775 on)

Kaskaskia River

DELAWARE
(1770 on)

Green River

CHEROKEE

SHAWNEE
(1750)

KASKASKIA

Missouri River

S O U T H E R N

Cumberland River

Little Tennessee River

CHICKASAW
(1753 on)

Savannah River

Duck River

Tennessee River

Tennessee River

CHICKASAW

Coosa River

N A T I O N S

UPPER
CREEK

Oconee River

Ocmulgee River

CHOCTAW

Tombigbee River

SHAWNEE
(1752-1760)

Alabama River

Tallapoosa River

LOWER
CREEK

Flint River

Chattahoochee River

Iroquois

Southern nations

Independent tribes

Algonquin

Present state lines

0   50   100
MILES

to surrender; that they should be well used, and if not the house should be burned down over their heads. As Capt. Jacobs could speak English, he said that he and his men were warriors, and he could eat fire; & when the house was in a flame, he and they that were with him came out in a fighting position and were all killed."

Smith, who later served as a colonel in the militia during the Revolutionary War, noted that Virginia riflemen had managed to fight Indians "one whole day at the mouth of the Great Kanawha" in 1774 and that small parties of Kentuckians "were equal to any Indians for a wood fight." He published his *Treatise on the Mode and Manner of Indian War, Their Tactics, Discipline and Encampments* to suggest that American Regulars, too, would benefit from using the tribesmen's hit-and-run methods of guerrilla combat in the new conflict with England.

Smith's memoir and journals implied a great many larger truths about these woodland people: they were far shrewder, far more sophisticated and far more admirable as human beings than most backwoodsmen ever acknowledged. Smith also sensed something else: Indian culture was so alien to that of Europeans and

---

DOMAIN OF THE FOREST DWELLERS, 1750-1775

In the mid-18th Century, the land between the Appalachians and the Mississippi was already populated by many tribes of forest Indians in three major groupings: the Iroquois, the Algonquins and the Southern nations. Though they roamed widely to hunt, the Indians lived in permanent villages, usually near rivers where they farmed the bottom land. Since tribal boundaries were fluid, the major areas of settlement *(left)* often overlapped and tribes peacefully shared hunting grounds.

But land became more precious as the first thrust of white settlement uprooted some of the easterly tribes. The Tuscaroras fled north to become the sixth nation in the Iroquois League. Delawares, crowded out of eastern Pennsylvania, migrated steadily westward. Bands of Shawnees wandered for 1,000 miles before falling heir to land north of the Ohio River abandoned by Miamis. Tribes farther west, still little touched by the advancing frontier, were expanding their territories. Only the southern Chickasaws moved east to be nearer the white men and their trading posts. The arrows trace these movements, and the dates indicate when they occurred.

their values so weighted by a belief in magic, personal glory and the worth of other forest creatures that they would become the inevitable victims — since they could not be conquerors — of white civilization.

British and American Indian policy underwent innumerable changes, produced innumerable truces and moved spokesmen for both races to innumerable sonorous protestations of peace during the first two centuries of white settlement in the New World. Whites and Indians were locked in an uneasy state of interdependence from the beginning. The Iroquois were so useful a bulwark for the colonies against the French in Canada that Queen Anne entertained four of their chieftains in London during the early 1700s. And the Mohawk Joseph Brant made himself so ferocious an ally of the Crown during the Revolution that he was later courted socially by the Prince of Wales.

Indians were so deeply drawn into the fur trade, meanwhile, as to exercise a kind of economic leverage — at least by proxy — in France and England as well as in Canada and the colonies. They became such heavy consumers of blankets, knives, guns and rum, which they received as trappers and mercenary soldiers of both countries, that they made themselves forever dependent on the white intruders from Europe.

Withal, the Indians remained a fighting race that subordinated every aspect of existence to a quest for ascendancy and eminence in war. And the whites never ceased to lust for the lands these warriors coursed and guarded, as George Washington put it, "like wolves — both being beasts of prey." Both sides agreed in their souls with the summation of this dilemma by an early royal governor of Virginia: "Either we must cleere them or they us out oft the country."

Indians believed, for a long time, that they were capable of doing the "cleereing" — at least west of the Appalachians. They were far more difficult foes than the hapless Aztecs and Incas — or the equally hapless natives of Africa. Forest Indians of the Eastern tribal confederations were as deeply steeped in tradition as the white colonizers, were as fully conscious of worth as any Englishman or Frenchman, found the foe as outlandish in many of his habits as the foe found them and were so successful at border warfare during the half century after Braddock's terrible defeat in 1755 that

Four Iroquois who were lionized in London

JOHN (WOLF CLAN)

HENDRICK (WOLF CLAN)

"They feed heartily, and love our *English* Beef before all other Victuals that are provided for 'em. They seem to relish our fine pale Ales before the best *French* Wines. They are not afflicted with Gout, Dropsy or Gravel; and notwithstanding their Intemperance here, they are not feverish upon any occasion, or troubl'd with Loss of Appetite."

The hale specimens thus described by a London observer were four Iro-quois chiefs brought to England by colonial officers in 1710 to meet Queen Anne. England and France, at war in North America, were constantly devising schemes to win the fealty of the ferocious Iroquois. And now the colonists hoped to cement an alliance by exposing the sachems, as they put it, to "as much of the Grandure and Magnificence of Brittan as possible." Moreover, a demonstration of Indian loyalty might help persuade Queen Anne to open the royal treasury and provide additional ships and troops to a proposed invasion of French Canada by colonial forces.

Well primed by their mentors, the Iroquois chiefs made the official request for assistance at an audience with the Queen, and as evidence of their unswerving loyalty, they then proceeded to ask her for Christian instruction — a boon she immediately granted by calling upon the Society

BRANT (BEAR CLAN)   NICHOLAS (TORTOISE CLAN)

for the Propagation of the Gospel in Foreign Parts.

Meantime, she entertained her noble guests with a royal tour of London, including the opera, a Punch-and-Judy show, bear-baiting and cock-fighting exhibitions as well as a gala round of receptions and banquets.

Gawkers followed the Indians everywhere, and the audience at the Haymarket held up a performance of *Macbeth* until they were made visi-

ble, in seats on stage. The Queen even commissioned Dutch artist John Verelst to paint their portraits *(above)* for her personal collection.

Through it all, the chiefs were said to exhibit "exquisite Sense and a quick Apprehension," but their specific comments were not recorded.

In any case, their visit served its purposes. The fleet that brought them home included a number of vessels manned by British marines, who on

arrival helped capture the French colony of Acadia, soon renamed Nova Scotia. The chiefs were impressed enough to remain allies for the rest of what became known as Queen Anne's War.

But hopes of their conversion to Christianity were doomed. Once home, a writer later lamented, "they sunk themselves into their old brutal Life, and tho' they had seen this great City they were all Savages again."

they fought with confidence in spite of a continuous and obvious increase in the number of white settlements on the frontier.

The tribes of forest Indians were grouped in three distinct regions of wilderness between the Appalachians and the Mississippi River. The Six Nations of the Iroquois occupied the area below Lakes Ontario and Erie in northern New York and Pennsylvania. The somewhat looser array of Algonquin people occupied land from Tennessee and Virginia in the South to Canada in the North. And the Appalachian confederacy of five Southern Indian tribes spread across North and South Carolina, Tennessee, northern Georgia, Alabama, Mississippi and Florida. All three of these groups tilled the soil and inhabited permanent villages, and two in particular—the Iroquois and the five Southern tribes—enjoyed civilizations far more complex than those ever achieved by the horse Indians of the Great Plains.

The Iroquois tribes (Mohawks, Oneidas, Onondagas, Cayugas, Senecas and Tuscaroras) lived in villages with populations ranging from a few hundred to more than a thousand. The central feature of these villages was the long house—a single-story building as much as 100 feet in length, sealed externally with elm bark and containing public corridors (where the occupants used a common cooking fire) and separate apartments for up to 20 families. The Iroquois towns were protected with high stockades of up-ended logs and were surrounded by fields where communal crops were grown. The Southern nations (Creeks, Cherokees, Choctaws and Chickasaws, which eventually became allied with a conglomeration of broken tribes called Seminoles) also constructed stockaded towns. They lived in wooden frame dwellings covered with thatch, which were usually grouped around a larger central temple or council house.

The Algonquins (Shawnees, Delawares, Miamis, Potawatomies, Ottawas and several related tribes) existed, for the most part, in flimsier tipi-like structures with outer shells of hide, matting or bark, but they sometimes built log cabins as well.

Most of the Indians were better agriculturists, by far, than the frontiersmen who invaded their hunting grounds. The Iroquois hybridized corn and grew more than a dozen varieties. They planted five kinds of

Algonquin villages north of the Ohio River consisted of crude conical tipis covered with overlapped segments of bark or hide, rarely stitched together and easily dismantled. A loose flap served as a doorway.

The most sophisticated of the woodland Indian dwellings, the Iroquois long house held as many as 20 families in apartments ranged along a central corridor. A matriarch ruled each long house and the occupants were all related on the female side.

The Creeks of Alabama and Georgia readily assimilated the log cabin construction of white frontiersmen. The single-family dwelling featured a low-eaved roof made of split wood slabs and an external chimney of logs sealed by clay mixed with moss.

Dead and dying animals litter the forest floor near Hinkley, in present-day Ohio, as settlers stage a glorious hunt in 1818. The slaughter, ostensibly to remove dangerous beasts, included 17 wolves and 21 bears, plus pheasants, turkeys and 300 deer.

squash and more than 10 varieties of beans. They burned or turned under the dead stalks and vines in the autumn to renew the earth, and augmented their crops, as did all the woodland people, with scores of varieties of roots, nuts and fruits from the forests. The Southern Indians farmed tobacco, rice, melons and sunflowers as well as the maize, squash and beans of the North.

The Cherokees learned quickly, on contact with whites, to import and breed cattle, horses, poultry and swine. And the Creeks put aside tracts of land rich in haws, persimmons and chestnuts as "beloved bear grounds" ("beloved" being a word they used for anything admirable) where ursine populations could feed and propagate without molestation until harvested by

tribal decree. The Creeks divided themselves socially between "red towns," or "red sticks," devoted to war, and "white towns," or "white sticks," devoted to peace. But all celebrated the ripening of crops with the Green Corn Dance, during which they extinguished and relighted their fires, downed a bitter "Black Drink" (brewed from leaves of special shrubs) and declared their personal quarrels at an end.

The Algonquins grew pumpkins, peas and watermelons as well as the standard maize. Those near the shores of Lakes Erie and Huron, reported a French soldier at Michilimackinac, enjoyed "the great abundance of fish" that "is daily manna that never fails"— whitefish, trout, sturgeon and pike, and all from "the purest water, the clearest and most pellucid you could see anywhere."

Almost all woodland tribes believed in life after death, for animals as well as themselves, though not in the "Happy Hunting Ground" furnished them by white romantics. And they were far more rigorously involved in moral and religious taboos and beliefs than most white men on the frontier. Many Algonquin tribes believed that the world was created by a magic Great Rabbit—a rather slippery fellow who overcame opposition by trickery and deception. But, like other Indians, they also allied themselves spiritually with purer and more personal deities (the sun, a tree, an animal) and sought counsel from them in dreams or in periods of hallucination induced by fasting. Whites often felt that Indian priests or medicine men were shameless charlatans, but many were rude medical botanists of some accomplishment and, beyond that, seemed as convinced as their followers that they had the ability to communicate with spirits and thus influence events. Almost all Indians believed in a mysterious, supernatural overforce (*Orenda* to the Iroquois) by which every man's soul mingled with those of all animals and plants in existence.

Indians were outraged again and again, because of this sense of symmetry in nature, by the slaughter of forest animals that inevitably followed heavy white settlement on the advancing frontier. This seems to have been true even of those who aped the white man and harvested beaver pelts and deer hides to satisfy their newborn lust for trade goods. None forgot that when they were left to their own devices they killed only what game they needed. All felt spiritually akin and grateful to the animals they felled. And because they had always lived in enormous, empty forest spaces before the white invasion, they conceived of ecological balance as the natural, even sacred way of things on earth.

The Pennsylvania tribes were provoked to bitter retaliatory ambushes after a rare backwoods lout named Black Jack Schwartz, "the wild hunter of the Juniata," staged a grand animal drive at West Mahantango Creek in about 1760. The "wild hunter" and a group of kindred spirits who called themselves the Panther Boys killed 109 wolves, 112 foxes, 41 panthers, 114 mountain cats, 17 black bears, 1 white bear, 198 deer, 111 buffalo and more than 500 smaller animals, and then—after laboriously piling timber over this mountain of flesh—set the whole vast heap afire to celebrate their prowess. Schwartz was an unusual sort of maniac, even for the frontier, and local whites were almost as enraged as the Indians—though only because the smouldering pyre stank so horribly for so long thereafter. But he reflected the white view of game—it existed to be killed—and, by implication, the European concept of personal property, which separated the races in such irreconcilable fashion as the frontier moved ever westward.

Formal ownership of land was a completely foreign concept to the Indians. They believed that land was there to be shared by all. This is not to say that powerful tribes like those of the Iroquois did not hold sway at times over large areas, but this was control by force of arms—the kind of influence a country with a big fleet might exercise over the oceans. But the land titles so coveted by speculators were beyond the Indians' comprehension. As time passed, certain chiefs were wily enough or were eventually so browbeaten as to convey great areas of wilderness they did not own in return for guns, blankets, hatchets and mirrors.

Such agreements and treaties tended to be sources of friction rather than of amity. Whites broke the pacts almost as a matter of course as the inexorable pressure of settlement made them obsolete. And Indians who made themselves party to these agreements did not own the land in question (as other tribes continually complained) and seldom had any real right to speak for their fellows (as competing chiefs were loud to announce) in the first place.

Indians were so outnumbered by white expansion to the Mississippi that they were doomed, no matter what the circumstances. But the process was accelerated because they were widely incapable of sustaining large-scale organization. A few charismatic chieftains attracted large followings, at times, by wit, eloquence and reputation but almost always for temporary military adventure. Broad intertribal cooperation, even in war, was more often than not the work of whites—French or British planners who bought such alliances with trade goods. Indian society rested most strongly on families and clans; real loyalties were usually confined within these blood relationships, and Indians had

A world of meaning in bits of seashell

Ceremonial wampum was not the "Indian money" of popular imagination. It is true that early English and Dutch colonists used wampum beads as a substitute for currency, which was always in short supply, and Indians later followed their example. But originally the Indians attached far too much importance to the spiritual power of these white and purple bits of shell to use them as objects of barter.

They would "do anything and part with everything they possess" in order to obtain wampum, according to an 18th Century account. They preserved it and made it into strings and belts that symbolized their laws and tribal history. Most wampum beads were acquired by trade with coastal tribes, which fashioned white beads

from portions of whelk shells and the more precious purple beads from the violet spot on certain clam shells. Bits of shell were worked into tiny cylinders and bored through with stone or metal awls. Some beads were painted with red ocher. Individual strands could be used separately or combined into belts, which were often of elaborate design.

Wampum played an especially vital role in the ceremonies of the Iroquois League; the Six Nations used it as a means of diplomacy and communication. The Onondagas, for example, sent belts to Senecas, Mohawks, Cayugas and Oneidas inviting them to council meetings and indicating the topic to be debated. Each color had symbolic meaning: white stood for peace, purple for grief or condolence,

red for war. The design on a wampum belt conveyed a message as well: an oval figure might be the tribal council fire, a white line a path, a row of diamonds the chain of friendship.

Belts were used to ransom captured warriors, install chiefs, declare war or ratify treaties. Wampum was the Iroquois equivalent of the court Bible: "What Indians say with hand upon the wampum belt is true," a chief told a white chronicler.

Lacking a written language, Iroquois statesmen used wampum to refresh their memory and sharpen their eloquence. Belts eventually passed into the hands of "Keepers of the Wampum," living libraries who could recite the meaning of each of their belts. As each of these sachems died, bits of Iroquois history died with him.

At an Iroquois council, the presiding chief displays a wampum belt, also seen close up in the foreground of this contemporary print.

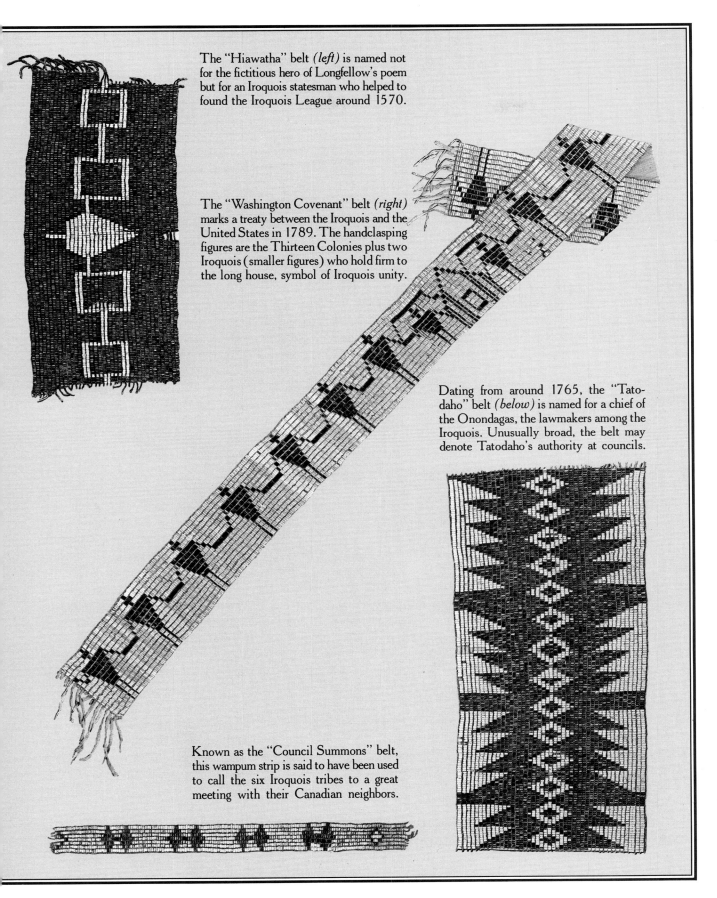

The "Hiawatha" belt *(left)* is named not for the fictitious hero of Longfellow's poem but for an Iroquois statesman who helped to found the Iroquois League around 1570.

The "Washington Covenant" belt *(right)* marks a treaty between the Iroquois and the United States in 1789. The handclasping figures are the Thirteen Colonies plus two Iroquois (smaller figures) who hold firm to the long house, symbol of Iroquois unity.

Dating from around 1765, the "Tatodaho" belt *(below)* is named for a chief of the Onondagas, the lawmakers among the Iroquois. Unusually broad, the belt may denote Tatodaho's authority at councils.

Known as the "Council Summons" belt, this wampum strip is said to have been used to call the six Iroquois tribes to a great meeting with their Canadian neighbors.

no duty to obey a chieftain unless they felt moved in spirit to do so.

Almost alone among the Indian nations, the Iroquois achieved a measure of unity and employed it with devastating effect in dealing with whites through the 17th and 18th centuries. The Iroquois used their geographical position and their ferocity as warriors to play the French and British off against each other with astonishing arrogance and certainty. While they, too, were organized into clans, they were able to accomplish a measure of solidarity through a sort of democratic consensus that rewarded ability by raising up leaders regardless of birth and background who were known as Pine Tree chiefs. The Iroquois were relentless and murderous fighters—and they terrorized all other forest peoples for a century. They compensated for their terrible losses in men, as did the Romans, by adopting their prisoners and making these outlanders Iroquois, too.

They dealt with Europeans from a posture of armed neutrality, and though generally favoring the British, they bargained "only with those who seem to us good" and resisted both threat and blandishment with haughty dignity. Emissary after emissary, both French and British, "cursed and raged" at the implacable independence—and guile—of these people, whom one outraged Jesuit defined as "those subtle, adroit and arrant knaves." There were few chieftains of any sort, including leaders of the most hapless tribal remnants later on, who did not display some of this instinct for intrigue and who were not—since their positions often depended on it—political orators with a wonderful grasp of metaphor and symbolism. Whites, it is fascinating to recall, were almost always moved while dickering with the Indians to accept and imitate Indian ceremonial while doing so.

But war was the real Indian response to the white frontier—war and the hideous tortures that accompanied it and that moved so many backwoodsmen to retaliatory excesses of their own when they found the opportunity for revenge.

There was never an accurate count of the Indians who existed east of the Mississippi in the early 18th Century. At the time the whites reckoned their numbers in scores upon scores of thousands. But there almost certainly were far fewer: perhaps 10,000 Iroquois, possibly 20,000 to 30,000 Southern Indians and a like number in the Algonquin tribes. It is doubtful, moreover, that any of the three groups ever boasted more than 3,000 full-fledged warriors. No such numbers ever marched as one army—no more than a thousand warriors of allied tribes ever fought in concert, and then only on the rarest of occasions. Most of the Indians' successes on the frontier were accomplished by war parties of fewer than 100 men. But these bands "approach like foxes, fight like lions and disappear like birds," as one Frenchman put it. They were seldom bested by the canniest of frontier militiamen and toyed with Regulars on most occasions.

The white man fought in the New World as he had fought in Europe—for land and, incidentally, to protect himself and his people after establishing himself upon it. He believed in meeting an enemy face to face and in enduring losses if necessary to wear down the foe and to achieve final victory—ideas that died hard even after he adopted Indian tricks in forest warfare. Such concepts seemed idiotic to Indians, who hunted men as slyly as they hunted animals, fought not for possessions but for personal glory, on which their very acceptance in society depended, and—by their savage code—for the opportunity to demean and mutilate an enemy, and thus to wreak vengeance for the loss of kinsmen. The idea of dying for a cause was as utterly alien to the Indian (although he was prepared to die in demonstration of his bravery) as was the idea of risking death if outnumbered and in danger of defeat rather than disappearing to fight another day.

Every war party hoped to achieve total surprise, to slaughter men, women and children caught thus unawares, to seize captives for torture or concubinage and to melt away into the forest to avoid retaliation by the infuriated enemy. They retreated as artfully as they attacked and tomahawked captives who were unable to keep a proper headlong pace. The captured white or enemy warrior had to expect torture after pursuit had died down or display as an entertaining exhibit after the party's triumphal return to its home village.

There are few clues to the incorporation of torture in the culture of American Indians. Some authorities suspect it may have sprung from the Aztecs' rites of human sacrifice and speculate that the ritual may have spread slowly north through the ages (like the cultivation of maize), shedding its religious overtones along the way. One can argue as to whether it proved the Indian more barbaric than the instigators of the Spanish Inquisition—or a crowd of Dutchmen who flayed an Indian alive in New Amsterdam in 1643 while the Dutch governor "laughed right heartily." Torture of the foe was accepted without question by most Indians—victim as well as victor—as a means of revenge and an expression of triumph after battle.

Torture was not, at least in theory, a completely one-sided process, for the helpless warrior took enormous pride in taunting his captors until he died. Selection of victims varied, but many tribes left the choice up to women, who could accept the captive as a replacement for a relative lost in war or—as was usually the case—order him to the stake. Women were often allowed to act as torturers as well and took particular delight in the successive removal of finger joints and hideously painful attention to genitals. Warriors sometimes brought such rites to a conclusion by lifting up a small boy and urging him, amid applause, to dash the victim's brains with a tomahawk.

The memoirs of Antoine de la Mothe Cadillac, a French lieutenant who was commandant of the French post at Michilimackinac near Lake Huron in the late 17th Century, suggest that both martyr and inquisitor thought such grisly ceremonial to be the most dramatic theater. "First the women caress them and take them to their cabins. They anoint them and give them food, urging them to conserve strength to suffer the longer and more courageously. Suddenly their feminine sweetness changes into despair and diabolical fury; and this is the way the woman who has demanded a prisoner's death informs him of the fate that awaits him. She calls upon the shade of her husband or son, who has been killed or burned, and speaks:

" 'Come hither my son; today I have a feast of fresh meat for you; accept this sacrifice I am making of this brave warrior. Rejoice, my dear son, he will be roasted and his genitals will be torn out; we will drink from his skull, we will tear off his scalp.' One of the warriors now enters and says, 'Take courage, my brother. You are to be burned.' The other replies: 'All right and thanks for the news you bring me.' At the same moment a horrible cry is raised throughout the village.

This cry is called a *Sakakua*. They seize him, take him away and fasten him to the stake. These sinister preparations, which should make the man shudder, only serve, however, as a means of showing his scorn for his tyrants. He chants his death song in a bold voice, recounting all the warlike deeds he has done during his life and the manner in which he has burned his prisoners, encouraging those around him not to spare him, and to put him to death like a warrior. I do not think that all this talk is entirely sincere; it is certain, however, that his gaze is steadfast and countenance tranquil.

"But it is time to open the ball and see how the chief actors are made to dance. The first step the prisoners are put through is tearing the nails from their hands, one after another, with the teeth. They then put the victim's fingers in the bowl of the pipe and thus smoke the ten fingers, one after another. After this little feast, five or six workers take up burning firebrands; they apply them to his ankles, wrists, and temples, and do not take them away until nerves and flesh are burned to the bone. The third is a necklace of glowing hatchets, made red hot in the fire over the shoulders. Each of them cuts off a piece of the buttocks with his knife, which he broils and eats without any seasoning. The women have kettles of boiling water ready, which they pour over these wounds. From time to time they pierce his neck and armpits with red-hot irons. They burn his genitals with birch-bark, which gives a very hot and penetrating flame.

"It might also be thought that anyone tortured in this way must shed tears or utter pitiful cries. But most of them taunt their tormentors, calling them cowards and women who lack the courage to cut them up into bits; and if any part of them has escaped being burned, they point it out themselves and speak to them like this: 'if you are ever taken prisoner by my tribe and are burned in my village, do not weep or cry out: a true warrior should die as I do.' Last of all they take off his scalp and throw hot ashes and sand upon the raw and bleeding flesh, and cut off his head, while all the village resounds with shouts of joy and delight, as if they had won a great victory. Whoever reads this short description may perhaps have difficulty in believing that anyone can bear such suffering without dying—they do not leave him a nerve or an artery which has not been subjected to the fire or the knife—but it is absolutely true. This terrible practice is especially common with the Iroquois, who burn their slaves by inches for four or five days on end."

White men who came to know Indians intimately were uniformly astonished after witnessing such grisly scenes at the warmth, even nobility, the same ferocious people could reflect, at times, in relations with those of their own blood.

Few were as privy to this side of the Indians' character as James Smith, the Pennsylvania border soldier who spent five years among the Indians as a captive. Smith was taken prisoner by tribesmen allied with the French while he was working on a road being constructed as an adjunct to Braddock's ill-fated advance in 1755. After his capture he was beaten savagely while running the gantlet and was taken to Fort Du-

quesne, where a French army physician tended to his injuries. The Indians permitted him to watch from a wall of the fort as the first of a dozen men from the broken British army was burned to death on the opposite side of the Allegheny River. Smith, who had every reason to fear for his own life, was appalled at the torture of the captured soldier as "they had him tied to a stake, and kept touching him with red hot irons etc. and he screaming in a most doleful manner!" But for some inexplicable reason the Pennsylvanian's life was spared. Instead of being killed, he was taken to a town on the Scioto River and made a member of the warlike Caughnawagas, an Iroquois people who had migrated west to Ohio.

At his initiation into the tribe, his captors plucked out most of his hair, pushed him into a river where a group of women scrubbed him as if to remove his

Pontiac's rebellion: resistance by a majestic chief

At the end of hostilities in the French and Indian Wars in 1760, Major Robert Rogers was sent to take formal British possession of France's wilderness forts beyond the Alleghenies. Rogers, a noted backwoods fighter, was unawed by what he found on the frontier, but years later he wrote admiringly of Pontiac, the Ottawa chief he had met on the trip.

The major may have sensed then, behind the chief's "air of majesty and princely grandeur," the fires that made him, three years later, the instigator of the most formidable Indian resistance the British ever faced—a rebellion that saw the fall of all but three of the dozen forts that the British had taken from the French.

Scarcely had Rogers raised the Union Jack above these Western outposts when the rigid and disdainful conduct of other British officers began

to grate on the region's tribes, accustomed to the free and easy French. By the spring of 1763, British arrogance had reached such a point that Pontiac found it intolerable; in late April he sent runners to arouse the tribes to lift the hatchet against the intruders.

Pontiac himself laid plans to strike at heavily garrisoned Fort Detroit. He proposed to enter the stockade for talks, with his warriors carrying guns and hatchets under their blankets. At Pontiac's signal, they were to attack.

Legend has it that on the eve of the assault a young Chippewa woman named Catherine learned of the plot and warned the man she loved—the fort's commander, Major Henry Gladwin. By whatever means, Gladwin was certainly wise to the ruse, for when the Indians entered the stockade, Pontiac found the garrison on full alert. Enraged, the chief stormed out

without giving the signal. He sent for Catherine and beat her almost to death. Two days later he returned and laid siege to the fort.

Other rebellious bands overran nine British outposts from the Allegheny River to Lake Michigan, so alarming Sir Jeffery Amherst, the British commander, that he offered £200 for Pontiac's scalp. He even suggested to an aide that it might "be contrived to send the small pox among the disaffected tribes."

But by autumn, the rebellion began to wane. Pontiac's siege crumbled as warriors left for the winter hunt, and the British retook their lost forts. Pontiac acknowledged King George as his "father" and retired to Illinois. In 1769 he was murdered by a Peoria tribesman though to have been incited by the British, who still feared the aging chief's seditious charisma.

skin—to wash out his white blood they said—and "bored my nose and ears" for the insertion of rings. Having done so, and having dressed him in an elaborate fashion, they "seated me on a bear skin, & gave me a pipe, & tomahawk," gathered around in "profound silence" and directed an interpreter to translate a speech by one of their chiefs: " 'My son, you are now flesh of our flesh, you have nothing to fear, we are now under the same obligations to love, support and defend you, that we are to love, support and defend one another.' At this time I did not believe this fine speech, but since that time I found there was much sincerity in said speech. If they had plenty of clothing etc. I had plenty, if we were scarce we all shared one fate."

Smith experienced something akin to awe at the wisdom and character of an old chief named Tecaughretanego. He "was no common person, but was among the Indians, as Socrates in the ancient heathen world; & it may be, equal to him—if not in wisdom and learning yet perhaps in patience and fortitude." The old chief was crippled by rheumatism in the winter of 1758 and won Smith's lifelong admiration by the dignity and unselfishness with which he endured starvation during a period when no game could be found.

Tecaughretanego believed humans were subject to control by the Great Spirit and gave an inspiring lecture on his faith when Smith returned "faint and weary" from an unsuccessful hunting trip. Tecaughretanego "commanded Nunganey his little son to bring me something to eat, & he brought me a kettle with some bones & broth. I speedily finished my allowance, such as it was, and when I had ended my sweet repast, Tecaughretanego asked me how I felt? I told him that I was much refreshed. He then said he had something of im-

Major Robert Rogers, the British forest fighter, extends his hand to Pontiac after the French and Indian Wars. Rogers later wrote that the Ottawa chief "was far from considering himself as a conquered Prince."

portance to tell me. He said that he had deferred his speech because few men are in a right humor to hear good talk, when they are extremely hungry, as they are then commonly fretful, but as you appear now to enjoy serenity of mind, I will now communicate to you the thoughts of my heart: *'Brother,'* he said, 'I have been young and now am old. *Owaneeyo* sometimes suffers us to be in want, in order to teach us our dependence upon him. Be assured that you will be supplied with food—be strong and exert yourself like a man and the great spirit will direct your way.' "

Smith decided to "run off to Pennsylvania my native country" the next morning instead. "I had but a poor prospect of making my escape: but my case appeared desperate. If I stayed here I thought I would perish with hunger, and if I met with Indians they could but kill me." He found buffalo tracks after 10 or 12 miles of plunging through the snow, was able to kill "a very large cow," and after eating some meat "almost raw ... began to be tenderly concerned for my old Indian brother and the little boy I left in a perishing condition. I made haste and packed up what meat I could carry. As it was moon light, I got home to our hut, and found the old man in his usual good humor. He thanked me and bid me sit down, as I must certainly be fatigued. I immediately hung on the kettle with some water, and cut the beef into thin slices, and put them in:—and when it had boiled a while, I proposed taking it off the fire, but the old man replied, 'let it be done enough'; this he said in as patient and unconcerned a manner, as if he had not wanted a single meal. He commanded Nunganey to eat no more raw beef at that time; but told him to sit down, and after some time he might sup some broth.

"When we were all refreshed, Tecaughretanego delivered a speech upon the necessity and pleasure of receiving the necessary supports of life with thankfulness, knowing that *Owaneeyo* is the great Giver. Such speeches from an Indian, may be thought incredible; but when we reflect on the Indian war, we may conclude that they are not an ignorant or stupid people, or they would not have been such fatal enemies."

Tecaughretanego was not alone among old chieftains with patience and judiciousness. There were a good many, indeed, who were admired for leadership in war but still came to feel that continued conflict with settlers was shortsighted or who tried, out of a sense of honor, to abide by the terms of truces forced upon them by circumstance. They could seldom, however, control hotheads among their own tribes who felt bound in their deepest beings by the traditions of their warrior-ancestors and sensed—correctly—that war was the only logical response to intruders bent on driving them from their hunting lands. Peacemakers usually came upon evil days as a result, since frontiersmen, who had seen the bodies of pregnant women slit open by war parties and the fetuses of unborn babies left impaled on poles beside them, were not inclined to consider the political attitudes of any Indian if granted an opportunity for revenge.

The Shawnee chieftain Cornstalk (as whites translated Keigh-tugh-qua) doomed himself when he opted for peace after leading Algonquin warriors against a large force of frontier militia in Lord Dunmore's War, a forest campaign that was instigated, in 1774, by the royal governor of Virginia to open the way for settlement. The war's one clash at arms, known as the Battle of Point Pleasant, is remembered as the first large-scale combat (about a thousand men were engaged on each side) in which backwoods riflemen were able to stand against a comparable number of Indians for hours on end and to claim a victory when darkness concluded hostilities. But even though the Long Knives did well pitted against the yelling foe in scores of confused little combats fought from tree to tree, it was Cornstalk who dictated most of the conflict's tactical dimensions and he, rather than the Virginians, who brought it to its conclusion at dusk.

The Indians pinned Colonel Andrew Lewis and his 1,100 militiamen onto a point of land between the mouth of the Kanawha and the Ohio rivers on the morning of October 10 and kept them there—killing 75 and wounding 140 of them—from early morning until nightfall. "The enemy," wrote William Preston, a militiaman, "behaved with bravery and great caution; they frequently damned our men for white sons of bitches. The head men walked about in the time of action, exhorting their men 'to be close, shoot well, be strong of fight.' "

Cornstalk, as he ranged through the battle, became increasingly aware that the Virginians would not break, though they were having, in the words of rifle-

A Mingo chieftain known as Captain John Logan finds his family murdered by white hooligans in 1774. The terrible discovery, depicted in this 19th Century engraving, drove the once-friendly Logan to take to the warpath until his death in 1780.

man Isaac Shelby, "a very hard day; sometimes the hideous cries of the enemy, and the groans of our wounded men lying around, was enough to shudder the stoutest heart." The backwoodsmen, in fact, drove back the Indians for a while during the afternoon and pursued them through the tangled underbrush. "The action continued extremely hot," said Shelby, "and the bravest of their men made the *best* use of themselves, while others were throwing their dead into the ohio, and carrying off their wounded." Cornstalk's losses were less than those of the whites—40 men—but he decided on a strategic retreat, engineered a silent withdrawal across the Ohio after dark and marched to the Scioto. He called a council of his peers.

"Shall we kill all our women and children," he asked, "and then fight until we shall be all killed ourselves?" The chiefs were silent. "Since you are not inclined to fight, I will go and make peace," said Cornstalk. He thereupon arranged a meeting with Lord Dunmore, who was advancing with a second force, and talked him into a truce, which spared the Shawnee towns from a two-pronged attack.

Cornstalk felt duty bound to this alliance with Virginia even after the outbreak of the Revolution. In 1777 he traveled to an American fort that had been raised on the Kanawha and warned its commandant, a captain named Arbuckle, that the British were bent on launching dissident Shawnees against the frontier settlements. Arbuckle held him as a hostage for his pains and made one of his sons, Elinipsico, a hostage as well when the youth called to inquire about his father. That was the end of both of them. Troops of the garrison overawed their officers, burst into the room where the pair was being held and shot them down to avenge a comrade who had been ambushed outside the stockade. As they were about to be killed, Cornstalk said to the boy: "My son, the Great Spirit has seen fit that we should die together, and has sent you here to that end.

91

During a missionary campaign David
Zeisberger, a Moravian, preaches to a band
of Delawares in Pennsylvania in 1776.
This sketch, drawn a century later, formed
the basis of a painting commissioned by
Moravians to commemorate the event.

It is his will and let us submit—it is all for the best."

Friendship with settlers in those same years cost the Mingo chief Tahgahjute—known as Captain John Logan—almost equally dear. Logan, a tall, grave and commanding figure, had a way of impressing the roughest of backwoodsmen he met on the Pennsylvania frontier; one white familiar called him "the best specimen of humanity he ever met with, either white or red." He was rewarded, on drifting west to the Ohio River, by a backwoods lout named Greathouse who plied members of his tribe, including his brother and sister, with drink at a white man's house on Yellow Creek, rendered them insensible and murdered them all. Logan retaliated by leading border raids in which he boasted of personally taking 13 scalps. He eventually fell prey to melancholy and rum and was killed by a nephew during a quarrel—but not without leaving a bit of prose that kept his name alive.

Though Logan had played no active role in the Battle of Point Pleasant, he was so important a chief-

tain that he was invited by Lord Dunmore to attend the peace negotiations with Cornstalk. He refused and dictated an impassioned explanation, which a messenger-interpreter, John Gibson, scribbled down in English and carried back to the governor and his officers. The mournful and indignant Logan erred in his facts—confusing Greathouse with a border soldier named Cresap—but his soliloquy electrified the peacemakers, was printed and reprinted by colonial newspapers, fascinated Thomas Jefferson and endured as a gem of popular oratory that generations of American schoolboys were forced to memorize and recite for solemn gatherings of their elders.

"I appeal to any white man to say, if he ever entered Logan's cabin hungry, and he gave him not meat; if he ever came cold and naked, and he clothed him not. During the course of the last, long and bloody war, Logan remained idle in his cabin, an advocate for peace. Such was my love for the whites, that my countrymen pointed as they passed, and said, 'Logan is

the friend of the white man.' I had even thought to have lived with you, but for the injuries of one man. Col. Cresap, the last spring, in cold blood, and unprovoked, murdered all the relations of Logan, not sparing even my women and children. There runs not a drop of my blood in the veins of any living creature. This called on me for revenge. I have sought it: I have killed many; I have fully glutted my vengeance. For my country, I rejoice at the beams of peace. But do not harbour a thought that mine is the joy of fear. Logan never felt fear. He will not turn on his heel to save his life. Who is there to mourn for Logan?—Not one."

And no Algonquin forgot the fate of a band of Pennsylvania Delawares, one of the Algonquin tribes, who were converted to Christianity by German missionaries of the United Brethren—a sect known to outsiders as the Moravians and bound to a Quaker-like creed of passivity and nonviolence. The missionaries worked a marvelous change in their savage converts. By 1771, when their white teachers led them west of the Ohio River to farm, they were very probably the most peaceful, industrious and wholly Christian beings on the continent. The Moravian Indians, as they were called, dwelt in neat villages that had such names as Salem and Gnadenhutten, bred horses and cattle, cultivated orchards, tilled the soil, gathered daily to worship God and meekly turned the other cheek to persecutors of both races.

During the Revolution the British urged warriors allied to the Crown to drive the Moravian Indians out of their homes, and the Iroquois obligingly responded with raids and contemptuous threats to "make broth" of the Moravians. An increasing clamor for the destruction of the Moravians rose at the same time among American backwoodsmen, who believed—quite wrongly—that the villagers were harboring hostile Indians. The peaceful Indians clung stubbornly to their farms through all of this. There were 90 of them in Gnadenhutten one day in March 1782 when a ferocious rabble of American militiamen, led by Colo-

A dream of confederacy shattered in battle

The last great effort of the forest Indians to wrest back their land began in 1808 under the charismatic Shawnee chief Tecumseh and his brother Tenskwatawa *(right),* known as the Prophet. From their base at Tippecanoe, in what is now Indiana, the brothers traveled as far as Florida to rouse tribes against the frontiersmen.

Watching the confederacy take shape at Vincennes, General William Henry Harrison described Tecumseh as "one of those uncommon geniuses, which spring up occasionally to produce revolutions." But Harrison broke the back of the alliance. In 1811 his troops overran and burned Tippecanoe. Then, in 1813 he led 3,000 militiamen to victory over 600 Indians on the banks of the Thames River in Ontario, Canada, where Tecumseh was slain.

Harrison's victory is commemorated by a gold medal *(inset)* and a fanciful print that shows him killing Tecumseh.

Tecumseh's one-eyed brother, Tenskwatawa, won thousands of Indians to their cause when he accurately prophesied a solar eclipse.

nel David Williamson, descended upon them, herded men, women and children into the church and announced that all were to die. The hapless Indians merely asked for a few minutes to kiss each other farewell and to sing to "the most High." This—their reward for good deeds in a naughty world—was reluctantly granted, after which they were all slaughtered.

This brutal deed prompted waves of indignation and remorse among some Americans. But it also exacerbated American horror at the ferocity of the Algonquin tribes—since the Algonquins pillaged along the upper Ohio in response to the massacre of the Moravian Delawares and roasted a captured colonel of the militia, William Crawford. Crawford was innocent of any connection with the killings but had the ill fortune to have taken over the command of Williamson's troops on a later expedition from Fort Pitt. Crawford asked a Delaware chieftain named Wingenund—an old friend—to intercede for him before he was taken to the stake. Their conversation, as reconstructed by a Moravian missionary, John Heckewelder, tells a great deal about the hopeless ambiguity of American-Indian relations in the 18th Century:

Crawford: Do you recollect the friendship that has always existed between us?

Wingenund: I recollect all this. I remember that we have drunk many a bowl of punch together. I remember also other acts of kindness that you have done me.

Crawford: Then I hope the same friendship still subsists between us.

Wingenund: It would, of course, be the same, were you in your proper place and not here.

Crawford: And why not here, Captain? I hope you would not desert a friend in time of need. Now is the time for you to exert yourself in my behalf, as I would do for you were you in my place.

Wingenund: Colonel Crawford! you have placed yourself in a situation which puts it out of my power and that of others of your friends to do anything for you.

Crawford: How so, Captain Wingenund?

Wingenund: By joining yourself to that execrable man, Williamson and his party; the man,

who, but the other day murdered such a number of the Moravian Indians, knowing that he ran no risk in murdering a people who would not fight.

Crawford: Wingenund, I assure you, that had I been with him at the time, this would not have happened . . . I went out with him later to prevent him from committing fresh murders.

Wingenund: This, Colonel, the Indians would not believe were even I to tell them so.

Crawford: What do they intend to do with me? Can you tell me?

Wingenund: I tell you with grief, Colonel. Williamson and his whole cowardly host ran off, and as they have taken you, they will have revenge on you in his stead.

Crawford: Can you devise no way to get me off?

Wingenund: Had Williamson been taken with you, I and some friends might perhaps have succeeded to save you, but as the matter now stands, no man would dare to interfere in your behalf. The king of England himself, were he to come to this spot, with all his wealth and treasures could not effect this purpose. The blood of the innocent Moravians calls aloud for revenge. The nation to which they belonged will have revenge. All the nations connected with us cry out: Revenge! Revenge!

Crawford: Then it seems my fate is decided, and I must prepare to meet death.

Wingenund: Yes, Colonel! I am sorry for it; but cannot do any thing for you. Nothing now remains but for you to meet your fate like a brave man. Farewell Colonel Crawford! they are coming; (weeping) I will retire to a solitary spot.

Crawford's inquisitors cooked him alive. He was attached to the stake by a long leash and roasted for two hours before he fell down and died.

Such melancholy episodes stiffened the resolve of white soldiers and treaty makers who dealt with Indians after the Revolution, but neither hastened nor delayed the inevitable reduction and dispossession of the forest tribes. The Indians were regarded as nuisances, certain to have been washed away under any circumstances as the rising and relentless tide of white settlement flooded their hunting lands. The once-mighty Iroquois were first to capitulate. Great throngs of Mohawks, Onondagas, Cayugas and Senecas, having supported England in the Revolution, retreated into Canada when the 13 states achieved independence, leaving fewer than 6,000 men, women and children behind. These weakened people surrendered large areas of countryside in western New York to a state commission in return for small cash settlements and the promise of annual annuities. By 1800 they had faded into a doleful, reservation-bound obscurity from which they never emerged.

The Algonquins of Ohio, Indiana and Illinois were not so easily dislodged. Backwoods settlement in the Northwest was still largely contained below the Ohio River after the Revolution. Canada—and the British with their supplies of arms and hopes of territorial incursion—lay conveniently to the north, and vast areas of Indian hunting lands were still untouched. The Northwest Indians had little reason to feel their own condition altered by the distant settlement of some quarrel between the American colonies and the English King, and they pursued their own policies of raiding across the Ohio as before. But the pressures of white civilization ground remorselessly upon them, forcing them, year by year, into ever-dwindling corners of their domains or into strange country west of the Mississippi, where those surviving disease, drink or death in battle were expected to live happily ever after.

The new government in the East spoke piously and unrealistically of its concern for Indians. Henry Dearborn, Thomas Jefferson's secretary of war, expressed with perfect sincerity his plans for the "introduction of the arts of civilization," which would "ultimately destroy all distinctions between Savages and civilized people." Congress authorized Indian agencies early and listened with satisfaction to members who expected Christian missionaries to assist them in achieving alterations in Indian behavior. "The Settlmt. of the Western Country," wrote George Washington, "and making a Peace with the Indians are so analogous that there can be no definition of the one without involving considerations of the other." Neither "Settlmt." nor "Peace" was achieved, however, by the benign means

he may have in good conscience anticipated. The Northwest Indians wanted no part of either, and few of the whites who dealt with them were concerned with the "arts of civilization."

The erosion of Indian holdings in the Northwest began with General Anthony ("Mad Anthony") Wayne's victory at the Battle of Fallen Timbers. A few months later the general treated 1,000 assorted Delawares, Potawatomis, Wyandots, Shawnees, Miamis, Chippewas, Ottawas, Weas, Piankashaws, Kickapoos and Kaskaskias to 50 days of feasting, and having combined intimidation with hospitality, presented them with the Treaty of Greenville in 1795. He promised them $20,000 in goods and, at the same time, relieved them of Ohio (minus a strip along Lake Erie) and a slice of Indiana.

William Henry Harrison continued the process after he was appointed the territorial governor of Indiana in 1800. He made a practice of inviting tribal chieftains to tell him their woes—or of listening to two sets of chiefs complain about each other—and of exacting land at low prices as a kind of by-product of official commiseration. Over 100 million acres of it had been transferred by treaty to the federal government and made available to the more daring of settlers by the winter of 1809.

This erosion of Indian space and Indian power did not go unopposed. A Shawnee named Tecumseh—one of the forest chieftains who deserves to be remembered for statesmanship—began declaring land treaties invalid as he grew into his middle 30s in the early 1800s and called for a confederation of Indian tribes, both North and South, as a mechanism for making the disavowal stick.

Tecumseh was a magnificent figure of a man—tall, erect, muscular, light copper in complexion—and he had a reputation as a warrior, having fought as a youth in many border battles. But he was far more than a warrior. He had a formidable mind, saw the inevitability of white government of the continent and envisaged his confederation as an independent buffer state between Canada and the United States. He demanded the maintenance of Indian lands within this state as a means of staving off the disintegration of tribal stability and tribal tradition. His sway among the Indians was remarkable: he was able to argue against torture and other cruel practices without losing an iota of influence.

Harrison, his most implacable foe, spoke of him with something like awe: "The implicit obedience and respect which the followers of Tecumseh pay to him is really astonishing. If it were not for the vicinity of the United States he would, perhaps, be the founder of an Empire that would rival in glory Mexico or Peru. No difficulties deter him."

Tecumseh was not above recourse to the white man's legalisms. He maintained that no land could rightfully be sold or ceded unless all tribes agreed to the deal. He pointed out that Anthony Wayne's Treaty of Greenville was, in fact, the best proof of this view, since the government had negotiated with the assembled tribes and had specifically guaranteed them, as a whole, title to all land not ceded to the whites. Tecumseh's argument failed, not because it was deemed false but simply because later American treaty makers ignored this precedent. Tecumseh responded—while visiting tribe after tribe in the Northwest and through the South—by urging Indian people to refuse further treaties and to make themselves party to a confederation so strong as to make their resistance a feasible method of dealing with the American government.

The exhortations achieved religious overtones—even a quality of magic—through the machinations of Tecumseh's brother Tenskwatawa, a one-eyed epileptic who became famous as The Prophet. Tenskwatawa launched a career as a kind of super medicine man after falling unconscious, apparently because of an epileptic seizure, and announcing, on regaining his senses, that he had been conducted into the spirit world and had been made the messenger of new revelation by the Master of Life. Harrison, aware of Tenskwatawa's increasing influence, wrote sardonically to the Delawares: "If he is really a prophet, ask him to cause the sun to stand still, the moon to alter its course, the rivers to cease to flow." The Prophet accepted the challenge with alacrity (since he had heard from white friends that a total eclipse was predicted to occur on June 16, 1806) and lent Tecumseh's plans a quality of jihad by turning day into night at the appointed hour.

It is hard to think that Tecumseh could have succeeded in his grandiose schemes, for all his credibility among the tribes. The oncoming waves of white settle-ment would surely have rolled over the strongest of Indian civilizations in the end. It was Tenskwatawa, though, who brought the confederation down, after Harrison—hoping for an excuse to take military action against it—camped with a thousand men on the outskirts of the two brothers' capital, Prophet's Town, near the juncture of the Wabash and Tippecanoe rivers. Tecumseh was campaigning among the Southern tribes and crying, with his face painted the black war color, for their pledges of armed assistance: "Burn their dwellings. Destroy their stock. War now. War forever. War upon the living. War upon the dead; dig their very corpses from the grave; our country must give no rest to a white man's bones."

In fact, Tecumseh wanted war only as a last resort and only if the whole Indian world was joined in it. The Prophet, however, having performed magic rites and having promised the young warriors that no bullet could harm them, launched them upon Harrison's sleeping soldiers at dawn on November 7, 1811.

The attack prospered for only a few minutes. Harrison's flanks were protected by a deep marsh and by a creek and heavy woods. He had hardened soldiers, a contingent of Regulars among them, and once awakened—even though they lost 38 men and 150 wounded—they poured murderous volleys into the attacking Indians and broke them completely with a cavalry charge from two directions. Harrison doubted, for 36 hours, that the Battle of Tippecanoe was his and kept his men alert for new rushes until the evening of the following day. But The Prophet's reputation—and a great deal of Tecumseh's, too—lay with the bullet-riddled corpses that magic had failed to protect when the white soldiers had begun to fire. Harrison finally sent out scouts who found Prophet's Town deserted; he burned it to the ground.

Tecumseh then turned to the British for assistance in carrying out his plans for confederation. After his brother's disastrous defeat at Tippecanoe, he traveled to Canada, where he became a brigadier general for the British. When war began, he led the Indians of the Great Lakes and Ohio Valley against the Americans, believing that his English friends would drive the settlers off Indian lands. But when the British abandoned plans to invade the Ohio Valley, Tecumseh denounced the British general: "You always told us that

you would never draw your foot off British ground; but now, father, we see you are drawing back. We must compare our father's conduct to a fat animal, that carries its tail upon its back, but when afrighted, he drops it between his legs and runs off."

Eventually, the British and their Indian allies pulled back into Canada, hotly pursued by troops under his old foe, Harrison. The forces clashed in the Battle of the Thames River on October 5, 1813. Tecumseh and 33 of his warriors were killed, thus shattering all the plans for a confederation.

The Prophet, meanwhile, had moved to Canada as well and spent his remaining days living on a British pension. The pair's disheartened followers resigned themselves to government ukase, left their villages behind and accepted life on reservations.

The final fate of the Southern Indians was more doleful yet. They, too, had pillaged and murdered in white settlements—on flatlands below the Appalachians as well as in the mountain valleys of western Georgia, the Carolinas, Alabama and Tennessee. They had served as mercenaries of England and, for many years, as Spain's bulwark against American designs on the lower Mississippi and the Gulf Coast. But no Indians embraced the "arts of civilization" with such enthusiasm and success as did the peoples of the Southern confederacies when they finally resigned themselves to the customs, laws and behavioral taboos that were thrust upon them.

The Cherokee Nation was a peaceful and prospering agricultural society by the mid-1820s. It possessed a growing school system, and its 15,000 people owned 22,000 cattle, 2,000 spinning wheels, 10 saw mills, 8 cotton gins, 31 grist mills and 700 looms (and, incidentally, 1,300 black slaves). A Cherokee genius, Sequoyah (for whom California's giant redwoods were later named), invented a written tribal language of 82 characters during the decade, and it was utilized in publication of a newspaper, *The Cherokee Phoenix*. Tribal police were appointed to keep order. In 1827 tribal delegates drew up a constitution modeled on that of the United States, and tribal elections produced a principal—Chief John Ross—of a self-governing tribal republic.

None of this ensured them the slightest protection against the land speculators who were crowding in upon them from the East. The State of Georgia appropriated their lands; the Supreme Court refused (in *The Cherokee Nation* v. *The State of Georgia*) to grant them legal redress; and the federal government exiled them in masses (with a quarter of their number dying on the way) to the wilderness of what is now Oklahoma. The Creeks, Choctaws and Chickasaws were pushed west by the same devices, and all were left to survive as best they could the summer dust storms, winter snows, cholera, smallpox and squalor that greeted them at the end of *Nuna-da-ut-sun'y* (The Trail Where They Cried).

As the moving frontier bore down upon the woodland Indians, they were treated as mercilessly by whites as they had treated the first backwoodsmen who ventured into the passes of the Appalachians a century before. Fate seemed, in retrospect, to have allotted them but one important role in the evolution of the new American nation—a tempering, by bloodletting, of the people who would possess the continent—and seemed to have been bent on destroying them when the role was played. There was an inevitability about the tragedy into which they were drawn on confrontation with the white invader: two such diverse and irreconcilable cultures have seldom been juxtaposed with so little warning and so little chance of resolving their conflicting aspirations and responses.

"A number of instances, such as the conduct of the Georgians to the Cherokees," wrote Theodore Roosevelt in his *The Winning of the West*, "are indelible blots on our fair fame; and yet, in describing our dealings with the Indians as a whole, historians do us much less than justice. The tribes were warlike and bloodthirsty, jealous of each other and of the whites, and the young warriors were always on the alert to commit outrages when they could do it with impunity. On the other hand, the evil-disposed whites regarded the Indians as fair game for robbery and violence of any kind; and the far larger number of well-disposed men resented the action of the government which, in their eyes, failed to protect them and yet sought to keep them out of waste, uncultivated lands which they did not regard as being any more the property of Indians than of their own hunters. With the best intentions, it was wholly impossible to evolve order out of such chaos without resort to the ultimate arbitrator—the sword."

A Seneca mother sits uncomfortably in a white man's chair in this poignant 1807 sketch drawn by a visiting French baroness.

4 | Key to the Great Lakes

"The skies are always serene," wrote Antoine de la Mothe Cadillac in 1701 of an idyllic meadow on the strait (*le detroit*) linking Lakes Huron and Erie. But it was not the beauty of the place that attracted him so much as the strait's potential as a "door of passage" to "vast seas of sweet water."

The fort he built there so dominated the Great Lakes that France was able to control the fur trade for more than half a century, until Britain took the prize in 1760. The British found an-other use for it: during the Revolution-ary War they made the fort their base for attacks, often with Indian allies, on American frontier settlements.

After the war they were obliged by treaty to give up the fort, but it was not until General Anthony Wayne's defeat of the Indians — who had kept up hos-tilities — left the British garrison un-shielded that they agreed to leave. In 1796 the Americans took over the small outpost that was still, in Wayne's words, "the centre of the wilderness."

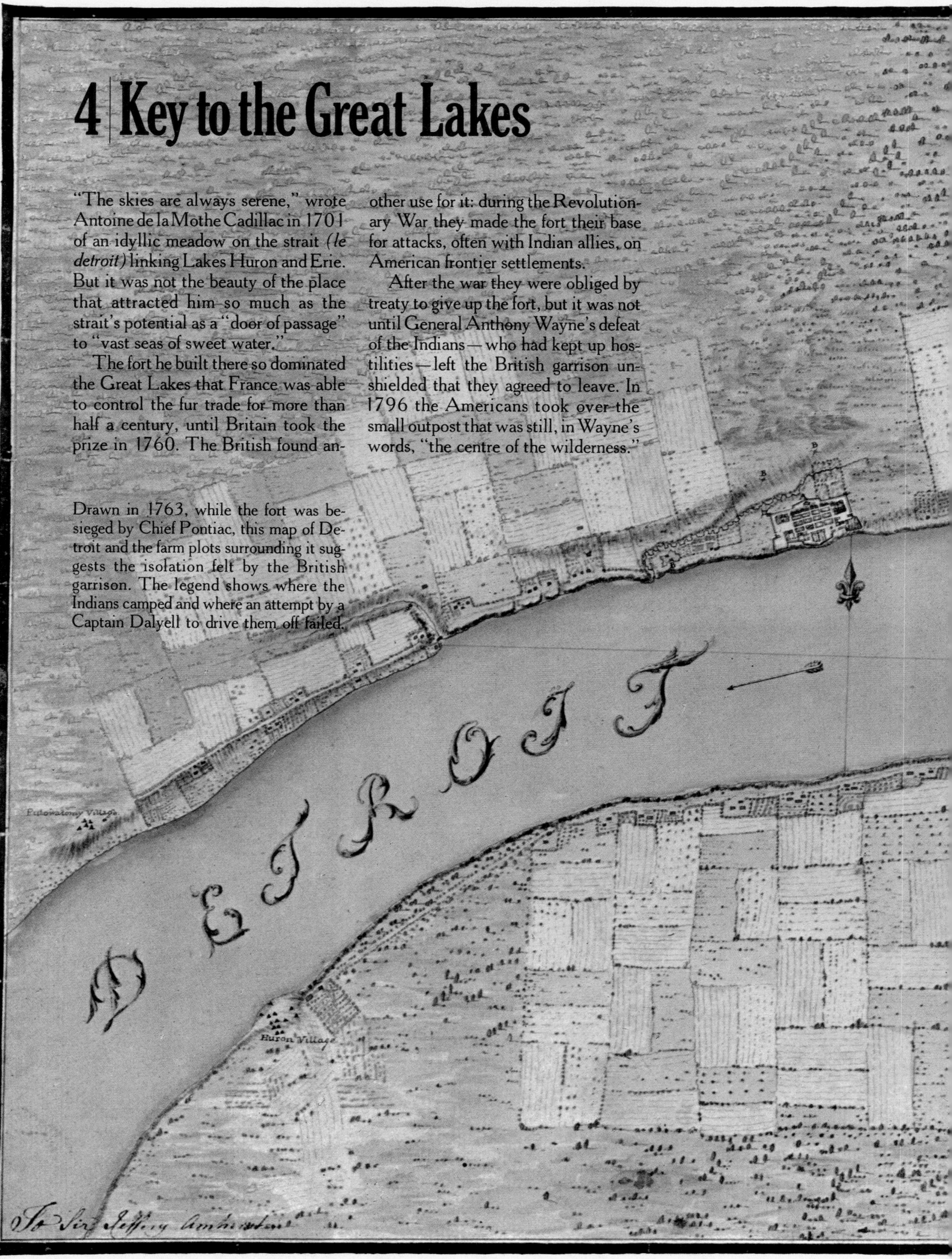

Drawn in 1763, while the fort was be-sieged by Chief Pontiac, this map of De-troit and the farm plots surrounding it sug-gests the isolation felt by the British garrison. The legend shows where the Indians camped and where an attempt by a Captain Dalyell to drive them off failed.

Potowatomy Village

D E T R O I T

Huron Village

To Sir Jeffery Amherst

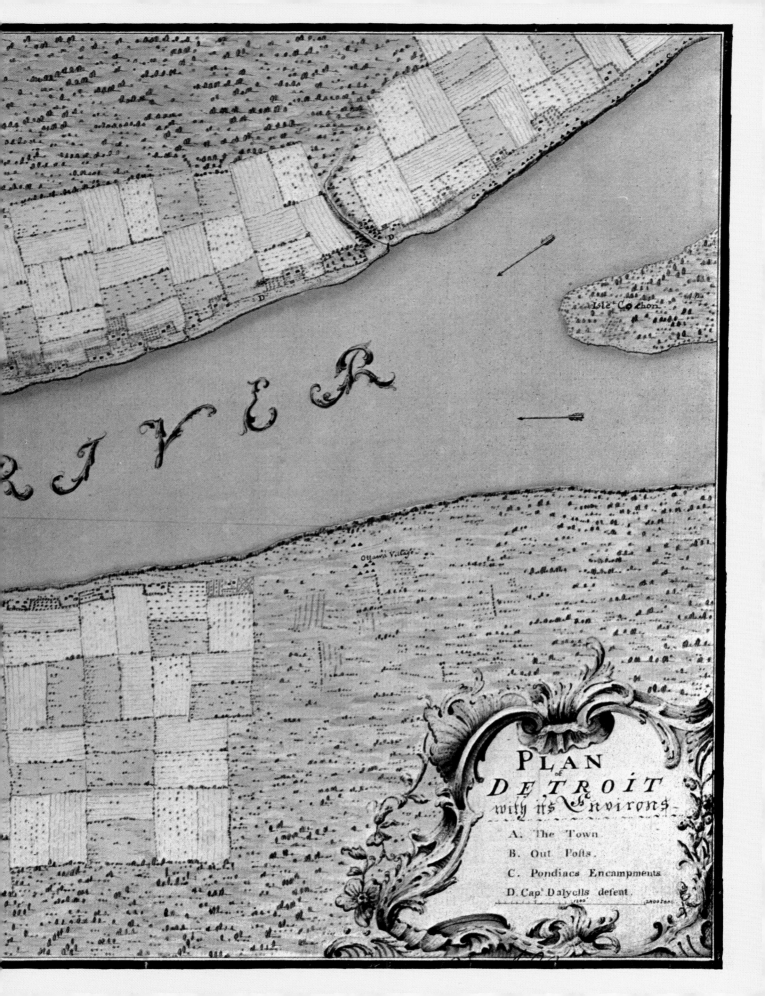

RIVER

Isle Cochon

Ottawa Village

PLAN
of
DETROIT
with its Environs.

A. The Town

B. Out Posts.

C. Pondiacs Encampments

D. Capt. Dalyells defeat.

"The fort is much better than expected," a British captain reported after the French surrender in 1760, the year in which this plan was drawn. Within the fort's walls stood 300 buildings, including a public bakery (labeled E in the key). The insets include the stockade's design *(upper left)* and a "View from the West" *(bottom center)*, the earliest known picture of Detroit.

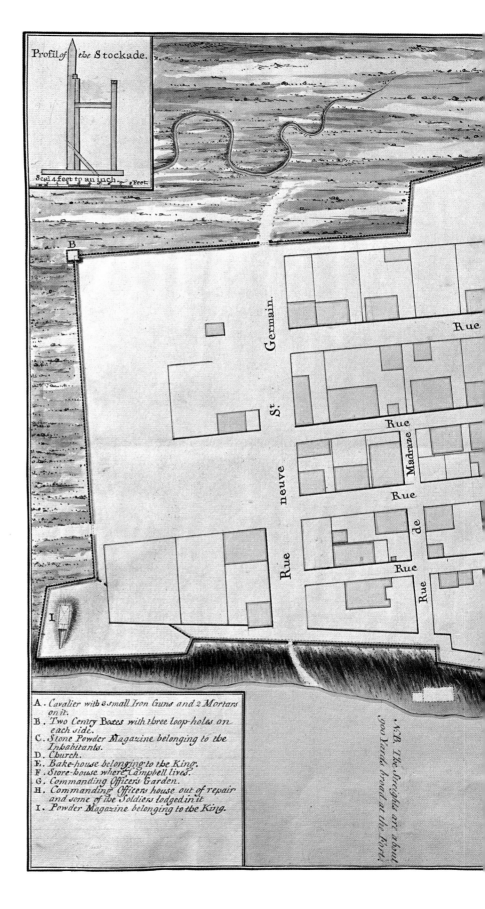

Profil *of* the Stockade.

Scal 4 feet to an inch   8 Feet.

St. Germain.

Rue

Rue neuve

Rue Madraze

Rue de

Rue

Rue

A. Cavalier with 3 small Iron Guns and 2 Mortars on it.
B. Two Centry Boxes with three loop-holes on each side.
C. Stone Powder Magazine belonging to the Inhabitants.
D. Church.
E. Bake-house belonging to the King.
F. Store-house where Campbell lives.
G. Commanding Officer's Garden.
H. Commanding Officer's house out of repair and some of the Soldiers lodged in it.
I. Powder Magazine belonging to the King.

N.B. The Streights are about 900 Yards broad at the Fort.

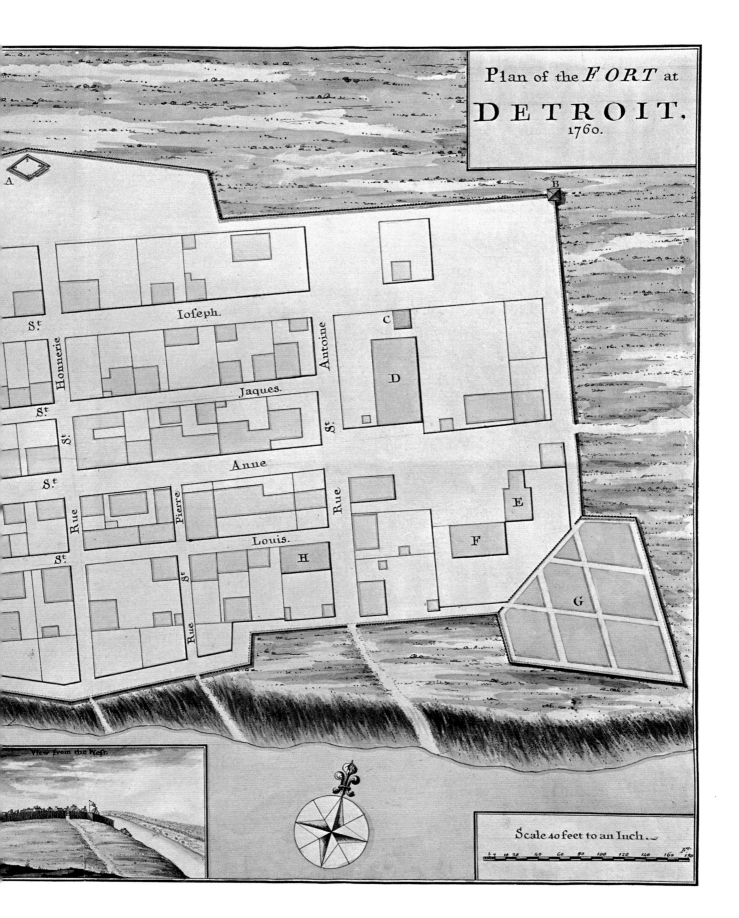

Plan of the *FORT* at

DETROIT,

1760.

A

B

Iofeph.

Honnerie

St.

St.

St.

Antoine

C

D

Rue

Jaques.

Anne

Pierre

Rue

St.

Louis.

Rue

St.

E

F

G

H

View from the Weft.

Scale 40 feet to an Inch.

5 10 20   40   60   80   100   120   140   160   Ft. 180

105

A detailed census report sent to London during Detroit's British period lists the 1,367 residents in nine categories and livestock in five. The population was rebuilding after a sharp fall in 1764, caused by a rush to newly founded St. Louis.

A General Return of all the Inhabitants of Detroit their Possessions Cattle, Houses, Servants and Slaves taken by Phillip Dejean Justice of the Peace for the said place the 2?d day of September 1773.

	Men	Women	Young men from 16 to 60	Boys from 10 to..	Girls from..to 15	Girls from 1 to 10	Servants	Men Slaves	Women Slaves	Oxen	Cows	Heifers	Sheep	Hogs	Acres of Land in Front	Acres of Land in Depth	Acres of Land cultivated	Houses	Barns
South side of the Fort	107	81	33	112	30	76	27	6	3	222	203	117	21	390	228	..	1429	93	63
North Row of the Fort	124	107	45	137	24	134	36	26	22	211	306	241	424	662	284	40	1175½	117	93
The Fort	66	36	6	35	4	30	27	14	14	20	83	22	62	45	..	..	..	68	..
On Hog Island	1	1	..	..	..	..	3	..	..	20	17	32	121	30	.	..	..	2	1
Total	298	225	84	284	58	240	93	46	39	473	609	412	628	1067	512	40	2602½	280	157

N.B. The Troops & Naval Departm.t with their Cattle &c are not included in the above, Th[e]ir men &c are generaly more Numerous Several being now hunting and at the Indian Villages altho' all the farms are Calculated at 40 Acres in depth eight of them acres 80 and one 60.

Signed P. Dejean

The British began building star-shaped Fort Lernoult as an adjunct to Detroit in 1778, anticipating an attack by George Rogers Clark. Clark needled the British with a letter of thanks for sparing "the Americans some expense in building" their own fort, but he never reached Detroit.

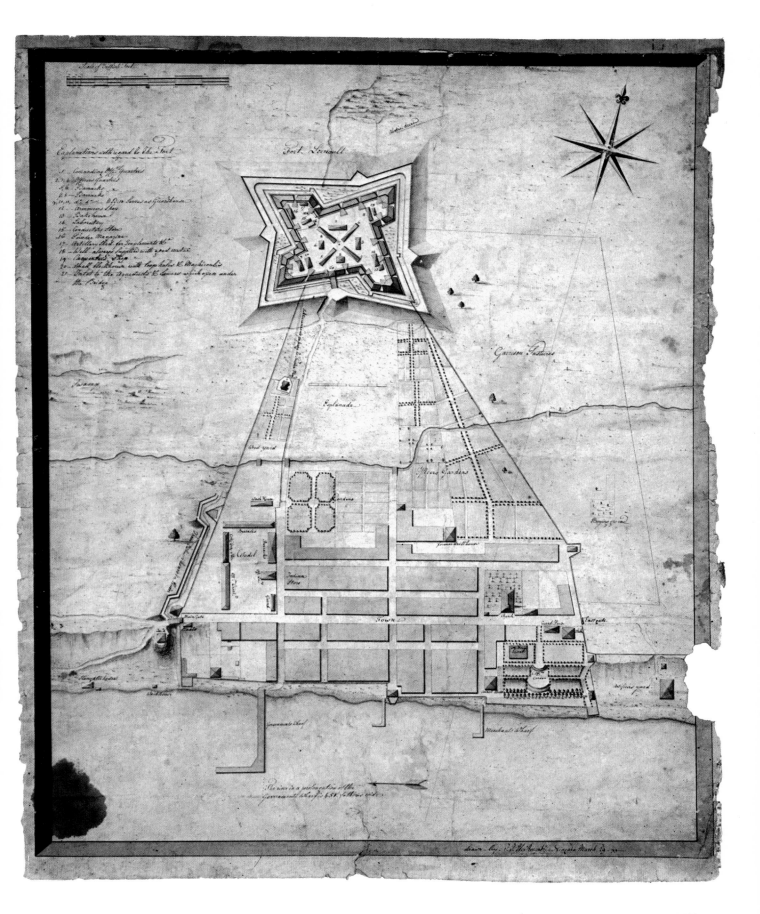

Warships of the Royal Navy dominate a riverfront bustling with smaller craft in this 1794 watercolor, which evokes the frontier heritage of Detroit's early history. Although a British flag flies over the walls, the gabled, pitched-roof houses reflect the village's French origins. At the river's edge some Indians land their canoe to barter furs for trade goods. Two years later, Detroit became an American town.

Bold leadership north of the Ohio

Dozens of border captains had a hand in securing the advancing frontier against the Indians and their allies, the British, but none were as crucial to the territorial integrity of the new United States—and to its intentions in the West—as were George Rogers Clark, the hero of Vincennes, and Anthony ("Mad Anthony") Wayne, the hero of the Battle of Fallen Timbers. Each man broke the enemy—in one case the British, in the other the Algonquin Indians—in wildernesses north of the Ohio River, and each did so in desperate circumstances that imperiled the very existence and honor of the young nation.

They were men of disparate background and disparate method, though each conquered by improvising on accepted military concepts of his day. Clark flew in the face of tradition by using a handful of backwoodsmen to confound and defeat well-armed Europeans in fortified towns. Wayne employed masses of Regulars, fortifications and methodical advances to confuse and intimidate the Northwest tribes. In addition to their military acumen, the two leaders had one other dazzling trait in common: each dominated men and mastered events by sheer force of character.

Clark, a big, redheaded Virginian, was the first of the pair to engage England and its allies in the Northwest in 1778. Although only in his twenties, he had concluded, early in the Revolution, that he could personally nullify the enormous strategic advantage Britain enjoyed through its alliance with forest tribes in what are today Ohio, Indiana, Illinois and Michigan.

The odds, at first glance, were awful. The English base at Detroit was linked by water with the trading center of Montreal; its southern approaches were protected by friendly villages of Shawnees, Delawares, Mingos, Ottawas and Piankashaws, who swapped furs and scalps for the guns, powder, war paint and trade goods that this line of easy communication with the North afforded its warehouses.

But Clark believed in surprise. He used it to capture three strategic towns, and by the time he was finished, he had overawed the tribes, captured the British commander, Henry Hamilton, and thwarted a grand design by which the British hoped to wipe out the scattering of American stations in Kentucky and to seal off the 13 rebellious colonies east of the Appalachian wall.

Clark's accomplishment might, nevertheless, have gone for naught if Wayne—a former Revolutionary general and a Regular to the core—had not been called back to service in 1792, had not reshaped the lamentable postwar army into the disciplined Legion of the United States, and had not led it to victory against the tribes in Ohio. England had great hopes of wrecking the shaky confederation of American states after the Revolution and did its utmost to turn the Northwest into a continuing problem that would strain the confederation's resources and undermine its resolve. The British ignored the treaty by which they had ceded the territory to the United States in 1783, encouraged the Algonquins to go on raiding from their forest fastnesses, and used them for a full decade to ravage American settlements in the West and to demean the Congress and the President before the world.

Wayne's and Clark's forays northwest into the wilderness were remarkable in themselves. Clark's invasion of Illinois in 1778 with his ragtail army of backwoodsmen was one of the nerviest and most improbable military adventures in the history of American arms. Wayne's dogged and disciplined advance into Ohio, 15 years later, demonstrated at last that

---

An 1821 memorial portrait of George Rogers Clark lends a sober dignity to the image of the brash colonel who had taken the Northwest by storm 43 years before.

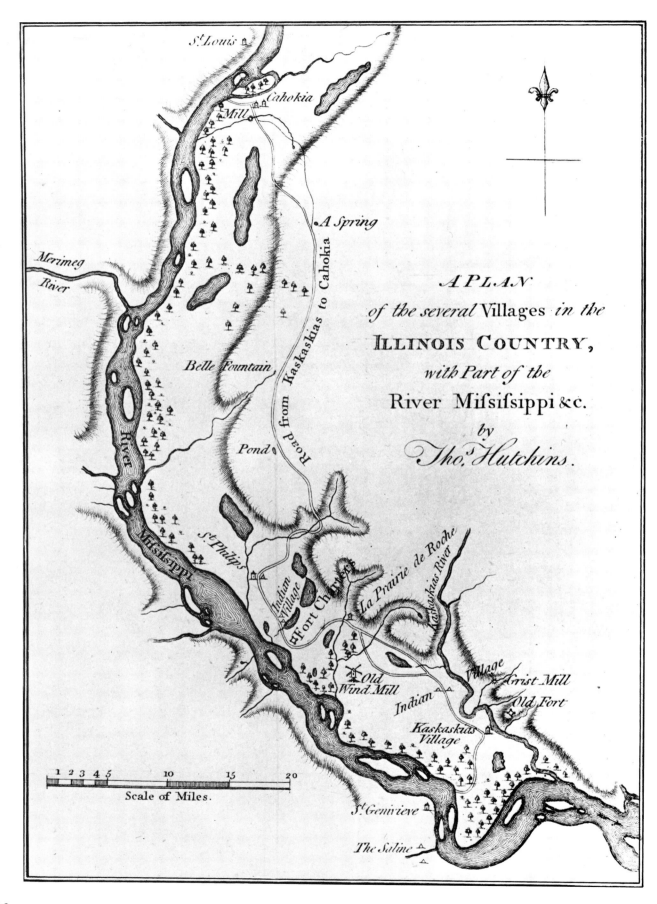

St.Louis

Cahokia

Mill

Merimeg
River

A Spring

Belle Fountain

Pond

River

Mifsifsippi

St.Philips

Road from Kaskaskias to Cahokia

A PLAN
of the several Villages *in the*
ILLINOIS COUNTRY,
with Part of the
River Mifsifsippi &c.
by
Tho.ˢ Hutchins.

Indian
Village

Fort Chartres

La Prairie de Roche

Kaskaskias River

Old
Wind Mill

Indian

Village

Grist Mill

Old Fort

Kaskaskias
Village

1 2 3 4 5   10   15   20

Scale of Miles.

St.Genivieve

The Saline

Regulars could fight Indians—and with a remorselessness seldom exercised by forces of frontier militia. But both expeditions involved larger considerations: Clark and Wayne shaped the future of the American West when they set out, each in the nick of time, to do battle north of the Ohio.

George Rogers Clark—the son of a well-to-do Virginia planter and the elder brother of William Clark, who was to explore the far West with Meriwether Lewis—could have been forgiven if he had abandoned his whole mad scheme before it was launched. He was no stranger to peril; he had made his way to the frontier as a surveyor when hardly out of his teens and had evolved into a hard-bitten roughneck who knew the wilderness as well as any of the backwoodsmen with whom he traveled and hunted.

Young Clark was also a man with important connections at Williamsburg, Virginia's capital. He had helped to sustain the Kentucky settlements against Indian attacks in 1776 by getting them 20 kegs of gunpowder from the Virginia Council, and by delivering the stuff down the Ohio himself. Virginia's Governor Patrick Henry received him warmly in the autumn of 1777 when he rode east again and offered to personally save the West from England and the tribes. But fate seemed bent on negating both his daring and his political influence in the months that followed.

Clark wanted to seize Detroit, the linchpin of British influence in the Northwest. But he correctly sensed that such an ambitious proposal would be rejected in Williamsburg, "as it was a general oppinion that it would take several thousand to approach that Place." Instead he urged a preliminary campaign, arduous enough in itself: the capture of the old French towns of Kaskaskia, Cahokia and Vincennes, which Britain had inherited after the French and Indian Wars and now used as bases for Indian raids south into Kentucky. Once he had stripped the British of these bastions, he privately hoped to march against Detroit.

Governor Henry and his friend Thomas Jefferson were fascinated by Clark's proposal to take the three towns. But the governor felt all secrecy would be lost by laying the plan before the politicians of the Virginia Assembly. And without the assembly's approval nothing could be done. Henry was unwilling, more-over, to strip Virginia—already strained by the demands of the war east of the mountains—of the 500 militiamen Clark believed essential to success.

The governor resolved these dilemmas by issuing two sets of orders. The first, which the assembly duly approved, granted Clark a colonel's commission in the Virginia militia and the right to recruit 350 riflemen for a three months "relief" of Kentucky—although to avoid erosion of manpower on the coast he was limited to seeking them in backwoods hamlets west of the Blue Ridge. Virginia also agreed to supply boats, stores and ammunition to sustain the expedition. Henry then augmented these vague and euphemistic instructions with a second, secret document specifically authorizing Clark to attack the British post at Kaskaskia, a river town in what is now southwestern Illinois. "If you are so fortunate therefore as to succeed in your expedition," his orders read, "you will take every possible measure to secure the artillery and stores and whatever may advantage the State."

Clark was rapidly submerged in sloughs of frustration. His recruiters were hampered by hostile local leaders, and by the reluctance of the settlers to leave their wives and clearings. He had fewer than 150 men aboard his tiny fleet of five flatboats when on May 12, weeks behind schedule, he finally set off down the Monongahela toward Pittsburgh and the Ohio River. He believed that four additional companies totaling 200 men were marching overland through Kentucky to join him at Corn Island—an isolated patch of wooded land lying amidst the falls of the Ohio River—which he had deliberately chosen as a staging area to discourage desertion by the less enthusiastic of his backwoods soldiery.

But only one of the four companies materialized at Corn Island and some of its members splashed away into the night after he broke the news of the expedition's real purpose. Clark had but 175 men when he set out at last into the wilderness of Illinois.

If none of his plans had gone right before, all seemed blessed by the gods of war thereafter. He had four tough and loyal lieutenants—William Harrod, John Montgomery, Leonard Helm and Joseph Bowman—and the services of a great woodland scout, Daniel Boone's old friend Simon Kenton. His four little companies of riflemen seemed invigorated, once they were plunged into the unknown, by the very audacity of the adventure on which they were embarked.

And fate quickly delivered them news of their quarry. They came upon a party of American hunters who advised Clark, as he told his journal, that in Kaskaskia "the militia was kept in good order, and there were spies on the Mississippi—and that all hunters, both Indians and others were ordered to keep a good lookout for Rebels—that the fort was kept in good order, as an asylum, etc.—but they believed the whole to proceed more from a fondness for parade than the expectation of a visit." Clark was also intrigued to hear that the town's French inhabitants had been taught by the British "to harbor a most horrid idea of the barbarity of Rebels, especially Virginians."

Clark's little band reached the Kaskaskia River at a point just a few miles above its juncture with the Mississippi at sundown on July 4. They were half starved, having jettisoned baggage "except as much as would equip us in an Indian mode," but they had come 120 miles, much of it across open prairie, without having encountered a soul.

They moved through trees along the riverbank as darkness fell, while their scouts searched out the ground ahead, and finally spotted the fort and peaked roofs of the town, a prize older than New Orleans, on a bluff across the Kaskaskia River. A startled farmer assured them, on being rousted from his house, that the local militia was not on guard. "I learned," wrote Clark, "that they had some suspicion of being attacked and had made some preparations, keeping out spies, but they making no discoveries, had got off their Guards." Clark's men found boats and canoes along the shore. It took Clark two hours to get all his troops across the stream and divided into two bodies—one to surround the town, one to follow him toward the fort.

At first, no sound save the creak of insects disturbed the hot summer night. Then the dogs of Kaskaskia discovered Clark's men as they climbed a bank above the water, and set up a frantic chorus of alarm. But, miraculously, no sentries materialized to challenge the intruders. The gate of the fort's stockade hung open. Clark and the scout Kenton burst into the quarters of Philip de Rocheblave, a French nobleman who had agreed to serve the British as Kaskaskia's commandant; they raised a lantern over his bed and told him that he and his wife were prisoners of Virginia. Backwoodsmen were loosed into the streets to tell the populace—at the top of their lungs—that the town was taken by the Long Knives, and to order all, "on pane of Death" to stay indoors until morning. The whole place was Clark's within 15 minutes. "Nothing," he wrote, "could excell the Confusion these People seemed to be in, being taught to expect nothing but Savage treatment from Americans."

"It was my Interest to Attach them to me," Clark reasoned. But he let them tremble "as if they were led to Execution" until Father Pierre Gibault, a Jesuit, called upon him with a committee of elders on the following day and asked permission—since all believed that at best they would be sent into exile—for a last gathering of friends and neighbors in the village church. He gave them permission and sternly warned them against any attempt to escape town.

When the elders called a second time, to plead that husbands not be separated from their wives and children, Clark rose ominously over them. He asked if they "mistake us for savages," and went on to explain "that our Principal was to make those we Reduced free instead of enslaving them, and that if I could have surety of their Zeal and Attachment for the American Cause, they should enjoy all the previledges of our Government." He had news, he added, that had not reached their distant prairies: France had joined the 13 states in their war with England. In that moment, as things turned out, Clark won all of Illinois.

The Kaskaskians not only trooped into their market square to swear allegiance to Virginia but sent emissaries along with Captain Bowman on the following day when he traveled to Cahokia and two smaller towns to arrange a similar mass conversion. Father Gibault rode to Vincennes and turned its people to the support of the American cause as well.

But Clark by now could count on barely 100 of his unruly backwoodsmen—the rest having refused to listen, on finishing their three-month enlistments, to his fervent promises of future pay. He sent Bowman to command at nearby Cahokia and Captain Helm east to Vincennes on the Wabash River. Their troops, however, consisted of the same local French militiamen who had been so recently pressed into the service of the English king. Moreover, Clark and his men were

encircled by large numbers of Indians who, as autumn approached, began to advance menacingly on Cahokia, to test his mettle for themselves.

They were encamped by the hundreds—chiefs, subchiefs and warriors from almost every Algonquin tribe between the Great Lakes and the Mississippi—by the time Clark left Kaskaskia and rode past their fires into Cahokia. Though greatly outnumbered, Clark managed to appear unconcerned. He believed there was but one way of dealing with Indians: as a conqueror who expected submission. Shortly after his arrival he met in council with the paramount chiefs. One of them offered him a belt of peace, but he coldly put it aside and told the tribal leaders he would give them their answer—peace or war—on the morrow.

That night, he ordered a gang of impudent young Winnebago warriors and their chiefs handcuffed and jailed after his guard caught them trying to break into his lodgings, and he rebuffed a delegation of other chiefs who called on him to plead for their release. But he spoke amicably enough when he rose the next day to address the chieftains of all the tribes—including the captives, who had been temporarily released.

The Long Knives and the "Red People" were very much alike, he said. Both had been victimized by the English. But the Long Knives had finally sharpened the hatchet, and the English, having become frightened "like deer in the woods," had hired Red People to do their fighting for them.

Did they wish to go on with war against him? He would let them leave the town in safety to take the bloody path. "I am a warrior, not a counsellor." But he warned them to think of their women and children if they opposed him. "I am ordered to call upon the Great Fire for Warriors enough to darken the land that the Red People may hear no sound but of birds who live on blood!" This speech, Clark noted later in a letter, "did more good than a Regiment of Men." Every tribe entreated him for peace—and pleaded for the release of the prisoners. When he refused this entreaty, two young men were offered to Clark as a sacrifice to atone for the Winnebagos' acts. Sitting down before him, their heads covered by blankets, the Indians awaited death by tomahawk.

Clark was speechless with surprise and admiration for the silent courage of the two young warriors at his feet. He ordered them to rise, and told them that their bravery had won peace and friendship for all their people. A great celebration then closed the council, and the Indians melted back into the woods. The British commander, Henry Hamilton, had been denied great numbers of his principal allies, and Clark now held sway, if only by bluff and bombast, over a wilderness larger than France.

All this was simply prelude, however, to vicissitudes that tried the very souls of Clark's remaining riflemen and drove him to the apex of his career as a border soldier. In Detroit, Hamilton was both startled and appalled—if only because he was gathering arms and stores for an attack on American-held Fort Pitt—at news of Clark's successes. He wasted little time, however, in responding to the unseemly presence of Americans in Kaskaskia, Cahokia and Vincennes. He left Detroit for Vincennes on October 7 with a force of more than 200 men, including three dozen Regulars, French and English volunteers and 70 Indians.

Hamilton's expedition moved slowly. It took him 71 days to cover the 600 miles separating him from his goal—in part because low water in the Maumee and the Petite Riviere (a tributary of the Wabash) continually grounded his boats, which were laden to the gunwales with 97,000 pounds of supplies and weapons. But the goods and a six-pounder cannon—which he fired off as he progressed to impress the inhabitants of every Indian village—won him back tribesmen who had defected. He had about 350 Indians in his train when he retook Vincennes, disarmed Clark's hapless Captain Helm, and induced the town's French burghers to renounce their "treachery and ingratitude," kiss a silver crucifix and resume their allegiance to the king with a written oath.

Next Hamilton sent Indians toward Kaskaskia to capture Clark, should he be found off guard, and to bring him back alive. But this plan came to naught when the would-be kidnappers quit after becoming bogged down in snow. Hamilton then ceased operations, released his volunteers and Indians with orders to rejoin him after planting their crops in the spring, and settled comfortably in Vincennes to contemplate the sure defeat of his tormentors within a few months.

Clark did not get firm news of Hamilton's victory until January 29, 1779, when one François Vigo, an

Italian-born Spanish trader, arrived in Kaskaskia and described the recapture of Vincennes. Clark pondered. Cold rain and melting snow had turned the prairies to bogs and had raised every river above its banks. Still he saw no other recourse but "to attack the enemy in his stronghold."

Nothing, he felt certain, was to be gained by retreat across the Ohio to Kentucky, for "all the men in it, united to the troops we had, would not suffice, and to get succor in time from the Virginia and Pennsylvania frontiers was out of the question. We saw but one alternative, which was to attack. If we were successful we would thereby save the whole American cause." Clark was encouraged "by the thought of the magnitude of the consequences that would attend our success." And he was convinced that the season of the year was "favorable to our design, since the enemy could not suppose that we would be so mad as to attempt a march of eighty leagues through a drowned country in the depth of winter."

Hamilton boasted two three-pounders on truck carriages as well as his six-pounder at Vincennes' Fort Sackville. Clark prepared to counteract this artillery by mounting two four-pounders and four large swivels captured from the French on a large riverboat he called the *Willing;* he loaded the bulk of his supplies aboard the boat and sent her on a roundabout course up the Ohio and the Wabash with orders to await him some miles below Vincennes. The *Willing* set off on February 4 with Clark's cousin, Lieutenant John Rogers, in command and with 40 of his precious soldiers to serve her oars and guns.

Clark talked to the people of Kaskaskia—as he noted in a letter—"as though I was sure of taking Mr. Hamilton," and his confidence caused "the Ladies also to be spirited and to interest themselves in the Expedi-

A brigade of frontiersmen led by George Rogers Clark slogs through icy floodwaters to surprise the British at Vincennes on February 23, 1779. "No provisions yet, lord help us," wrote one famished soldier after three days of forced march. But then the men came across an Indian woman with a canoe full of buffalo meat, which fortified them for the attack.

tion which had great effect on the Young men." Thus he managed to augment his remaining riflemen with two little volunteer companies of French militia. Nevertheless, he reflected, he had only 200 men, and had "set out on a Forlorn hope, indeed." He wrote wistfully: "I would have bound myself seven years a Slave to have had 500 troops."

On February 5, the day after the departure of the *Willing,* Clark broke camp and set out at the head of his column for Vincennes. The route he was to follow stretched 240 miles and was "flowing with water" over much of its length. Yet, for all his misgivings, Clark could hardly wait to visit astonishment on his foe: "I cannot account for it but I still had inward assurance of success; and never could, when weighing every Circumstance doubt it." His confidence became the sole sustenance of the expedition; his energy and ebullience were all, in fact, that kept his despondent force moving when, after several days of brisk marching, it began to encounter miles of quagmire, and stream after flooding stream.

Clark made a point of "running through the mud and water the same as the men themselves." He was hard put to hide his own perturbation, nevertheless, as they sloshed up to the first of two rivers they called the Little Wabashes. Both were over their banks and a lake "frequently four feet in depth" covered the five miles of plain between them.

Clark forced himself to fight down "irresolution" by ordering a large canoe hacked out of a big log and by telling himself that his men, once on the other side, would "abandon all thought of retreat, preferring to undergo any difficulty which offered a prospect of success, rather than to attempt a retreat involving the certainty of encountering all they had already endured." The swollen rivers exacted four days of suffering "too incredible for any Person to believe." Every man, every pound of baggage had to be ferried across both streams. The men built platforms on which to pile stores along the way and, between rivers, men and horses alike were forced to wade in frigid water, sometimes to their chins.

Their hardships multiplied thereafter. They found no dry land except for that on a few little rises and knolls; they had no provisions left after the 18th; they could find no sign of their gunboat; and much of their powder was ruined by the incessant rain. "Hard fortune!" wrote Joseph Bowman in an understatement.

Clark and his men were within sound of Hamilton's morning gun on the 23rd — having abandoned their horses and crossed the Wabash itself in two canoes. But a freezing night had laid a skim of ice on four miles of breast-high water that lay between them and a rise of ground just south of Vincennes. All were weak with hunger. Men began refusing to go on, but they forced themselves forward in shivering and reluctant knots after Clark blacked his face with gunpowder, "raised the war whoop" and plunged into the awful lake alone.

He still entertained "some suspicion of three or four of them," however, and ordered Bowman to "fall into the rear with 25 men and put to death any who refused to march, saying we wished to have no such person among us." What followed was pure nightmare. Men stumbled in the icy water, went down, and were saved from drowning only by those still active enough to pull them back to their feet. The feeblest were rescued by the party's two canoes. Some men attempted to husband their strength by pausing to cling to logs, but most splashed steadily along in staggering knots, with the weak in the arms of the strong and with every man's vitality draining away into the numbing water as the morning wore on. The sight of dry ground, gained after hours of this suffering, undid many of them; they fell on the bank, legs still in the water, unable to move another inch. But all, miraculously, were alive. And now, having survived when survival seemed impossible, they found cause for hope once more.

The sturdiest dragged up dead wood and built fires. They soon had some chunks of buffalo meat cooking in a blackened kettle, taken from an Indian woman who came upon them in a canoe. Bleak winter sunshine warmed them a little, and showed their foremost lookouts Vincennes at last — a sprawl of little farms, a few log buildings, a log church and the blockhouses of Fort Sackville on high ground.

The scouts waylaid a duck hunter who came out from the town during the afternoon. Determined "to be as daring as possible," Clark decided to risk sending him back to town with a message for the French inhabitants: "Being now within two miles of your village I request such of you as are true citizens, and willing to enjoy the liberty I bring you, to remain still in your houses. Those that are true friends to Liberty may depend on being well treated. But every one I find in arms on my arrival, I shall treat as an enemy."

This rashness proved to have been the course of wisdom when the little army picked up its weapons and marched into the town after dark without waiting for the *Willing* and its artillery.

All but the fort was Clark's on arrival — including precious gunpowder that the French had cached underground against discovery by the British and had dug up in haste after receiving his message. Indeed, Vincennes citizens had kept the secret of his presence so well that Hamilton, locked serenely in his fort, believed drunken Indians were celebrating in the streets when Clark's riflemen first began sniping at glimmers of light behind the fort's gun ports. The fort eventually erupted with answering musket and cannon fire, but Clark's hardbitten sharpshooters, who rolled or dodged to new cover after every shot, were too much for its defenders. Hamilton's artillery was noisy but ineffective; the Americans picked off his gunners whenever they exposed themselves to aim and fire, and by early morning had wounded a number of them.

Clark called a halt to firing at midmorning and sent a man with a white flag up to the fort with a letter: "Sir: — In order to save yourself from the impending storm that now threatens you, I order you immediately to surrender yourself, with all your garrison, stores, etc., etc., etc. for if I am obliged to storm, you may depend upon such treatment as is justly due to a murderer." Hamilton refused to be saved — at least immediately. He wrote in return: "Governor Hamilton begs leave to acquaint Col. Clark, that he and his Garrison are not disposed to be awed into an action unworthy of British subjects."

This was true enough — in part. Hamilton's 36 stolid redcoats had assured him that they "would stick to me as the shirt on my back." His French volunteers, on the other hand, had "hung their heads" and murmured that their own countrymen had gone over to the Americans. Hamilton raised a white flag after a few more hours of noisy fusillading and sent Leonard Helm, the American officer he had captured during the retaking of Vincennes, to Clark with a counterproposal: three days of truce and secret negotiations that "may be to the honour and credit of each party." ◉

The gentleman they called the "Hair Buyer"

To American settlers in the Ohio Valley, the real coup in taking Vincennes in 1779 was the capture of British Commandant Henry Hamilton, otherwise known as the "Hair Buyer." In his role as lieutenant governor of Detroit, Hamilton organized and financed ferocious Indian raids on settlements all along the frontier, and he was universally believed to have paid bounties for American scalps gathered during the raids.

So despised was Hamilton that Thomas Jefferson, then governor of Virginia, found it impossible to accord him the usual courtesies of rank when the captive commandant was brought to Williamsburg. Instead, Hamilton was ordered shackled in irons and clapped into a cramped, foul dungeon. When the British protested his treatment, Jefferson retorted sharply that it was "justified on the general principle of national retaliation."

Whether Hamilton was actually as villainous as the Americans believed is a matter of dispute. There is no question that he encouraged his Indian allies to raid, supplied their needs and rewarded their successes. But he vehemently denied that he ever paid for scalps and insisted that he did everything possible to mitigate the horrors of that "deplorable sort of war."

In Hamilton's own eyes he was merely carrying out a disagreeable but necessary mission in attempting to deny the West to American settlers. And most Americans who came before him as captives were astounded at the civil treatment they received from the notorious Hair Buyer. Daniel Boone, who was briefly Hamil-

ton's prisoner in Detroit in 1778, was so impressed with the governor's "great humanity" that he later paid a special visit to the incarcerated Briton in his Williamsburg cell.

In 1781, Hamilton was released in a prisoner exchange and quickly resumed his career, first as the lieutenant governor of Quebec, later as the governor of the island colonies of Bermuda and Dominica. Despite all the odium the Americans had heaped on him, Hamilton was regarded in the

Colonial Office as a superior civil servant and "a gentleman of great honor and integrity."

Indeed, Jefferson and the frontiersmen might have been surprised to learn that the blackguard they held responsible for "acts of the most wanton barbarity" was a remarkably civilized man. Born to a noble Scottish family with a distinguished record of public service, Hamilton had spent 20 years as an army officer before he was posted to Detroit in 1775. At

Detroit he quickly alienated the original French settlers by cracking down on sharp trading practices with the Indians—and he just as quickly earned the respect of the tribes for his fair dealings.

Hamilton made an effort to learn Indian languages and recorded detailed observations of Indian customs and local geography in his journal, which he illustrated with sketches, some hasty, some elaborately detailed. Skill in drawing was not an uncommon accomplishment for an 18th Century gentleman, but several of Hamilton's efforts show artistic talents well beyond the call of social obligation. In addition, his portraits of Indians reveal an eye for ethnographic minutiae that makes them a rare record of tribal dress in the Revolutionary War period.

Of the eight known portraits, all sketched in pencil on gilt-edged postcards, the most detailed is of a Miami chief named Pacane, whom Hamilton met on his way from Detroit to Vincennes. The chief's wealth is evident from his silver arm bands, earrings and nose rings, and the cowrie shells that decorate his shoulders. Hamilton noted on the back of the portrait that he had presented Pacane with a silver-mounted knife in honor of the chief's father, who once had "taken down from a stake when he was to have been roasted Cap. T. Morris," an officer described by Hamilton as "a friend of many years standing."

Hamilton's portrait of Otcheek, "a respected warrior of the Mohawk nation," depicts the characteristic Iroquois raven-feather headdress; the portrait of Quooquandarong, "a wise and moderate Sachem of the Huron nation," shows the chief carrying a decorated calumet and wearing his

PACANE

hair curled on copper worm screws.

Tzenoritze, a dissolute Huron prince, Hamilton dismissed as "easily led, given to liquor." Pepiquenne, of the Nipissins tribe, whose name Hamilton translated as "the Flute," he described as having "but little character or authority . . . nearly a silent flute." Even these offhand remarks indicate what set Hamilton apart from most of his contemporaries on the frontier, both British and American. He regarded Indians as individuals, not, like his eminent superior Lord Jeffery Amherst, as "the vilest race of beings that ever infested the earth."

PEPIQUENNE

TZENORITZE

QUOOQUANDARONG

OTCHEEK

Ferrying his troops down the Wabash to Vincennes, Hamilton sketched the passing scenery from his boat and went ashore to note geological curiosities. He spent hours examining fossils in this crumbling bluff, near present-day Logansport, Indiana.

Hamilton probably made this careful ink drawing during a layover on the same river expedition. Later, as a prisoner, he remained an indefatigable sketcher, snatching moments even on his 700-mile march to Williamsburg to depict the countryside.

lark refused the three-day truce proposed by Hamilton, perhaps suspecting that his adversary expected an expedition from Detroit, but agreed to talk if Hamilton was willing to meet him, forthwith, in the French church near the fort. In the meantime, Clark's men ambushed a war party as it hurried toward the fort to present scalps it had taken at the Falls of the Ohio. They took four surviving warriors captive. Clark ordered these "Poor Devils" tied to a fence and tomahawked, one by one, in full view of those waiting in the stockade for the outcome of the cease-fire. This was Clark's harsh way of demonstrating to the Indians that the British could no longer protect them, and of presenting the British troops with gruesome evidence of his own obduracy.

The "Hair Buyer" was moved to an orotund indignation when he described this episode in his official report. "Colonel Clarke yet reeking with the blood of these unhappy Victims came to the Esplanade before the Fort Gate, where I had agreed to meet him and treat of the surrender of the Garrison — He spoke with rapture of his late achievement, while he washed off the blood from his hands stained in this inhuman sacrifice." But Hamilton agreed to surrender for all that — though not without a great deal of face-saving argument — since he was told that "not a single Soul should be Spared," and because "half of our number had shewed their poltronnerie [cowardice] and treason, and our wounded must be left at the mercy of a merciless set of Banditti. At ten o'clock in the morning of the 25th, we marched out with fix'd Bayonets and the Soldiers with their knapsacks — the colors had not been hoisted this morning, that we might be spared the mortification of hawling them down."

Clark spent most of a month dealing with problems that rose out of his victory and preparing — this time with genuine military leverage rather than simple audacity — to ensure American domination of Illinois. He sent Helm and a party of soldiers hurrying up to the Wabash to capture seven boatloads of stores on their way from Detroit and clothed and otherwise enriched his soldiers by dividing the cargo among them. He welcomed the crew of the *Willing,* who arrived, to their embarrassment, two days after Fort Sackville had fallen. Clark won the gratitude of Hamilton's French volunteers by sending them home to Detroit under

parole, and, intent on divesting himself of more dangerous prisoners, he sent Hamilton, his officers and 18 of his Regulars off under guard to be jailed in Williamsburg. Eventually, they would be included in a prisoner of war exchange.

Clark's astonishing descent upon Vincennes dashed British hopes of dominating the American West, and his victory there — for all his failure to take the ultimate prize, Detroit — encouraged the flow of migration over the Appalachians. Something like 5,000 people settled in Kentucky during the year, and 30,000 by the end of the Revolution.

Clark was — at least temporarily — master of all he surveyed north of the Ohio. Kaskaskians presented him with 54,600 pounds of flour and Cahokians with a fifth of their cattle to promote his military ambitions. Virginia promised him 500 men, and Kentucky 200 to 300 more. The Piankashaws, Chippewas, Potawatomis and Miamis all "begged to be taken under the cover of our wings," as he put it. But Clark — though he was only 26 years old — had reached the apogee of his military career and, indeed, the climactic moment of his life. His dreams of ascendancy and American hopes of peace north of the Ohio were both subject to slow but inevitable dissolution in the years that followed.

Virginia made him a brigadier general and sent him a handsome commemorative sword — which he is supposed to have thrust into the ground and broken in a fit of rage over the fact that the state provided but a handful of the promised soldiers. Kentucky did no better by him. His hopes of marching on Detroit and of excising the last seat of British harassment on the frontier were stifled and stifled again, partly by official indifference, partly by the frustrating problems of holding what he had in Illinois and of maintaining a fort he built on the Kentucky side of the Ohio (at the site of present-day Louisville) in 1779.

His reputation and his control of his little garrisons were both eroded by the increasing worthlessness of Continental currency: his soldiers, some in rags, complained that one Mexican dollar was worth more than a thousand in American scrip, and merchants who had given him fortunes in supplies on credit wrote bitterly to say they had ruined themselves by backing him.

Clark struggled fiercely to rise above this chaos. He impoverished himself for the sake of his backers by

Colone Clarks Compliments to Mr.
Hamilton and begs leave to inform
him that Col. Clark will not agree
to Any Other Terms than that of Mr.
Hamilton's Surrendering himself and
Garrison, Prisoners at Discretion —

 If Mr. Hamilton is Desirous of
a Conferance with Col. Clark he will
meet him at the Church with Captn
Helms —

Feby 24th 179   G R Clark

In a note to Henry Hamilton, commandant of the besieged British garrison at Vincennes, Clark demands unconditional surrender but offers to talk about the matter at a log church *(below)* 80 yards from the fort. Hamilton, who had been holding out for "honorable" conditions before capitulating to Clark's "motley Banditti," met the Virginian and they agreed on terms. But after the surrender ceremony Hamilton and several of his officers were ordered clapped in irons. Outraged, he railed at Clark: "You must renounce all pretentions to the character of an officer or a gentleman."

selling and mortgaging property of his own. In 1780 and again in 1782 he organized and led expeditions of militiamen and volunteers on raids against Indian towns in Ohio—at one point closing the land office at Harrodsburg, Kentucky, to distract settlers from their fever for property and keep them at hand for his recruiters. But as Indian atrocities multiplied in Illinois and Kentucky, he grew increasingly discouraged at the apathy in Virginia to his demands for men and money. And, finally, he was reprimanded for failing to provide Virginia's bookkeepers with an accounting of notes he had drawn on the state while campaigning.

He was relieved of his commission in 1783 at the age of 30—having failed to receive a cent of pay for his years of service in the West—and began a long, twilight existence as a civilian. He served as chairman of a Virginia commission that allotted free land to soldiers of his Illinois expedition (his own 8,049 acres were immediately attached by creditors). He picked up the sword again, briefly, in 1786 and was demeaned in so doing; a campaign by Kentucky militia against the Indians along the Wabash was bogged down by shortages of food and supplies after he took command and ended with a mutiny of disgruntled troops. Clark became a conspirator in dubious political plots (among other things he agreed to lead a French expedition, which never materialized, against Spanish Louisiana). Drink became his companion in the end; he spent many of his declining years holed up in a cabin overlooking the Ohio. But, meanwhile, another star had risen—that of Anthony Wayne.

The area north of the Ohio had become a hotbed of problems which seemed to grow more insoluble with the passage of time. The new Congress essayed a dual program calculated to make the Algonquins' country a seat of orderly white civilization and to meet the nation's war debts partly through the sale of land to settlers. Congress set out to persuade the tribes to cede land to the government by treaty, and dispatched surveyors to lay out townships of thirty-six 640-acre sections in present-day Ohio. These subdivisions were then offered for sale at Eastern auctions.

But dickering with the tribes was an uncertain business. The Shawnees, for one, refused to have any part of the process, and a great many whites as well were critical of the government, and interfered with its hopes of orderly transition from the beginning.

Large numbers of squatters ignored the section system, which valued land at one dollar an acre, sold it in lots no smaller than 640 acres and in the process put it out of reach of all but speculators. The frontier people firmly believed, in the words of an army officer given the task of driving them out, that all Americans have "an undoubted right to pass into every vacant country and there form their own constitution." The squatters swarmed on Indian land as well as treaty land and fought for it with desperation thereafter. Meanwhile, tribe after tribe was attacked by raiding parties of riflemen from Kentucky bent on vengeance for depredations that the more hostile of war chiefs still visited on border stations south of the Ohio.

These trying domestic problems were exacerbated by continued British attempts to weaken the uneasy new confederation of American states. The British refused to abandon posts by which they had controlled waterways along the Canadian border since the French and Indian Wars—Dutchman's Point, Point-au-Fer, Oswegatchie, Oswego, Niagara, Mackinac and Detroit—although all lay well south of the line drawn by the 1783 Treaty of Paris, which supposedly spelled the end of the conflict between the former colonies and Britain. They justified this obstinancy by accusing the new states of violating the treaty in turn (a charge that was true enough) and failing to recompense American loyalists and British merchants for losses and debts incurred during the Revolution. And from the disputed posts, the British sent forth agents to urge a confederation of Algonquin tribes to resist further American encroachments.

This intervention divided the Indians in the beginning. The Shawnees, Kickapoos and Miamis pledged themselves to demand a border at the Ohio; however, the Delawares, Wyandots and Senecas were reluctant to involve themselves in a scheme that seemed so certain to induce war with the Americans. But raids and counterraids kept the territory seething with unrest; the squatting remained uncontrolled despite American efforts to check it; and the Indians rebuffed all American efforts to negotiate treaties for their land.

The most indecisive of Indians were emboldened, in 1790 and 1791, when two American expeditions—

LITTLE TURTLE

A CHIEF WHO MASTERED TWO GENERALS

The worst defeats suffered by American frontier forces came in 1790 and 1791 at the hands of a confederation of Algonquin tribes under the Miami chief Little Turtle. A master of woodland warfare, Little Turtle staged a mock retreat in 1790 that lured an expedition led by the overconfident General Josiah Harmar into a bloody ambush in which 183 militiamen died. The following fall, the Miami chieftain organized a dawn attack in the dense forests near present-day St. Mary's, Ohio, and overran a larger army commanded by the high-minded but inept General St. Clair. Unable to repel the tide of settlers, Little Turtle was finally reconciled to their presence in Ohio and earned the praise of President Washington in 1797 by counseling peace to his tribesmen.

GENERAL ARTHUR ST. CLAIR

GENERAL JOSIAH HARMAR

one under General Josiah Harmar and one commanded by Territorial Governor Arthur St. Clair—were repulsed in spectacular fashion when they attempted to enforce the government's will in Ohio.

Both armies—Harmar had 1,500 men and St. Clair 3,000—included some dependable troops but were largely composed of undisciplined militiamen or newly recruited Regulars who had not the slightest understanding of forest war, or of any war for that matter. Harmar, a veteran of the Revolutionary War, was appalled at the militia he received from Pennsylvania and Kentucky: mobs of boys and old men who arrived without equipment and seemed eternally bent on questioning rather than obeying the orders of their officers. As he moved north with this noisy multitude the Indians fell back into the forest—stealing and killing more than one third of his pack horses.

A small command under Colonel John Hardin was massacred when half of his men deserted just before an Indian attack. To avenge their deaths, Harmar sent 400 men (of whom 60 were Regulars) back against the villages. Warriors under a Miami chieftain named Little Turtle struck from ambush, however, when Harmar's unruly militiamen left the formation to hunt Indians on their own. Little Turtle's warriors then descended upon the Regulars and slaughtered most of them before the dismayed survivors could extricate themselves and rejoin their comrades in a doleful retreat to the Ohio.

Governor St. Clair, an aging Revolutionary general who enjoyed the confidence of President George Washington despite a lingering reputation for military ineptitude, was now commanded to succeed where Harmar had failed. St. Clair deserves a certain commiseration denied him by history. His opponent, Little Turtle, was a wily and daring tactician; the Algonquins were savagely efficient woodland guerrillas; and his own troops were as unreliable, for the most part, as those that had gone north with Harmar. But St. Clair made lamentable mistakes as he advanced to the Maumee country in the autumn of 1791. He weakened himself by sending a regiment of Regulars chasing after deserters and left his remaining 1,400 men strung out through the woods with the militia isolated from the rest when he camped on the night of November 2. St. Clair had his men stand to arms at dawn the following day, but as the enemy failed to materialize he then dismissed them to their tents and fires.

The militia was thrown into instant confusion, as a result, when Little Turtle's warriors burst, shrieking, from the trees shortly after sunrise. The fleeing men carried terror with them as they dashed into the encampments of the Regulars. Gangs of Indians bounded among them and hacked at them with tomahawks. The uneven battle went on for two hours, with Indians firing from behind trees into masses of disorganized and bewildered soldiery. St. Clair, who was so ill he had been carried on a litter, rose bravely and ordered bayonet charges in an attempt to organize an orderly retreat. But his troops fled in panic through the gap he created, throwing down their muskets as the Indians pursued. St. Clair survived, but before the Miamis, Shawnees and Wyandots were finished, 630 of his men were dead—more than the Indians had killed in the massacre of Braddock's column in 1755, more Americans than had fallen in any battle of the Revolution.

St. Clair's defeat not only restored the wildest hopes of the Algonquin tribes—which began, forthwith, to terrorize Western settlements anew—but convinced the British that the United States had been proven incapable of defending the territory. This was a logical assumption: Eastern Americans were against further military adventures and the Algonquins were now prepared to fight for the Ohio boundary if it was not granted to them by treaty. But both the English and the Indians failed, in their new euphoria, to consider President George Washington's capacity for indignation—and resolution.

Washington received word of St. Clair's awful defeat during a formal dinner in Philadelphia. He suppressed his feelings throughout the long, quiet meal, but flew into a monumental rage immediately after his guests had departed: "To suffer that army to be cut to pieces, hacked, butchered—tomahawked by surprise—the very thing I guarded him against!" He resolved to find a commander capable of reorganizing the American Army and of using it—if the Indians would not have peace—to end forest warfare forever.

Washington hesitated for weeks before finally making "Mad Anthony" Wayne commander in chief of the new army, which was to be called the Legion of the United States. He feared Wayne's impetuosity—

This somber broadside, published in Boston, spread news of the rout, on November 4, 1791, of General St. Clair's army in Ohio. The Algonquins killed over 600 Americans, including 39 officers whose names are printed over the coffins at top.

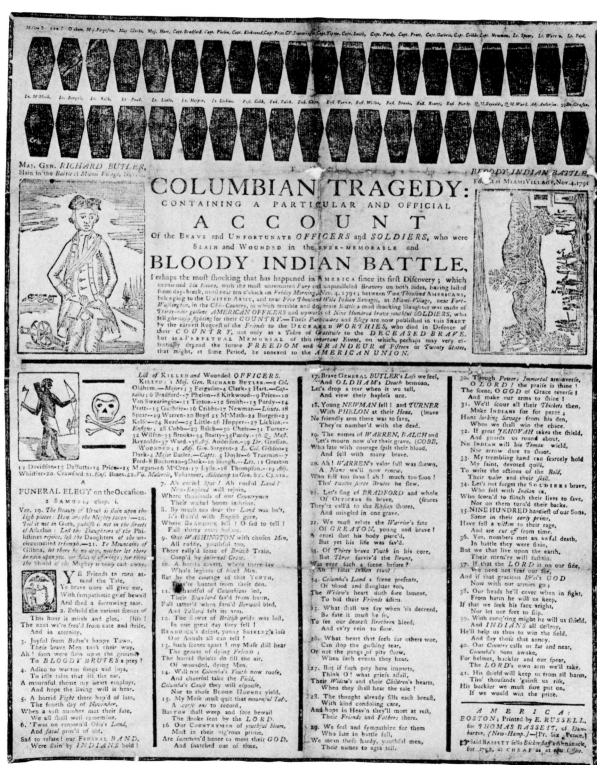

and with reason. A rugged, dark-eyed and animated Pennsylvanian, Wayne believed there were few exigencies in war that could not be overcome by headlong attack, preferably with the bayonet. This rashness had exposed him to entrapment on occasion, and had cost him heavy losses in battles at Paoli and Brandywine. But no Revolutionary general had fought like Wayne. It was he who had driven the Hessians back to Germantown, who had led the attack at Monmouth and who had captured the British bastion at Stony Point with a surprise assault at midnight. Soldiers trusted him. And time, it turned out, had tempered his belligerency with patience and judiciousness.

Wayne made it plain from the beginning that he did not propose to take the field before creating an army capable of fighting any troops in the world. This was a formidable task. The hapless survivors of St. Clair's expedition formed the nucleus he found waiting for him at Pittsburgh, and such men as recruiters could scrape up for him were often the same ne'er-do-wells, felons, drifters and bar flies who had joined the army for food and shelter in the years since the Revolution. "The offscourings of large towns and cities; enervated by Idleness, Debaucheries and every Species of Vice," said one disgusted officer. A good many of these newcomers ran off as soon as they had drunk up their bounty money in the town's saloons. Wayne dealt with such malingerers with a heavy hand. He offered rewards for deserters and had them shot when returned, or subjected to 100 lashes on the naked back. But he also abandoned Pittsburgh, marched his troops 22 miles west along the Ohio and put them to work with saws and axes at raising a new encampment he called Legionville.

The levies of Legionville were subject to incessant drill, incessant practice at targets, incessant instruction in use of the bayonet — and to endless and exhausting mock skirmishes in which the enemy was always presumed to be firing from the cover of stumps and trees. Winter came. The troops drilled in snow, learned to reload while charging at the dead run — and to splash on into the icy river if not halted by direct command. Discipline was harsh; but the men walked with a new confidence. They were leavened by robust volunteers — 101 from Virginia, 30 from Maryland, 164 from Westmoreland County. To boost morale further,

Wayne sent men into the country to shoot bears. He presented his cohorts with bearskin caps adorned with plumes — some red, some white, some yellow, some green — representing the army's four sublegions.

All through the spring and summer the army drilled while the government attempted to arrange a last-ditch meeting with the Algonquins. The suspense ended in August: the Indians notified three United States land commissioners (in a note written by functionaries of the British Indian Service) that there would be no conference and that the Ohio must "remain the boundary line between us."

Wayne, having spent so long "endeavoring to make the rifleman believe in that arm, the Infantry in heavy buckshot & the bayonet, the Dragoons in the sword, and the Legion in their United prowess," warned his men they might have to march at a moment's notice. "We now," scribbled an excited young lieutenant named Thomas Underwood, "have but one alternative left and this is we must meet the savage foe; the Emortal Washington at the Head of our Government, and the Old Hero, Gen'l Wayne and his well disciplined legion. We have little to fear, accept our god and fear him in love."

But if the army envisioned some dramatic dash into Indian country it was soon disappointed. It moved no faster than its vulnerable wagon train and it did not camp at night without felling trees for hours to create encircling barricades. It was treated to some humbling excitement on the sixth day. Wayne sent Colonel John Hamtramck, an experienced Indian fighter, ahead of the main body with men of the 1st sublegion to create a mock ambush and watched in austere displeasure as it entrapped his advance guard. Seventy miles from Cincinnati, he halted, set the army to building blockhouses, stockades and row on row of log huts, and — having created a 53-acre stronghold he called Fort Greenville — settled down to yet another winter of molding the army in his own image.

There was grumbling among young officers at Wayne's deliberation — a good deal of it prompted by the second-in-command, Brigadier General James Wilkinson, a self-serving veteran of the Revolution who would eventually prove himself one of the greatest rascals in American history. The commander in chief remained unperturbed. He proposed to use Regulars as they had not been used in forest warfare, to dictate the terms of battle in so doing, and thus to deny the Indians the initiative they had always enjoyed in their own country. Fort Greenville was a base from which he would sally forth in his own good time.

"Give me authority to make these Arrangements," he had written to Secretary of War Henry Knox, "and I will pledge my reputation as an Officer to establish myself at the Miami Villages, or at any other place on the Miami River that may be thought more proper in the face of all the savages of the Wilderness that can be brought against me. Shou'd they Collect in force & approach within striking distance in the night — with a View of surprising, or attacking me in the Morning — Our *Indians* guides, scouts, spies and Cavalry, *who shall always patrol & hover widely round me will* not suffer the savages to advance undiscovered, nor shall I wait their attack — on the Contrary they shall feel the effects of a Nocturnal charge — and I know *that they are a contemptable enemy in the Night.*"

But Wayne gave the Indians pause from the beginning by his very deliberation. There was something ominous, something remorseless about his army's ponderous and disciplined advance and about the labor it expended so prodigally on the construction of Fort Greenville. The Algonquin chieftains — Little Turtle, Captain Pipe, Red Pole, Blue Jacket, Blackhoof — kept scouts on the periphery of his route from the moment he left the Ohio River. None had seen soldiers so responsive to their officers or so constantly wary of attack. A delegation of lesser sachems — whom Wayne admitted to talk to him of peace — had never seen a military establishment run as was Fort Greenville. And Wayne soon offered the tribes a deliberate provocation. Eight companies of his troops marched to the scene of St. Clair's defeat; they buried the skulls and bones of the dead, and spent weeks building a satellite stronghold called Fort Recovery.

It was Wayne's — and Washington's — assumption that the Indians' boundary dispute masked something far more crucial to the expectations of the United States than the boundary: an unspoken clash of nerve and will with England that might well undo the very fabric of the new nation.

"The Savages," Wayne wrote to Knox in one breathless sentence, "have become confident haughty

General Anthony Wayne signals a charge as his infantry-men begin to overrun their Indian adversaries in the decisive Battle of Fallen Timbers in 1794. The fighting lasted just 40 minutes and less than half of Wayne's 2,100 men saw action, but his display of overwhelming force persuaded the tribes to surrender enormous areas of land north of the Ohio.

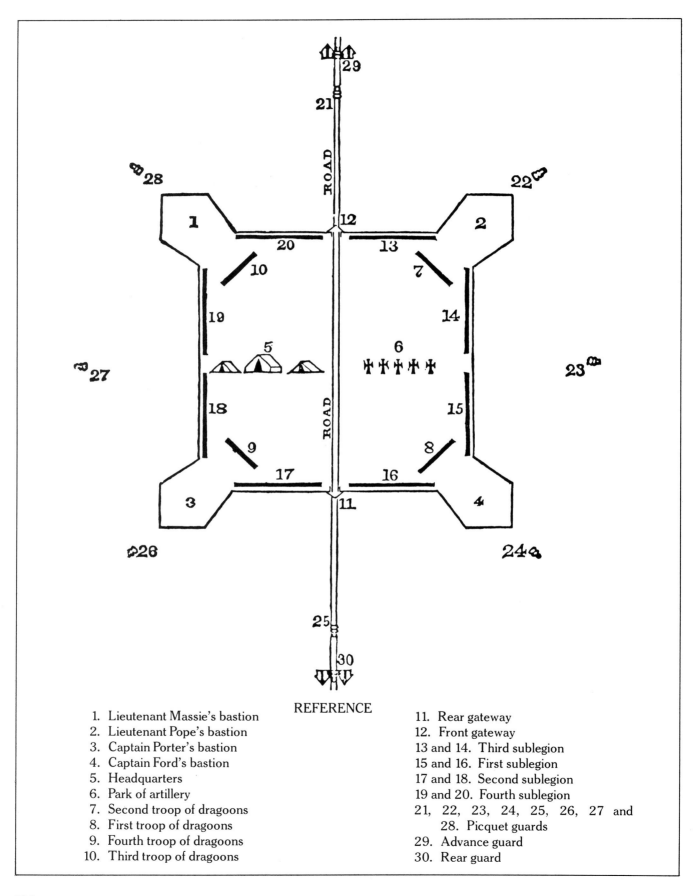

REFERENCE

1. Lieutenant Massie's bastion
2. Lieutenant Pope's bastion
3. Captain Porter's bastion
4. Captain Ford's bastion
5. Headquarters
6. Park of artillery
7. Second troop of dragoons
8. First troop of dragoons
9. Fourth troop of dragoons
10. Third troop of dragoons

11. Rear gateway
12. Front gateway
13 and 14. Third sublegion
15 and 16. First sublegion
17 and 18. Second sublegion
19 and 20. Fourth sublegion
21, 22, 23, 24, 25, 26, 27 and
    28. Picquet guards
29. Advance guard
30. Rear guard

& Insolent from reiterated success; which they have evinced by a Wanton & deliberate Massacre of our flags, an enormity that can't be permitted to pass with impunity unless the U S of America will sacrifice National Character & Justice to Mistaken prejudice & mean Economy, particularly whilst British are in possession of our posts on the Lakes for atho' they may not directly—I am convinced that they do indirectly stimulate the Savages to continue the War, nor can all the sophistry of British Embassadors Agents or state spies convince me to the contrary until they surrender up those posts."

The English ceased all sophistry in February. Lord Dorchester, Governor General of Canada, gave a delegation of chiefs from Northern tribes to understand that British soldiers would soon be fighting at their sides against the Americans. "Children, from the manner in which the people of the United States push on and act and talk, I shall not be surprised if we are at war with them in the course of the present year; and if so a line must then be drawn by the warriors. We have acted in the most peaceable manner and borne the language and conduct of the people of the United States; but I believe our patience is almost exhausted." The chiefs were galvanized, the more so when the speech was printed and distributed along the border and British officials were directed to read it aloud to the gatherings of eager Indians.

"His Excellency Governor Simcoe has just now left my house on his way to Detroit with Lord Dorchester's speech to the Seven Nations," wrote the Iroquois

---

AN AMBITIOUS DAILY ENCAMPMENT

General "Mad Anthony" Wayne's laborious advance into Indian territory was marked by nothing so much as the absence of the impetuosity he was celebrated for. In addition to the half-dozen strongholds he constructed from Legionville to Fort Wayne, he ordered his men at the end of each day's march to set up a fortified camp roughly along the lines of the plan at left. A square site that could be as large as 75 acres was surrounded with breastworks of logs and tangled branches, and four solid redoubts were built at the corners. While the infantry dug in, the dragoons cut grass for their horses so that the animals could be kept inside the camp. Not surprisingly, the Indians were too intimidated to attack.

Joseph Brant to the Secretary of Indian Affairs for Canada, "and I have every reason to believe when it is delivered that matters will take an immediate change to the Westward, as it will undoubtedly give those Nations high spirits and enable them by a perfect union to check General Wayne." John Butler, a British lieutenant-colonel, read the speech aloud to a large council of Indians gathered near Buffalo and added: "You have heard great talk of our going to war with the United States, and by the speech of your Father just now delivered to you, you cannot help seeing there is a great prospect of it."

Dorchester soon sent Governor Simcoe into American territory with workmen, tools and artillery to build a fort at the foot of the Maumee rapids. The result, which Simcoe named Fort Miami, was impressive: a system of stockaded blockhouses fringed with rows of spiked poles and surrounded by a moat. Three companies of scarlet-coated English Regulars and one of Canadian militia marched through its gate to a rattle of drums when it was complete. It became a storehouse for rifles, gun locks, powder, vermilion war paint and tobacco that an Indian agent, Alexander McKee, parceled out to Miamis, Shawnees and Delawares as the spring wore on. Dorchester's speech and Dorchester's fort were to prove colossal blunders—incontrovertible evidence of British duplicity—but they persuaded 2,000 Northwest Indians to strike at the Americans in Fort Recovery.

Seventeen columns of warriors, led by the Shawnee Chieftain, Blue Jacket, and by British officers in Indian dress, converged on the fort at dawn on June 30. They were presented with instant booty and instant victims: 360 pack horses that had carried stores the 25 miles from Fort Greenville the day before, and whose impatient drivers had been allowed to begin the return journey before their escort was ready. The commander of the fort immediately ordered out dragoons and riflemen. But 21 officers and men were killed in the first confused and noisy melee. The survivors fell back, firing, and returned safely inside the fort as hundreds of warriors devoted themselves to chasing frightened horses. That evening the Indians were repulsed with heavy losses when they tried an assault, en masse, across open ground around the stockade. They issued forth later in the night only to recover their dead; the

"I have an insuperable bias in favor of an elegant uniform," admitted Anthony Wayne, who cared enough about appearance to hire barbers to keep his troops, as well as himself, properly clipped and shaved during their frontier campaigns.

next morning, after some desultory firing, they withdrew as silently as they had come.

Wayne drew a great deal of satisfaction from the outcome of this defensive action—not only because his troops had been invigorated and the foe obviously discouraged but because it seemed to have been an act of folly by his British counterparts. "There were a considerable number of armed white men in the rear," he wrote Knox, "who were heard talking in our language & encouraging the Savages. Their faces were Generally blacked except three British Officers who were dressed in scarlet & appeared to be men of great distinction." Wayne speculated that it "wou'd appear that the real Object of the Enemy" was to have taken the American fort by surprise, and he boasted that they "were ultimately compeled to retreat about One O'Clock of that day with loss & disgrace from that very field where they had upon a former Occasion been proudly Victorious."

Wayne now had a well-trained army of 2,500 men, with mounted dragoons, detachments of artillery and riflemen (who could shoot as accurately as backwoodsmen) to augment the infantry—armed with musket and bayonet—which made up the bulk of his forces. He spent July immobilized at Fort Greenville, nevertheless, while General Charles Scott and 1,500 mounted Kentucky volunteers, who had spent the previous summer drilling with Wayne's Legion at Hobson's Choice, rode into Ohio to join him. While waiting, Wayne listened to reports from his scouts, considered the terrain that yawned before him to the north, and weighed ways and means of bringing the tribes to battle on ground of his own choosing.

Most of the Indians lived along the borders of two rivers—the Maumee to the west and the Auglaize to the east—which flowed together as they ran north and enclosed the wilderness before him in a great, open-bottomed triangle. The Miami villages lay along the Maumee; those of the Delawares, Ottawas and more distant Shawnees were in country on or east of the Auglaize. The wilderness within the triangle itself was dense, swampy and broken by innumerable small tributaries of the Auglaize. Both Harmar and St. Clair had avoided this region, and had thus exposed themselves by turning west over easier country toward the Miami towns. Wayne decided to plunge directly north through the heart of this difficult woodland. He thus meant to leave the tribes on either side guessing as to his eventual destination—and to draw them to him like a magnet when he emerged at the juncture of the two streams, just south of the British fort.

Wayne believed the country at the top of the triangle to be "the grand emporium of the hostile Indians of the west." The Legion set off for this heartland of the tribes on July 28; and began, once more, to subject the minds of the Algonquins to its will by the awesome efficiency with which it covered ground. Surveyors and axmen contrived a road for the artillery, wagons and livestock, building bridges over streams as they labored forward. The troops marched in double columns, with scouts and spies ahead and with dragoons in front, rear, and on both flanks, while the Kentuckians rode as a mobile guard of the rear.

"The Dragoons and Light Troops sustained considerable fatigue and injury from the thickness of the Woods and Brush thro which they passed on the flanks," wrote George Rogers Clark's younger brother William. "We proceeded with the usual velocity through thickets almost impervious, through Morasses, Defiles and beads of netles more than waist high & miles in length."

Wayne stopped for two days once he was at the entrance to the triangle, threw up a fort and spread conflicting rumors that he planned to march east and west, hoping to confuse the enemy as to his further intentions. The ruse worked. His scouts found no Indian sign for two days after the army resumed its march into the thick of the triangle. The Delawares discovered the army again as it approached the Auglaize River. Indian villagers fled in terror as the sweating troops reached the Auglaize and marched up the stream through great tribal gardens of vegetables and corn. The Indian towns "were just forsakin," wrote William Clark. "Some of the houses burning, they left every appearance of having gorne off with precipitation and the greatest consternation."

There was good reason for consternation as every chief, and indeed, every warrior was instantly aware. Wayne had not only placed himself in the very midst of the ultimate Algonquin stronghold, but had done so without losing a man, with arms, baggage, stores and livestock intact, and at a time of the year when his troops could utilize the ripening crops of the Indians themselves. He consolidated these advantages by marching to the confluence of the Maumee and the Auglaize and raising yet another stockaded strong point, which he named Fort Defiance, on easily defendable ground immediately between the two streams.

Would the Indians fight — or talk peace? Little Turtle, in whom opportunism was balanced by sagacity, had urged an attack on Wayne at his first encampment beyond Fort Recovery, had been overruled, and now viewed the position of the tribes with doleful realism. But the Shawnee Blue Jacket — urged to battle by English agents and confident of English support — still burned to repulse the invader. He felt that the Americans could be broken if lured into an awful tangle of fallen trees, left by some ancient cyclone, near the guns of the British at Fort Miami.

Wayne summoned a scout named Christopher Miller, a one-time captive of the Shawnees, and sent him off—despite the man's understandable protests—with a message urging the Miamis, Wyandots, Shawnees and Delawares to "experience the kindness and friendship of the United States of America and the invaluable blessings of peace and tranquility." Miller returned, astonished at being alive, on August 16: the Indians would consider the white captain's words for 10 days. If he advanced any sooner they would answer him with war.

Wayne had no intention of giving the foe 10 days in which to swell his numbers. On the following morning, he ordered the army up the Maumee. But he stopped 10 miles short of the great blowdown, camped again, and once more set the troops to throwing up earthworks — this time to facilitate protection of the army's stores and baggage, since he wanted his infantry unencumbered by backpacks or blankets when it went into battle at last. He lingered there through the 18th and 19th as well, knowing that Algonquin warriors always fasted before battle in religious preparation for the fray. Thirteen hundred of them had positioned themselves amid the fallen trees, with a British officer and 53 militiamen from Detroit. General Wayne, the strategist, decided to let the Indians starve until the morning of the 20th.

He had written Knox: "The fortuitious events of War are very uncertain. But this I can promise — that no conduct of mine will ever cause that great and good man Our Virtuous President to regret the trust & confidence that he was pleased to repose in me." Wayne was now 49 years old and corpulent; he had been sleeping on the ground with the troops and his left leg ached unbearably from an old wound. He rose early on the 20th, powdered his hair and had the offending limb wrapped in flannel from ankle to thigh. An aide saw tears of pain spring to his eyes as he mounted, after struggling into a ruffled cravat and a blue coat and lashing a sword to his middle with a leather belt. But he sat squarely in the saddle as the Legion moved up the bank of the Maumee with the Kentuckians riding in column on their left. And he spurred his mare forward at 10 o'clock, as an advance guard of the volunteers approached the Indian stronghold and provoked a furious fusillade.

One of his young lieutenants pulled up beside him and strove for words of gentle remonstrance: "General Wayne, I'm afraid you'll get into the fight yourself — and forget to give us the necessary orders." Wayne went on staring fixedly ahead; two long years of deliberation and restraint behind him and forgotten. "Perhaps I may," he said at length. "And if I do, recollect the standing order of the day is, 'Charge the damned rascals with the bayonets.'" But he rephrased this simple concept for his commanders after a few more minutes of surveying the menacing scene. He sent masses of the rifle-carrying mounted Kentuckians off to contain the Indians' right flank and his sword-swinging dragoons to a point on the left flank where the piles of tree trunks approached the river. He positioned his infantry in two ranks before Blue Jacket's defenses — the first to conduct the initial attack, the second to charge thereafter if circumstance dictated their inclusion in the fray.

Wayne believed in muskets — which would accommodate paper cartridges with one ball and three heavy buckshot placed before the powder charge. Such a load, though useless at a distance, was murderous at close range. And muskets — unlike rifles of the day — would also accommodate bayonets. He believed in cold steel above all. His infantrymen were told to endure the enemy's first fire while running into the timber, to attack with the bayonet while the Indians struggled to reload, and to fire only when they could shoot into the backs of a disorganized and retreating foe.

Wayne's orders were executed with an exactitude rare in war. The battle was over almost before the smoke of the defenders' first volley had drifted away in the hot summer air. Wayne noted with grim satisfaction that the "Savages with their allies abandoned themselves to flight & dispersed with terror & dismay." The Indians at each flank were penned off from open ground by the plunging, leaping horses and the sabers of the reckless American riders. Those in the center, scrambling back to avoid the bayonets of the yelling foe, were hampered by the very tangles of boles and dead limbs in which they had secreted themselves. The infantry exacted a high price for the several dozen men it had lost in entering the timbers. "The loss of the Enemy was more than double that of the Federal Army," wrote Wayne. "The woods were strewed for a considerable distance with the dead bodies of Indians & their white Auxiliaries, the latter armed with British muskets and bayonets."

Woodland rebellion was ended in Ohio when the Indians broke and ran at the Battle of Fallen Timbers. Wayne had confronted them with a display of force beyond their experience. And he had also, to their horror and dismay, faced down the British king. Survivors of the battle learned the bitter truth about their supposed allies as they burst out of the woods and crossed an open prairie toward the English fort. Its cannon stayed silent, its loopholes empty, and its gate locked fast as they ran up to its stockade calling for rescue from their pursuers.

Wayne wasted little time in dramatizing the perfidy that Lord Dorchester had visited upon the credulous Algonquins. On the day following the battle, the fort's commandant, Major William Campbell, demanded to know why forces of the United States had approached so near a fort belonging to His Majesty the King of England. As no war existed between the two countries, the British commander asked, what was he to make of the Americans' actions? Wayne answered by leading a body of troops to Campbell's stockade, inspecting it in leisurely fashion while within pistol range, and directing that the nearby house of McKee, the British Indian agent, be burned to the ground along with various other outbuildings. Wayne, eager to take

the fort, hoped to provoke the British into attacking him. However, the British commander held his temper and his men in check — neither side wanted to be responsible for igniting a second Revolutionary War.

Wayne spent the better part of the next two months in laying waste to Indian towns and to vast Indian gardens that stretched for 50 miles along the Maumee. He destroyed the Miami villages against which so many other expeditions had failed, and built one more log fortress — which its commandant immediately named Fort Wayne — near their smouldering ruins before returning the remainder of the Legion to Fort Greenville for the winter.

A procession of chastened, embittered and impoverished chieftains called upon him in February and solemnly sued for peace. "Hence it follows," he wrote with satisfaction, "that the Legion are excellent oculists and Aurists, & that the bayonet is the most proper instrument, for removing the Films from the Eyes — & for opening the Ears of the Savages, that has ever yet been discover'd — it has also another powerful quality! it's *glitter* instantly dispeled the darkness, & let in the light." The chieftains trooped back the following summer and signed the Treaty of Greenville, by which great areas of Ohio were formally deeded over to the United States.

After 40 years of bloody resistance by the tribes, the Northwest was now opened for peaceful settlement and the British influence there permanently weakened.

Wayne died of an infected leg in the winter of 1796 — having taken possession of Detroit when the British consented, at last, to evacuation — with the plaudits of Congress and his grateful countrymen still ringing in his ears.

Fate was not as kind to the man who began it all, George Rogers Clark. He lingered on, a lonely and embittered victim of his alcoholism and tarnished dreams until 1818, when he died of a stroke at the age of 65. The old Indian fighter suffered several seizures during his declining years, an indignity that brought partial paralysis and, finally, a massive infection of his right leg. But he did not lose his courage — or his sense of style — when it became necessary to amputate the limb. Clark requested that a drummer and fifer be present, and tapped time to their cadence with his good hand as the surgeon performed his grisly chore.

Outside his fort at Greenville, Anthony Wayne, flanked by his officers, dictates treaty terms to the chiefs routed at the Battle of Fallen Timbers. In exchange for $9,500 in annuities to be distributed among the tribes, Wayne exacted two thirds of Ohio, a sliver of Indiana and strategic outposts in Illinois and Michigan.

5 | Stampede to the Mississippi

Frontier-bound Easterners snapped up a river guide called *The Navigator* in 1801, not only to study author Zadoc Cramer's tips on flatboating but to savor his patriotic enthusiasm for westward expansion. The frontier, Cramer wrote, was uniquely "watered with limpid streams and navigable rivers" and "no people better deserve these advantages" than Americans.

Restless Americans agreed. Migration had been halted for a generation by war with the British and the Indians. Southern farmland was wearing out, and rocky plots in New England fetched up to $50 an acre. Maps like the one at right showed prospective homesteaders the abundance of land in the West—available for a few dollars an acre. Tales of its richness drew 26,000 people through the Cumberland Gap in the summer of 1795.

Such overland travel was hard. The roads were narrow swaths cleared of brush and small trees. Larger trees were chopped off 18 inches aboveground—what remained often left wagons literally stumped. When it rained even those roads became quagmires. It was easier, when a river was handy, for a family to load their possessions onto a flatboat and pole downstream to a new home. But not all Western streams were "limpid"—rocks and rapids took their toll of the inexperienced.

Until the War of 1812 closed the frontier again, the West lured many thousands of migrants, including one old couple who joined the rush because their neighbors had all gone west, and they "felt sort o' lonesome" back home.

Westward expansion in the young nation of 18 states was pressing toward a temporary barrier, the Mississippi, when this map was made in about 1803. But newly acquired Louisiana lay invitingly beyond.

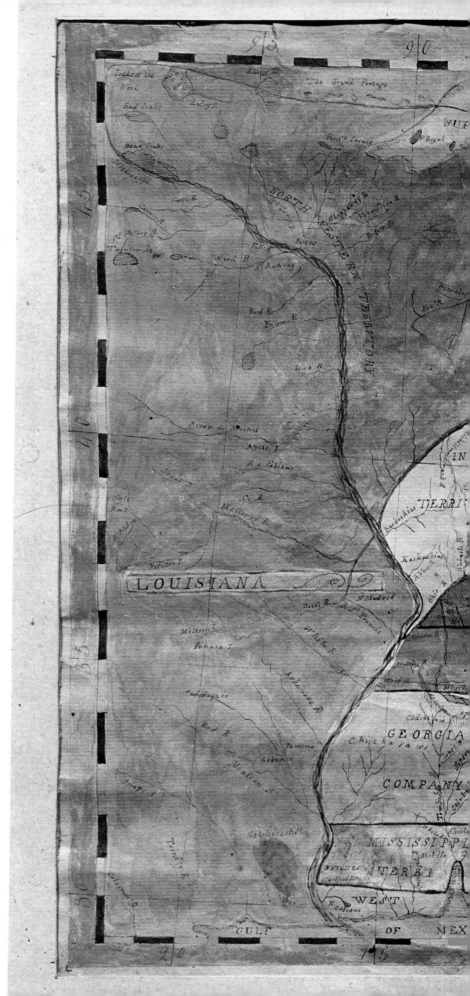

A rush of innocents and rascals to claim the land

"Ask these Pilgrims what they expect when they git to Kentuckey the Answer is Land," wrote Moses Austin of the gaunt and ragged throngs he encountered on the Wilderness Road in 1796. "Have you anything to pay for land? No. Ever see the country? No. Can any thing be more Absurd than the Conduct of Man? Here is hundreds. Travelling they know not for what Nor Whither, except its to Kentuckey . . . the Land of Milk and Honey. And when arriv.d what do they find?"

Neither Austin, who would later pioneer Texas, nor any other rational observer could have imagined that the hard-bitten hosts were going to find heaven itself there—that backwoodsmen of this new frontier would succumb to a religious hysteria so redolent of hell-fire as to start them groaning, groveling and engaging in spasmodic twitching called "jerking" by the thousands, and that they would foster a democratic concept of instant salvation so impelling as to make outdoor revivalism an enduring American institution.

These new settlers flooded west in streams as Indian raiding subsided after the decisive Battle of Fallen Timbers in 1794. Road systems were improved. Wagons were able to cross the Cumberland Gap into Kentucky on the Wilderness Road, penetrate Tennessee from the East on the Old Walton Road and branch away, in the late 1790s, on rutted lanes being hacked ever deeper into the backwoods. Zane's Trace carried overland traffic southwest from Wheeling into the Kentucky River Valley. Water-borne immigrants floated down the Ohio River on fleets of flatboats—

each peripatetic farmer's cows feeding on a huge haystack at one end of the craft while his wife and children tried to make do amid piles of furniture, a churn and clotheslines at the opposite end.

Kentucky boasted almost a quarter of a million people by 1800; there were nearly half that many in Tennessee, and newcomers crowded into Ohio at a rate that was to add 200,000 in the next decade.

These people behaved, for the most part, as their hardened predecessors had. They adopted the hunting shirt and moccasins of the frontier, cleared a few acres, planted corn and coped as best they could. But the new West underwent startling changes nonetheless. Corn prompted the establishment of dozens of little distilleries (whiskey being an eminently barterable product) and fed increasing herds of cattle and hogs, which were sometimes driven to Eastern markets over the new roads.

Wealthy planters—or their sons—moved to Kentucky with slaves, heavy furniture and the family silver and began clearing great tracts for tobacco. Doctors, printers, lawyers, blacksmiths and small merchants came over the mountains to seek opportunity in Louisville, Frankfort, Maysville, Knoxville and, above the Ohio, in Dayton, Xenia, Franklinton (now Columbus) and Fort Washington (now Cincinnati). To Lexington came a silversmith named Edward West, who facilitated house construction everywhere by inventing a machine for making nails—articles so precious, since they were banged out singly by blacksmiths, that many Americans burned their houses when moving to recover the hardware for the next house.

Not many towns, however, boasted more than a few hundred inhabitants. The new frontier was as predominantly rural and as rudely self-sufficient as had been the older frontier of the Eastern Appalachians, though its people were less confined and their social

James Kingsbury in 1796 became the first settler in Connecticut's "western reserve" on Lake Erie. He had grown stout and evidently prosperous by the time he commissioned this silhouette 25 years later.

JOURNAL
OF
DOCTOR JEREMIAH SMIPLETON's
TOUR TO OHIO.

CONTAINING

An account of the numerous difficulties, Hair-breadth Escapes, Mortifications and Privations, which the Doctor and his family experienced on their Journey from Maine, to the 'Land of Promise,' and during a residence of three years in that highly extolled country.

BY H. TRUMBULL.

Fearing depopulation, some Easterners spread discouraging tales about the West. This 1819 journal derided Ohio as a place without "shoemakers, tailors or hatters," where "the inhabitants walk on all fours."

pursuits more varied. Linsey-clad entrepreneurs promoted bearbaitings and cockfights, as well as rifle matches, and drew jeering, cheering audiences to gander pulls, in which mounted men spurred past a greased goose suspended upside down from a tree limb and tried to jerk its head off as they passed. Race "paths" materialized; "anything with four legs and hair" was eligible to run for prizes. Thousands took to litigation—mostly over land claims—with the advent of circuit-riding judges. Brawling tavern drunks still gouged and bit.

But Kentuckians missed something, if only subconsciously, for all that—the fear, horror, excitement and moments of bloody triumph they had known in a half century of conflict with the forest Indians.

This vacuum was partly filled by a preacher named James McGready, a "tall and angular" Presbyterian who could make Satan as real as a whooping Shawnee and hell more horrible than the stake. McGready had only the most rudimentary religious training, having simply studied with a farmer-preacher in western Pennsylvania until he felt "prepared for eternity." But he had dark eyes and a "bold and uncompromising manner," and he compensated for his lack of formal education with an instinct for exhortation, a circus ringmaster's command of audiences and a way of terri-

fying sinners to make them ready for "awakening."

McGready seems to have encountered resistance as an embryo preacher from congregations he bullied in western North Carolina—particularly for forbidding the consumption of whiskey at funerals. He lit out for Kentucky, according to legend, after he received a threatening letter written in blood. But his bellicosity struck like lightning, as the Presbyterian General Assembly described it, in the "Egyptian darkness of religious life in the West."

The new preacher, according to Presbyterian annals, "so arrayed hell and its horrors before the wicked" of Red River, Gasper River and Muddy River—three of Kentucky's more sin-filled areas—"that they would tremble and quake, imagining a lake of fire and brimstone yawning to overwhelm them, and the wrath of God thrusting them down the horrible abyss."

After being exposed to McGready's preaching, the "boldest and most daring sinners" began "covering their faces and weeping." He was so frightening at Gasper River in July 1799 that many took "to falling to the ground, groaning, praying and crying for mercy." This phenomenon was intensified when John McGee, a Methodist minister, attended McGready's next service and grew so overwrought that he jumped up amid the benches of the congregation and began shouting and exhorting, too. This dual assault had an astonishing effect on "profane swearers, Sabbath breakers" and others of similarly dubious sanctity: "the floor was covered with the slain in a moment and their screams for mercy pierced the heavens."

The Great Revival of the 1800s—which raged through Kentucky and Tennessee like a forest fire and smouldered along the trail of the pioneers into older Southern settlements—was born of these proceedings. So was its principal instrument, the marathon, multidenominational, outdoor camp meeting.

Churches just could not hold the throngs of people that began converging on McGready's services—and those of ministers who aped his techniques—once tales of "miracles" penetrated the backwoods. And no one preacher could properly exhort them, for McGready had decided that the process of warning sinners about the works of Satan could be intensified by applying it around the clock for three or even four days in a row. Volunteer laborers set the scene for

Everybody pitches in as a family clears a site and builds a cabin in Ohio. Many settlers avoided prairies and laboriously hacked farms out of forests since they mistakenly thought treeless land was infertile.

services by laying out streets for the tents and lean-tos, setting up rows of split-log benches, laying in wood for bonfires and creating speaking stands to accommodate the shifts of gesticulating preachers.

Great crowds attended these outdoor revivals in both Kentucky and Tennessee. Some people traveled on foot, some rode, but most arrived in wagons loaded with food and bedding and camped in family groups or with neighbors from their distant communities. Many were drawn by simple curiosity, the picnic atmosphere and the promise of excitement and change. Not a few came to jeer, look for fights and drink whiskey that surreptitious vendors ("Satan's emissaries" to the indignant clergymen) dipped from barrels hidden within earshot of the preaching.

But firelight, impassioned sermonizing and exhaustion induced real fear and wild exhilaration in thousands of these simple, hard-used and literal-minded souls. They were infected, at every meeting, by curi-ous forms of mass hysteria—though never so dramatically and in such numbers as during a monster revival that Barton Warren Stone, one of McGready's converts to Presbyterianism, held at Cane Ridge, Kentucky, from August 6 to 13, 1801.

The Great Revival reached its zenith at Cane Ridge. A count of teams and wagons suggested that from 20,000 to 25,000 people—one tenth of the population of the entire state—were there at one time or another during the week. They abandoned themselves to frenetic bouts of falling, laughing, singing, barking and jerking as the meeting wore on—"exercises," as the preachers called them, that had become hallmarks of the new backwoods evangelism and that were taken to reflect a cleansing penitence by the sinner and divine approval by the Holy Spirit.

This loosening of restraint was reflected in more erotic exercises as well. One John Lyle, an orthodox Presbyterian minister, concluded sadly that "more

Thousands gather to be "saved" in a Kentucky wood about 1800 in a frontier rite that produced its own music and hymnals *(below)*. Revivals so moved backwoodsmen to "wrestling with the Lord for mercy" that a preacher exulted, "Hell is trembling and satan's kingdom is falling."

THE

SPIRITUAL SONGSTER:

CONTAINING A VARIETY OF

CAMP-MEETING,

AND OTHER

HYMNS.

Be glad in the Lord, and rejoice ye righteous, and shout for joy all ye that are upright in heart.—Ps. 32. v. 11.

FIRST EDITION.

PRINTED AND PUBLISHED BY GEORGE KOLB, FREDERICK-TOWN, MARYLAND. 1819.

Preacher Barton Stone likened revivalism to "fire in dry stubble driven by a strong wind," and said the frontier penitents' "uncommon agitations" were needed because "nothing common" could save their souls.

souls were begot than saved" and noted later that "Becca Bell—who often fell, is now big with child to a wicked, trifling school master of the name of Brown." But Lyle also admitted to being "much melted" by seeing so many who were truly "under conviction."

"The noise," according to James B. Finley, a young Ohioan who had come vowing to "resist nervous excitability," was like "the roar of Niagara and people were agitated as if by a storm: I saw five hundred swept down in a moment as if a battery of guns had been opened upon them, and their shrieks and shouts rent the very heavens."

Hundreds were moved to responses even more dramatic. A Methodist named Jacob Young noted many "of the smitten gathering on their knees and barking and snapping to tree the Devil." Those driven to jerking were more spectacular yet. Finley saw peni-

tents bending spasmodically forward and backward, their heads nearly touching the ground at the end of each stroke; a movement so quick, observed a parson named Peter Cartwright, that women's kerchiefs were snapped off and "even the hairpins flew out."

The Great Revival left religion firmly rooted in the new West. The violent concepts of eternal suffering and promises of sudden salvation were exactly suited to a race of bear hunters and Indian fighters. But the revival ignited great quarrels among and within the churches that had joined at its inception. Presbyterians had believed, over the years, in a Calvinistic doctrine of "election"—that only a chosen few were predestined by God for heaven, that even these rare mortals were "brought to grace" by a slow process of calling, faith, justification, adoption and sanctification, and that no amount of shouting, rolling or jerking could alter God's view of the human who had not been picked for glory in the first place.

McGready and his followers veered recklessly from this orthodoxy; they believed that God could shower grace as he chose, having done so on the day of Pentecost. They felt that sermons should be aimed at "the joints and marrow" rather than the mind and that it was sheer folly, when gouging the Devil out of some shrieking wretch, to offer him smelling salts, quiet and time for contemplation.

McGready, under pressure from traditional Presbyterians, eventually made "due submission" to orthodoxy, stayed within the church and vanished from the public eye. The Methodists and Baptists, who took a democratic view of man's chances of salvation, inherited most of the fruits of the revival movement and captured thousands of the same Scotch-Irish who had brought Presbyterianism from Ulster. Both went on holding camp meetings—or "brush arbor" services as they were called in the Old South—but only, having recovered their contentious view of one another, for their own members, who defiantly sang either:

Baptist, Baptist, Baptist—
Baptist till I die.
I'll go along with the Baptists
And find myself On High!
or:
I'll tell you who the Lord loves best—
It is the shouting Methodist!

Corn likker: the drink that "every boddy" took

"It smells like gangrene starting in a mildewed silo, it tastes like the wrath to come, and when you absorb a deep swig of it you have all the sensations of having swallowed a lighted kerosene lamp." So lamented one imbiber after sampling a jug of Kentucky-made corn whiskey. But for every critic of the frontier brew, there were thousands of Western Americans who enjoyed its unique sour-mash flavor and hundreds who distilled it to pay for the goods they had to import from the cities back East.

Converting surplus corn into whiskey was the most practical way for homesteaders in the remote hills of Kentucky and Tennessee to get their grain to market. Shipping corn overland was difficult and expensive: a pack horse could carry only four bushels across the mountains. But the same horse was able to carry the equivalent of 24 bushels of corn when it was condensed into two kegs of distilled whiskey.

To make whiskey from corn the settlers first concocted a mashy liquid called still beer. They scalded ground cornmeal in homemade wooden tubs, then added barley malt, bran and yeast, and poured in a measure of pure spring water. After letting the mash ferment, they obtained a brew— about 7 per cent alcohol—that was ready for distillation.

A typical frontier still consisted of a pear-shaped copper kettle topped by a detachable head with a tapered neck that ended in a spiral of tubing called a worm. When the still was fired, alcoholic spirits vaporized upward into the head and through the worm. The worm was immersed in a barrel of cold water, which caused the heated vapor to condense into whiskey. Drawn off through the end of the worm, the "corn likker" was distilled a second time, or "doubled," to increase its alcoholic content. The spent "stillage" of corn mash was saved for hog feed.

A fanciful portrayal of distilling—from corn mash to corked jugs—was Douglass Hewitt & Co.'s trademark for Old '76 whiskey.

A corn-husking party in Kentucky is enlivened by swigs from a jug of home-brewed whiskey, "until out of those lusty throats swelled

By 1800 there were more than 1,500 family-operated stills brewing corn likker in Kentucky.

Frontiersmen brought out their convivial jugs at all social occasions. "Every boddy took it," recalled Ebenezer Hiram Steadman, an early chronicler of Kentucky life. "When we had a corn-shukin', a log-rollin', a house-raisin', or any such frolic, the whiskey just sloshed around like water." The local clergymen did not encourage whiskey drinking, nor did they all condemn it. The minutes of one Kentucky congregation for 1795 describe a debate on whether it was "consistent with true religion to carry on a distillery of spirits." After discussion, the congregation voted that it was "Not inconsistent."

Money was scarce on the frontier, and whiskey frequently took the place of hard currency. Teachers received corn-likker wages, and a gallon jug of whiskey passed for a quarter in practically any store in Kentucky. Thus in

1791, when Secretary of the Treasury Alexander Hamilton persuaded Congress to enact excise taxes on whiskey to pay off the nation's war debts, thousands of Western farmers protested, insisting that the whiskey tax was a tax on their own money. When Hamilton ignored these protests, suggesting that opponents of the tax should merely drink less, the outraged farmers rebelled. Mobs of frontiersmen in western Pennsylvania and Virginia assaulted tax collectors and tarred and feathered government agents who tried to enforce the law.

At the height of the Whiskey Rebellion, in July 1794, a motley army of 5,000 rebels occupied Pittsburgh. President Washington sent 15,000 troops across the mountains to restore order. In the face of this federal force, the Whiskey Rebellion collapsed. But a deep vein of resentment against the federal government's authority remained on the frontier, even after the tax was finally repealed in 1802.

A federal revenuer suffers a rough fate in this 1792 cartoon opposing the whiskey tax.

a song that could be heard in the deep woods."

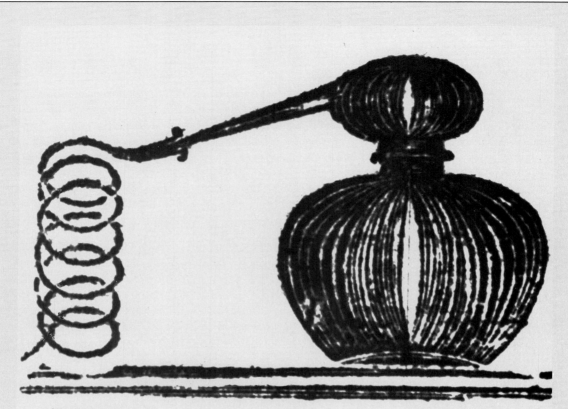

FISHEL AND GALLATINE,
COPPER AND TIN SMITHS,

INFORM their friends and the public, they have now on hands, a variety of STILLS of the best quality, and having laid in an assortment of Copper, and engaged workmen of skill, can with satisfaction complete any orders they may be favoured with.

TIN WARE of every description, by wholesale or retail; Copper Boilers, Hatter's Kettles, Copper Tea Kettles, Brass and Copper Wash Kettles, &c. &c.

Tin Ware and merchandise exchanged for old Copper, Brass and Pewter.

Lexington, 8th Sept. 1807.   tf

A compact copper still is featured in an 1807 advertisement placed in the *Kentucky Gazette* by a firm of Lexington metalsmiths.

The heresies, excesses and partisan emotions of Western religion only reflected the heresies, excesses and partisan emotions of Western society as a whole in the years between the Revolution and the War of 1812. The James McGreadys and Barton Stones of the revival movement were not the only leaders who were moved to a fierce pragmatism—some with the best of motives, but many for seditious and selfish ends—in responding to the challenges of opening the continent as far as the Mississippi. The first adventurers to cross the Appalachian wall had been able, like sailors setting forth on an uncharted sea, to turn their backs on the constrictions of civilization. But now the new Westerners felt constrained and threatened on all sides. Eastern legislatures taxed them, Eastern speculators jostled for control of enormous areas of Western land (particularly along Georgia's Yazoo Strip), the Creeks and Cherokees menaced them from the South, and Spain blocked their hopes of commerce on the Mississippi and the Gulf Coast.

All this deepened that sense of abused and angry singularity with which backwoodsmen had reacted, from the beginning, to interference from people on the Eastern Seaboard. The Revolution was hardly over before Westerners began scheming how to wrench free in order to court destiny on their own. It was a confused period, dramatized by two events. One was the founding of the Commonwealth of Franklin by John "Nolichucky Jack" Sevier—a hero of King's Mountain—and by other dissident Tennesseans bent on separating themselves from North Carolina. The other was the Spanish Conspiracy, hatched by that super scoundrel General James Wilkinson, the most flamboyant of the many intrigues in which Westerners plotted to break away from the confederation of American states and found separate little republics or ally themselves with Spain.

No post-Revolutionary phenomenon reflected the disorderly, if dogged, political aspirations of the new Western settlers, or the headstrong attitudes of their leaders, more accurately than the organization and collapse of the "Lost State of Franklin." This short-lived political curiosity had its beginnings when the North Carolina legislature voted, in June 1784, to cede its western territory (roughly corresponding to present-day eastern Tennessee) to the Continental Congress.

The backwoodsmen of this area, guessing that the congress might well leave them in an orphaned state for years, took matters into their own hands in August 1784. They sent two men from each local militia company to a convention at Jonesboro and established their own independent commonwealth. Many of them wanted to call it Frankland, after the hardy Franks of ancient Europe, but a majority decided to amend the final "and" to "in," hoping to gain Benjamin Franklin's blessing and, with it, admission to the confederation of original states.

Within a short time North Carolina decided to take its western lands back. But the Franks, as they had taken to calling themselves, paid no heed. They numbered perhaps 30,000 in eight counties, stretching roughly from the western border of North Carolina to the Tennessee River. In March 1785 they elected a legislature, named John Sevier governor and prepared to make their own way in the world.

Sevier, already famous as an Indian fighter and well remembered for his participation in the earlier Watauga government, is sometimes credited with having been the moving spirit in the creation of Franklin. The fact is, he seems to have been horrified at the idea when it was first presented to him. At the time he was involved, with a North Carolina speculator named William Blount, in the Muscle Shoals Company, which proposed to plant a colony near the great bend of the Tennessee River, and he was afraid that the new state might inhibit the development of this enterprise. Once Blount and company deduced, however, that control of such a government might be used to advance their scheme, Sevier accepted the Franklin legislature's call for his services and did everything he could to shape the new state in his own image.

This took a certain amount of doing, particularly since the more idealistic Franks sat down to write a constitution. Some of the attitudes reflected by this document sound odd today. No Frank could hold office, for instance, unless he was a Christian who believed in heaven, hell, the Bible and the Holy Trinity. Clergymen were also banned from office, however, and—reflecting the frontiersmen's deep suspicions—so were lawyers and doctors. But the proposed constitution was still ultrademocratic for its day: it called for universal male suffrage, voter registration, election by ballot and the resolution of some issues by popular referendum. In the end Sevier saw to it that the project was junked in favor of the more manageable North Carolina constitution, which provided that the governor and the five-man Council of State be elected by the legislature rather than the people.

Sevier instantly created a set of dissidents by this intrusion and by the highhanded, if easy, way he seized the reins of authority thereafter. The most vehement and capable of Sevier's critics was John Tipton, a tall, heavy, imposing fellow with a strong will and a jealous disposition. Tipton had fought as a soldier in Lord Dunmore's War and had served in Virginia's House of Burgesses before going over the mountains to farm near Sinking Creek. He made no secret of his resentment of Sevier's attitudes and was the governor's most hostile opponent from the beginning to the end of the political experiment in Franklin.

Still, the new state was launched in orderly fashion. Taxes were levied; the "promotion of learning" was ensured (the backwoods legislators even ordered Latin added to the curriculum); and a sort of ambassador — one William Cocke — was sent to present the Continental Congress with the Franks' hopes of inclusion in the federal union. The legislature took pains to devise a rudimentary scale of monetary exchange adapted to the barter system, the common means of paying debts. As the British monetary system was still in use, taxes were made payable with bacon valued at sixpence per pound; rye whiskey at two shillings, sixpence per gallon; sugar at one shilling per pound; and otter, beaver and deer skins at six shillings apiece.

Time was unkind both to Sevier's venture with the Muscle Shoals Company and to the Franks' hope of inclusion in the American union. Sevier got the Franklin legislature to authorize an expedition of some 90 settlers to the big bend of the Tennessee (his friend Blount having secured a title to the area from Georgia, which claimed considerable Western territory) and sent them off with high hopes under the command of his brother, Valentine. They arrived in the fall of 1785, set up a land office and took it upon themselves to elect Valentine to the Georgia legislature. They stayed only two weeks, however, before deciding to beat a hasty retreat, the Georgians having refused to grant them a legislative seat because they did not con-

stitute an official county and the Cherokees having suggested on general principles that they depart or sacrifice their hair.

Franklin itself fell prey to bitter, if ludicrous, civil strife as North Carolina — with Tipton acting as its principal agent — moved to re-establish its authority in Tennessee. Hotheads among the Sevierites were incensed. "The people here," one wrote, "condemn a certain Col. Tipton for being the instigator of our unhappiness. They have lately hanged him in effigy with a will in his mouth. A very extraordinary will, indeed! It bequeathed his ignorance, his perjury, his folly, and his ambition to be divided among his friends, and a wooden sword to the most deserving."

Despite such attacks, Tipton had a considerable following among citizens who favored reconciliation with North Carolina. In the spring of 1786 the Tiptonites elected representatives to the North Carolina legislature and duplicated Franklin's local sheriffs, judges and militia officers with similar officials of their own. Both the Franklin and the North Carolina governments tried to tax the populace — which responded, in many cases, by paying no taxes at all. Sevier, claiming to act for an independent Franklin, held trials at Jonesboro; Tipton, acting for North Carolina, set up court at Buffalo, 10 miles away.

Armed bands from each side disrupted the other's judicial proceedings. The Continental Congress ignored the renegade state, and Benjamin Franklin did nothing, on being apprised of the honor that had befallen him, except to urge friendship with the North Carolinians and, worse yet, with the Southern Indians. The commonwealth's short history ended when Sevier's term as governor ran out in March 1788 — though not before Sevier led his followers into a noisy little gun battle with the Tiptonites.

This climactic confrontation was provoked in February 1788 when Jonathan Pugh, a Tiptonite and high sheriff, rode to Sevier's home on the Nolichucky and — in the governor's absence — seized some of his slaves to satisfy a judgment for nonpayment of North Carolina taxes. Tipton assembled 45 followers, in anticipation of Sevier's wrath, and settled down in a log house on his farm to await developments.

Sevier was undeterred: he sent his son James off with a message ordering some of Franklin's militia into

Rough and ready lawyers on horseback

Circuit-riding lawyers, who traveled from county to backwoods county, were often regarded as meddlers, "quarrel-mongers" and worse by those they served. Nevertheless, the legal profession was the surest path to social prominence and political advancement on the frontier.

Any young man could get admitted to the bar, but only the hardiest survived for long in the backwoods. There, a strong constitution, common sense and a talent for storytelling were more important than a knowledge of law. Circuit riders spent half the year on horseback, carrying little more than a spare shirt and a copy of the statutes in their saddlebags.

In court, rolling quids of tobacco in their mouths to impress the homespun jury, the lawyers bullied and cajoled their way through as many as 17 cases a day. The judge—usually a local squire—often privately urged the lawyers to go at it full tilt, to make sure his constituents got their money's worth. And if the lawyers could not settle a case with speeches, the judge might let them clear up the matter with fisticuffs on the courtroom floor.

Stern-faced frontier lawyers with umbrellas stuffed in their bedrolls clop down a narrow path cut through an Allegheny forest.

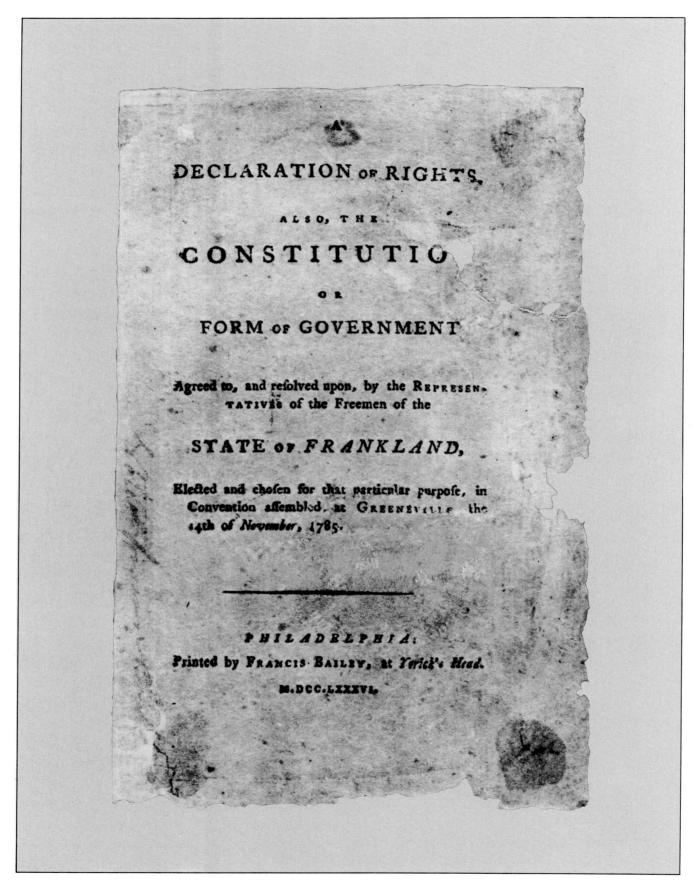

A

DECLARATION of RIGHTS,

ALSO, THE

CONSTITUTIO

OR

FORM of GOVERNMENT

Agreed to, and resolved upon, by the REPRESEN-
TATIVES of the Freemen of the

STATE of FRANKLAND,

Elected and chosen for that particular purpose, in
Convention assembled, at GREENEVILLE the
14th of *November*, 1785.

PHILADELPHIA:
Printed by FRANCIS BAILEY, at *Yorick's Head*.
M.DCC.LXXXVI.

service. "I am informed," the message said, "that the Tipton party has got very insolent and have been guilty of cruelties and barbarous actions. I have ordered fifteen men out of each company to turn out." Tipton sent hurriedly for reinforcements of his own from the North Carolina militia at Greasy Cove: "The rebels are again rising; Sevier is now making his last effort. I therefore request you to collect men with the greatest expedition and to march to my house."

Sevier led his little army of about 150 men to Tipton's home on February 27 and sent in a messenger demanding surrender within 30 minutes. Tipton refused. Sevier, distracted at this point as his men detected and drove off a company of Tiptonites who were trying to join their chief, made camp and installed a field gun on a knoll overlooking Tipton's house. He put off firing it, however—though Tipton again refused to surrender the next day—since a good many of his cohorts had gone off to try buying food with certificates drawn on the Commonwealth of Franklin. He lost the battle, such as it was, as a result of this delay.

It snowed heavily the next morning. Tipton's force of rescuers rode through the falling snow without being seen. Tipton's guard sallied forth to join them, and the resultant mob managed—after some noisy volleying in which Sheriff Pugh received a fatal wound and in which many men on both sides fired into the air—to put the Franks to flight for good.

Sevier fled to the southern border to escape writ servers and set out to re-establish himself by a tried and true device—bloodying the Chickamaugas and Cherokees for their resistance to white seizure of tribal lands. Outlying settlers fell loyally behind him. Sevier had long ago perfected a technique of surprising Indians with hard-riding mounted bands—he was, in fact, one of the first Southern cavalry captains, a forerunner of Nathan Bedford Forrest—and he now led long cross-country attacks on village after village.

His reward was dark, if only temporary, disgrace: one of his followers, John Kirk, lured several friendly Cherokees (including Old Tassel, a famous chief) into a cabin under a flag of truce and tomahawked them. The tale spread, horrifying men of reason everywhere. Worse was to come. Tipton and a posse tracked Sevier when he ventured near his home on the Nolichucky, clapped him in irons and spirited him off to jail

in Morganton, North Carolina, where he was charged with treason (having offered, in his extremity, to regain Franklin for Spain if given money and arms).

Thus ended his last hope—and that of other diehard Franks—of achieving nirvana in the wilderness. Sevier's own career, though seemingly smashed, had actually only begun. His trial for treason was never concluded. Some friends rescued him, according to dramatic legend, by sauntering into the courtroom with pistols under their coats, whisking him away from the bailiffs and hurrying him out of town at a gallop on his favorite mare. His son John Jr. told a more mundane story: friends met Sevier at a Morganton tavern after he was released on bail and they all spent an hour or so over some drinks before mounting up and heading west. But in any case there was no pursuit. Many North Carolinians admired his dash, charm and bravery, and the authorities dropped the matter, since the state shortly ratified the federal constitution and treason was no longer in their jurisdiction.

Sevier became a staunch Federalist; once official tempers had cooled, he was elected to the North Carolina Senate and was soon a brigadier general of the state militia. He was elected the first governor of the state of Tennessee in 1796, served five more terms in that office and was one of the most honored men of his era when he died in 1815, rich in land, slaves and children (18 by two marriages) at the age of 70.

Sevier was not the only Westerner of stature to consider turning away from the original 13 states for some kind of territorial alliance with Spain. Dozens toyed with the idea, even while dozens more plotted to take New Orleans (or Mexico, as was the case in Aaron Burr's ornate scheme of empire) by force of arms.

Some of this restlessness stemmed from Western impatience with Eastern Federalist politics and Eastern treaty makers, who ignored Western aspirations in negotiating with the European powers. But it was prompted, as well, by the Spanish governors of New Orleans—especially by Esteban Rodríquez Miró, a soldier-administrator who served from 1782 until 1791. Miró worried about the movement of rifle-packing backwoodsmen toward the Mississippi and responded with soft words, secret manipulation of the Southern Indians and attempts to lure Western leaders

A backwoods doctor who advanced the frontiers of medicine

DR. EPHRAIM McDOWELL

In December 1809, Dr. Ephraim McDowell of Danville, Kentucky, answered an urgent call to attend a woman 60 miles away who was struggling to give birth to overdue twins. Danville was a backwoods town with a population of only 300, but McDowell was no ordinary backwoods sawbones. The son of one of Kentucky's first judges and married to the daughter of its first governor, he had studied medicine at the University of Edinburgh and at the age of 38 was reputed to be the best surgeon west of Philadelphia.

McDowell arrived to find that the woman, Jane Crawford, was not pregnant after all but was suffering from an enormous ovarian tumor. He told her that, while the tumor would kill her eventually, the most eminent surgeons of the time held that to cut her open and remove it would mean "inevitable death" almost at once from "inflammation." But, he offered: "If you think yourself prepared to die, I will take the lump from you."

Mrs. Crawford consented and made the arduous ride to the doctor's crude operating room in Danville. McDowell scheduled surgery for Christmas so as to be aided by the local congregation's prayers. But, according to some accounts, by the time the operation began, the congregation had become a mob, ready to lynch the doctor if his experiment failed.

With McDowell's assistants holding her down, Mrs. Crawford recited

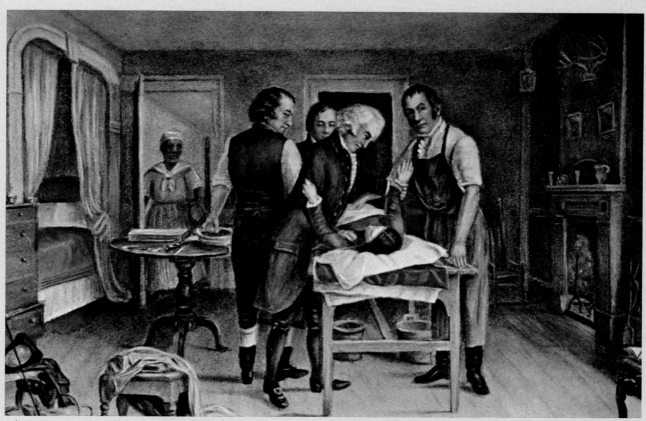

Assistants steady the patient as Dr. McDowell *(right)* begins his pioneering ovariotomy in a room adjoining his Kentucky home.

psalms as the doctor opened her abdomen, cut out a diseased ovary weighing 22½ pounds and sewed her up again in 25 minutes. Five days later she was on her feet, and three weeks after that she was on her way home.

McDowell's pioneering ovariotomy was a complete success. Mrs. Crawford lived 32 more years to a ripe old 78, and the operation itself was eventually recognized as a bold precursor to modern abdominal surgery. McDowell, however, appears to have been in no hurry to advertise his achievement. It is a measure of how far he was ahead of his time that when his brief account of the operation finally appeared in a Philadelphia journal in 1817, the reaction of

the medical establishment was divided between skepticism of his claims and censure for his recklessness.

Even among the learned doctors of New York and Philadelphia, surgery in the early 19th Century was confined largely to dressing wounds and amputating limbs — without benefit of anesthesia or antisepsis. Most internal disorders were treated with some combination of powerful purgatives, stiff doses of opiates and liberal bleeding ("even when symptoms of extreme prostration are present").

Scarcely one American physician in 10 had any formal training, and few of those were practicing west of the Appalachians, where a "doctor" might be anybody who called himself

one. Exponents of all kinds of dubious medical dogmas — "botanics," "homeopaths," "Indian" doctors — vied with one another and conventional practitioners for the frontier trade.

But if the backwoods doctor was cut off from the refinements of the Eastern medical centers, he was also free of their stifling orthodoxies. As a result, a few men like McDowell achieved remarkable medical advances. Undeterred by what they thought of his operation back East, the Kentuckian performed ovariotomies on 11 more women and, as he said later, "lost but one." In 1830, Ephraim McDowell died; the pioneer of abdominal surgery was a victim, ironically, of a ruptured appendix.

Dr. McDowell's mahogany chest holds the common frontier nostrums, often valued in proportion to how bitter they tasted. Most of them were used only as purgatives or emetics, but in pioneer households the cathartic Calomel, a mercury compound, doubled as an insecticide, and Squills, a stimulant, was also "a fine rat poison."

and Western territory into the embrace of Spain.

A succession of disgruntled or avaricious Western politicos were attracted to this proposition in the late 1780s, but none — for all their fevered correspondence — ever finally took the bait, and Governor Miró was left to become the dupe of General James Wilkinson, as wily a rascal as ever invited a bribe. Wilkinson came over the mountains after the Revolution to make himself "the Washington of the West." Sensing that the Spanish might be offering him opportunity from afar, he descended grandly on New Orleans and promised fulfillment of Miró's fondest dreams. Historians have labeled Wilkinson's long, devious and lucrative relationship with the credulous governor — and his successor — the Spanish Conspiracy, but it might better have been called the Kentucky Confidence Game.

The two Spaniards should doubtless be forgiven their susceptibility. Wilkinson was often suspected of venality by his peers — Henry Knox, Anthony Wayne and George Washington among them. But he possessed so open and hearty a mien, such energy and ambition, such sublime innocence of ethical standards, and so large and certain a view of his own place in the cosmos that they all seemed incapable of denying him the positions of authority into which he insinuated himself. He was handsome, cheerful and reckless, had the air of a gentleman (having grown up on a Maryland plantation and having studied medicine as a youth), seemed incapable of embarrassment or dismay, and demonstrated early, for all his flaws of character, that he was a natural leader.

Through his friendship with a ranking general, Wilkinson got himself commissioned as a brevet brigadier general in the Revolutionary Army at the tender age of 20 — and appointed secretary to the Board of War as well. But he lost his exalted positions within months for bad-mouthing Washington during a drinking spree. Nevertheless, within a year he had managed to wangle the lucrative post of clothier-general — and again was forced to resign, this time for gross neglect of duty.

Wilkinson was unabashed. He moved to Pennsylvania, and having married Anne Biddle, daughter of an important Quaker family, was duly commissioned a brigadier general of that state's militia. He also was elected to the Pennsylvania Assembly before he headed for Kentucky in 1783, at the age of 26, to undercut the influence of its old hero, George Rogers Clark, preach separation from Virginia and encourage local discontent. He rated himself "easy, prompt & eloquent in public debate." And he had other means of winning and influencing friends. He entertained lavishly in his big Lexington house and was generous with his whiskey, holding that "the way to men's hearts is down their throats." Within three years he had become the territory's most important politician.

A great part of Kentucky's discontent with Virginia (of which it was still a part) and with the United States as well hinged on the facts that Spain had closed the Mississippi to commerce in 1784 and that no Eastern politician seemed to understand the hardships this worked on Westerners, who were denied an outlet for their furs, tobacco, lumber and produce.

Wilkinson set out in 1787 to capitalize on this dilemma. He loaded a flatboat with tobacco, flour, hams, butter and two blooded horses and set off for New Orleans — assuring himself an untroubled passage by presenting the horses to the chief Spanish official at Natchez, who appreciated this sort of communication between gentlemen and understood the realities of diplomatic discourse. Natchez was the outpost at which American boatmen normally were turned back; Wilkinson was waved on south — and with a glowing letter of introduction to Miró himself.

He wasted no time, on arrival in New Orleans, in telling the governor a heady tale. Kentuckians, he said, were fearsome fellows who would take any measure "no matter how desperate" to get their goods to the sea, and they contemplated an arrangement with Great Britain that would "bind them to attack Louisiana," but they greatly preferred a friendly understanding with Spain. "Notables of Kentucky," he claimed, had "pleaded" with him to carry this word to New Orleans and suggested they would separate from the union to become "vassals" of His Most Catholic Majesty. He struck a more personal note when he added that he would, if allowed to bring cargos down the river, make the governor a silent partner in the business of selling two-dollar Kentucky tobacco at nine dollars a hundredweight in New Orleans.

Miró swallowed this tale whole and asked his new friend to take an oath of allegiance to Spain. Wilkinson agreed with alacrity and even went further — he insist-

A master intriguer, General James Wilkinson conned a fortune out of Governors Miró and Carondelet of Spanish Louisiana. The credulous viceroys granted him a fat pension and lucrative trading privileges in return for his supposed efforts to advance Spain's interests in Kentucky.

ESTEBAN RODRÍGUEZ MIRÓ

BARON HECTOR DE CARONDELET

ed on writing out a form of his own and giving it to the governor on paper. Miró was charmed, though Wilkinson, slippery as ever, filled the page with innumerable reasons to explain his changing allegiance without ever actually saying that he had done so or actually swearing fealty to Spain.

Miró granted Wilkinson the right to ship $30,000 of cargo into New Orleans annually as a means of rallying Kentuckians to the cause of Spain. The governor, in fact, did more; he "loaned" Wilkinson $6,000 in 1788 and another $7,000 in 1790 to facilitate his friend's work as an *agent provocateur*. Wilkinson, meanwhile, parceled out trading privileges to excited Kentucky merchants — at commissions that brought him a great deal of money — and promised to make them all rich when separation was achieved.

The scheme collapsed. Spain opened the river in 1789 — though charging a 15 per cent duty — to curry American favor in the event of war in Europe. Miró was relieved by a new governor, Baron Hector de Carondelet, in 1791. Kentucky became a state in 1792, and at last could make itself heard in Congress. And Wilkinson went broke after a reckless venture in tobacco speculation.

But the resilient rascal immediately turned to the Army again for "Bread & Fame" and got himself appointed commandant of Ohio's Fort Washington — thanks mostly to recommendations from men who distrusted him intensely and hoped he would be sealed away from mischief on the frontier. Such hopes were in vain. Citizen Edmond Charles Genêt, first ambassador to the United States from Republican France, contrived yet another plot in 1793, and Wilkinson, again a brigadier general, used it to renew his seditious and profitable relationship with Spain.

Americans, particularly in the West, were wildly enthusiastic about Revolutionary France. New Orleans was full of Frenchmen. Kentuckians hated paying duty to Spain on the Mississippi. Genêt, surveying all this, believed that he had at hand the elements of a personal triumph. He made George Rogers Clark, the embittered hero, general of an "Independent and Revolutionary Legion of the Mississippi" and set him to gathering and training American mercenaries as a prelude to an invasion of Spanish Louisiana. Thousands, including Thomas Jefferson, supported the scheme and,

Ready cash for a money-starved society

On the frontier few settlers saw more than a couple of dollars in cash a year. The young country's currency shortage left the isolated backwoods bereft of legal tender. Business limped along on a barter system under which lenient shopkeepers accepted payment in everything from grain to ginseng root. What money settlers did plunk down on the barrelhead was a motley assortment of coins minted in Europe and domestic issues of dubious worth. Even currency intended for use on the frontier (examples of which are reproduced here in their actual sizes) flowed back to the East to wholesalers who demanded cash.

The copper sou *(top, near right)* issued by France in 1767 for distribution in the colonies sifted into the Northwest Territory. One side bears the motto *Sit Nomen Domini Benedictum* (Blessed Be the Name of the Lord). The other has a crossed scepter and arm of justice, the mint mark "A" for Paris and "L.XV" for Louis XV, who ordered the coin.

The Myddelton halfpenny *(below the sou)* was minted privately in England for Philip Parry Price, who toured Britain from 1795 to 1796 recruiting yeoman farmers to emigrate to a large tract he owned in Kentucky. Price planned to circulate the copper token among his tenants and had it elegantly designed to show "Hope" presenting two children to America. On the reverse side Britannia sits with bowed head, grieving over the loss of her colonies. Price made the coin payable to his alias, P. P. P. Myddelton, but the British authorities were not fooled. Price's dream of

FRENCH COPPER SOU

MYDDELTON HALFPENNY

a frontier realm with its own coinage ended when he was arrested for draining Britain of its native talent.

The first small-change notes printed for the Northwest Territory *(below the halfpenny)* were inscribed in French and issued by the Scioto Company, an American firm that sold land in the Ohio Valley to French immigrants. When 500 such immigrants arrived in America in 1790, they discovered that their deeds were worthless. Nevertheless, the settlers pressed on to the frontier and forced the land company to reimburse them in coupons like the one shown here, worth three cents, which they cashed in for supplies at the company store.

The Northwest Territory's only official venture into money-making was a series of notes intended to facilitate federal land sales. The engraved note *(top right),* issued in Cincinnati from 1800 to 1803, promised the bearer five dollars plus interest. The eagle in the upper left-hand corner attests to the note's reliability, and a small hand points to a warning against counterfeiting. Writing on the face indicates that the bill was redeemed in 1806 by one Wm. McFarland.

Although some merchants offered banking services, the first attempt to establish a bank in the Northwest Territory came in 1806 when the Bank of Detroit got a charter for 101 years. The bankers imported a vault from Boston, sold stock and issued $1.5 million of ornate notes like the one at lower right. Most of them, however, were carried east by speculators, and the bank—which had received no deposits—closed in 1809.

SCIOTO COMPANY SCRIP

NORTHWEST TERRITORY NOTE

BANK OF DETROIT NOTE

The frontier's biggest land scandal erupted in 1795 when Georgia sold its Yazoo Strip — 35 million acres of land stretching from Tennessee to Spanish Florida — to the four land companies designated on this map for only one and a half cents per acre.

for a few months, had reason to believe that New Orleans might be captured.

None of the plotters reckoned, however, with the difficulties that befell anyone who caused George Washington to lose his temper. Washington was aghast at the scheme, not only because it violated American neutrality but also because he considered Genêt's direct appeal to American citizens an affront to his own authority as Commander in Chief. He complained to France and directed Anthony Wayne to build a fort on the Mississippi as a precaution against any "Revolutionary Legion" sailing down the river. Genêt was hastily recalled, and Clark's riflemen went back to raising corn.

Wilkinson sensed opportunity. He wasted no time claiming, through agents sent down the river, to have saved New Orleans — or inventing tales with which to extract money from the new Spanish governor, Baron de Carondelet. He had spent $8,640, he insisted, hiring informers and advancing bribes while personally breaking up Clark's projected attack on Louisiana, but he needed more money, much more money than that.

It was "absolutely necessary," he wrote to Carondelet, that he resign from the Army to devote full time to Spain; thus he needed an annual pension of $4,500. And it was his painful duty to warn the governor that His Most Catholic Majesty must now support a new separatist movement in Kentucky — one Wilkinson seems to have invented for the occasion — or face invasion by Kentuckians bent on erasing duties on the Mississippi. He needed $200,000 to head off this dread possibility, plus $12,000 in retroactive payment of an older pension that he maintained the previous governor, Miró, had promised but had failed to provide. "Do not," he entreated, "believe me avaricious as the sensation never found place in my bosom. Constant in my attachments, ardent in my affections, and an enthusiast in the cause I have espoused, my character is the reverse."

Carondelet was suitably alarmed and informed Madrid that he was about to be inundated by 60,000 hairy backwoodsmen. He had sense enough to ignore the request for $200,000 but agreed to hand out the $12,000, which he split into two equal portions for transmission by a pair of Wilkinson's agents, an Irish adventurer named Henry Owen and a certain Captain

Joseph Collins, who were on hand in New Orleans.

Collins took a roundabout route — by sea packet to Charleston, by land to Pittsburgh, by riverboat down the Ohio — frittering away all but $2,500 of Carondelet's $6,000 before he reached Kentucky. Owen took his $6,000 in three kegs up the Mississippi with a crew of boatmen who promptly murdered him.

Wilkinson was not a man to let such disappointments blunt his sense of cupidity, and he soon had new means of impressing the Spanish governor in New Orleans. He became ranking officer of the United States Army on the death of Anthony Wayne. And from that eminence he was able to extort $9,640, which Carondelet sent north in barrels of sugar. This disbursement brought Wilkinson's pay from Spanish sources to the ringing total of $32,000. But his advice and warnings were henceforth unheeded in New Orleans since Carondelet, for all his naïveté, concluded that he was being mulcted and ended the "conspiracy."

None of this inhibited Wilkinson's eye for the main chance. He squeezed $20,000 out of another Spanish official, Florida's Governor Vicente Folch, for writing his "reflections" on Spanish policy just before Louisiana was transferred to the United States. He then got himself appointed governor of a part of the new American territory, Upper Louisiana, after sending a copy of the document to Thomas Jefferson as evidence of his fitness for office. He was soon thickly enmeshed in Aaron Burr's ornate schemes of empire when that brilliant, if aberrant, lawyer-politician-intellectual — ruined in the East by killing Alexander Hamilton on the dueling ground — set out in 1806 to court fortune and power in the West.

Wilkinson outdid himself inventing and using ciphers during this period of scheming with Burr; the two used three different systems to mask the meaning of long-winded correspondence they conducted through messengers. One was based on hieroglyphs in which a list of arithmetic and punctuation symbols replaced such words as "president" and "vice president." Another code, an arbitrary alphabet cipher, consisted of simple substitution of new characters for the standard letters and numbers. The third system, known as the dictionary cipher, was keyed, through the use of numbers, to pages and positions of words in the 1800 Wilmington edition of *Entick's Pocket Dictionary*.

The conspirators scribbled combinations of words and numbers by the yard, as in the letter from Burr to Wilkinson of July 29, 1806: "14. will 297.37 420.26. 1.34.15.—never to 320.7." This cryptic sentence translates as "Burr will proceed westward 1st August, never to return."

Burr hoped to "revolutionize" Louisiana and Mexico with a force of volunteers and to set up an imperial government. He planned to march to New Orleans, seize two million dollars in its treasury and grab its "fine park" of French artillery; then with money and heavy weapons, he could move west to attack Mexico. Wilkinson, in his capacity as governor of Upper Louisiana, would in no way interfere with the theft of the territory's treasure and matériel. Rather, he would be helpfully absent when Burr's men arrived—by leading his American troops on a showy "peace-keeping" mission in Texas, which would have the added benefit of pinning down Spanish forces on the Sabine River.

But Wilkinson double-crossed Burr, having cannily concluded that his dubious ally was a loser. He stayed firmly in New Orleans and sent an armed force to arrest Burr when the expedition—only 60 men in 10 flatboats—reached Bayou Pierre on the Mississippi.

Burr fled, was captured by soldiers from a nearby fort and was taken to Richmond to stand trial for treason. Wilkinson presented himself there in full uniform—"swelling like a turkey cock," in the words of Washington Irving, a spectator at the trial—to testify for the prosecution. He was disappointed to hear a jury find Burr not guilty and, in fact, came within an ace of indictment himself—the famed John Randolph exclaimed, while presiding over the jury deliberations, "Wilkinson is the only man I ever saw who is from the bark to the very core a villain!" Wilkinson's career dwindled thereafter, but not his compulsion for intrigue. He was in Mexico City in 1825, conniving for options on Texas land and offering gratuitous advice to the short-lived Emperor Iturbide, when he died of chronic diarrhea at 68. He had traveled to Mexico as a representative of the American Bible Society.

If Wilkinson outdid all rivals for individual duplicity, a pack of Georgia legislators deserves the palm for skullduggery conducted en masse. They were party, in 1795, to the largest and, very probably, the most dubious land deal in history: the sale of 35 million acres in the Yazoo Strip—which embraced most of present-day Alabama and Mississippi above the border of Spanish Florida—for one and a half cents an acre. Not that they acted without precedent. Much of the Strip (named after the Yazoo River, a tributary of the Mississippi) had been sold six years before, at even lower prices, under conditions that dramatized the confused, claim-and-counterclaim post-Revolutionary struggle for territory north of the Gulf of Mexico among a variety of contestants: Spain, the Southern Indians, the federal government and the Eastern states.

In the late 1780s the Creeks inhabited most of Alabama and southwestern Georgia, the Choctaws claimed the southern two-thirds of Mississippi and the Chickasaws claimed the rest of it. Spain claimed western Mississippi, having established an outpost at Natchez. The federal government, which had theoretical control of the Indians—but not their land—pressed Georgia to cede its claim to the Yazoo Strip as other states had ceded claims west of the Appalachians.

Georgia politicos had long taken a casual view of unsettled land. For years the state's governors had been giving lavish chunks of it to speculators under a law authorizing grants to encourage farming. They often gave away land, in fact, that did not exist; 29,097,866 acres was granted in counties that contained only 8,717,960. In 1789 the legislators decided to squeeze what could be squeezed out of the Yazoo before the federal government eventually wrenched it away from them. They voted to sell three huge areas to hastily organized "Yazoo companies"—10 million acres for $66,964, 11.4 million for $93,741 and four million acres for $46,875.

None of these grandiose schemes of settlement ever came to fruition, in spite of the feverish plotting in which the principals were engaged. Most—including Patrick Henry, organizer of the Virginia Yazoo Company—gave serious thought to detaching themselves from the federal union. "The Law," wrote Henry, "is destructive of people's rights to chuse their form of government." And he condemned the government's campaign to take control of Western lands as "Injustice and Tyranny."

Neither Henry nor any of his contemporaries actually sought shelter under the Spanish flag, although Dr.

Georgia Senator James Jackson *(inset)* led the fight to repeal the Yazoo Act, which granted vast tracts of state land to speculators for a pittance. When the act was rescinded in 1796, legislators met *(below)* in front of the Statehouse to burn copies of it. Jackson, at far left, holds a magnifying glass, which, legend says, "called down fire from heaven" to start the blaze.

James O'Fallon, a rascally Irish physician who represented the South Carolina Yazoo Company, talked rapturously to Miró of doing so — when not threatening to invade western Mississippi with a fictitious militia "of 10,000 men." Neither approach worked.

Miró listened politely to the speculator's pleas for cooperation but prodded the Southern Indians into chasing off the few settlers who managed to establish themselves west of the Chattahoochee River. The federal government, meanwhile, instructed its new wards, the Creeks, to defend their land against intruding whites and made their remarkable chieftain, Alexander McGillivray, a brigadier general. The Georgia legislature, growing restive, finally delivered a fatal blow to the Yazoo companies by demanding debt payments in gold or silver, a condition none could meet.

Still, Yazoo fever smouldered on, and by 1794 a new set of speculators concluded that exploitation of the Strip was feasible at last. The invention of the cotton gin had set off galloping inflation in the prices of Southern land, and Indian claims that had hampered the earlier land grabbers had been "extinguished," in many cases, by treaties with the Southern tribes. Four new Yazoo companies were formed. Senator James Gunn, a Georgia demagogue who headed the largest one, rawhided state legislators into voting the companies vast grants — threatening recalcitrants with a whip and offering land or money to the more reasonable. The purchases thus validated were heralded as the biggest land sale in history: $500,000 in hard currency for 35 million acres west of the Chattahoochee.

But this phase of the Yazoo affair quickly escalated into a scandal that shook Georgia politics to its foundations and became a *cause célèbre* that inspired acrimonious debate in Congress for 20 years. Its legal ramifications were solved only by an interpretation of the Constitution that lent new power to the Supreme Court and that shaped an American view of contracts and property that endures to this day.

The whole elaborate and wonderfully shady enterprise blew up when Gunn's fellow senator, James Jackson, rising up against the speculators, branded the whole business a "vile blot" on the honor of the state and got a new legislature to cancel the sales with a statute known as the Rescinding Act. The enduring repercussions of this action dramatized the fact that

events in the distant West were becoming increasingly important to the settled East: the Yazoo companies had dumped great blocks of land on suckers in New England, and these dupes reacted with alacrity on being dispossessed by Georgia's sudden change of heart.

The Yazoo affair was played out, henceforth, in cities of the Seaboard, though not without displays of temper worthy of a frontier tavern. Congressman John Randolph of Virginia, who fought the idea of federal compensation for the Yazooists, smashed a wine glass over a Congressional opponent's head at a Washington dinner party and then went after him with a bottle. Chief Justice John Marshall stepped between the Yazooists and the anti-Yazooists in the end by putting aside legal niceties and agreeing in effect to let the Supreme Court resolve the issue.

The Court made history with its decision. It overturned the Rescinding Act — the first time it had ever struck down a state law — on the ground that a legislature could not unilaterally void a legal contract it had entered into during an earlier session. The original Yazoo grant legislation was declared legal — despite the impure motives of its framers. With that principle established, Georgia ceded the Yazoo Strip to the federal government, which paid $1,250,000 for the land. All that remained was to remedy the financial plight of the suckers who had purchased Yazoo land, and Congress attended to that detail by appropriating $5,000,000 in compensation. The only ones left holding the bag were the American taxpayers, who had to pay the necessary $6,250,000 to end the affair.

The long struggle over the Yazoo Strip was conducted as though the land were empty, but the Southern Indians were intimately involved — as they were also involved, if only as temporary obstacles or capricious pawns, in the schemes of men like Blount and Sevier and in the shifty diplomacy of Miró and Carondelet. They suffered from the beginning — as had the people of the Algonquin confederation — from the lack of a political system that might have unified their responses to these intruders in their tribal domains. But there was an exception: one man, Alexander McGillivray — a young chieftain of mixed Scottish and Indian blood — made the Creeks a force in international diplomacy during the era of intrigue after the Revolution and confounded the Spaniards and Americans in doing so.

The great Creek leader was the son of Lachlan McGillivray, a Scottish trader who established himself in the wilderness near the present city of Montgomery, Alabama, made a fortune, started a plantation and married a Creek girl named Sehoy, who was descended from aristocrats of the Wind Clan. After Alexander's birth in 1759, the elder McGillivray bowed to the Creek custom that a son should be educated by relatives of the mother's family, and the boy became the special charge of one of Sehoy's brothers, a chief named Red Shoes. As a result, Alexander had a dual upbringing; he absorbed the language and attitudes of the white world in his father's big house, and Indian tongues and customs from his uncles. Lachlan McGil-

livray sent him off to Charleston during his teens to study under a tutor and to learn something of manners and the mysteries of countinghouses.

The boy was bored by numbers but fascinated with history and language—subjects that illuminated his bent for power and his instincts for manipulating others and that equipped him to interpret and checkmate the designs of high-placed Americans and Europeans. He was a tall, thin youth with a bulging forehead and penetrating dark eyes. He had curiously long fingers and learned to scribble in English at very fast speeds—a practice that presaged his lucid and voluminous correspondence in dealing with allies and enemies.

Alexander's formal education ended with the onset of the Revolution. American patriots confiscated his

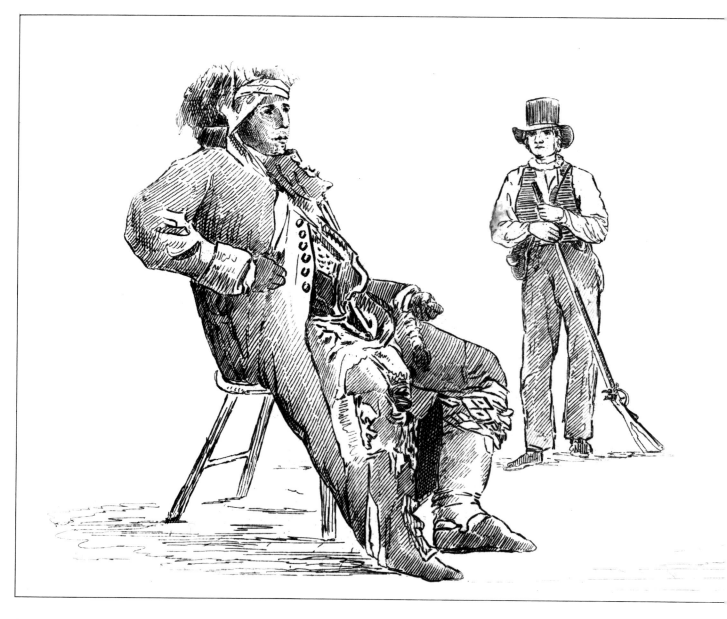

father's slaves and estate, and the elder McGillivray, a defiant Tory, went back to Scotland to end his days. Alexander retreated, burning with indignation and ambition, to Little Tallassie, a Creek town on the Coosa River near present-day Montgomery. He was received there as a chief, made himself an agent of the British and began, at 17, a career in tribal politics in which he emerged, during the early 1780s, as a kind of guiding spirit of the entire Creek confederacy.

McGillivray was an odd sort of chief. He was a coward who was perfectly willing to talk, with a kind of arrogant humor, about hiding in the bushes during the one battle he had steeled himself to "observe." He was not averse to personal gain and soon had three plantations, which he worked with black slaves. He wore white man's clothing or Indian garb as suited his fancy. He had several wives, drank to excess and suffered from venereal disease.

But the Creeks were being squeezed between the westward-thrusting Americans and the Spanish, and McGillivray played the two against each other as had no other Indian. He was incorruptible; he abrogated treaties by which two lesser chieftains, known as Tame King and Fat King, had ceded tribal lands to Georgia. He had an exquisite understanding of the uses — and limits — of war. He became, thus, an anomaly — an Indian politician who could dictate strategy to war chiefs and control a whole people.

In 1783 McGillivray went to Miró for aid in counteracting pressure from what he termed "the dis-

between himself and the American backwoodsmen — but friends who would not be so incautious as to involve him in a war with the United States. But there was very little he could do about the trade, and it flourished for years, with the Creeks growing increasingly well armed. McGillivray used the weapons to stage raids on settlers from Georgia. But he prudently sandwiched truces between attacks and limited himself, for the most part, to preventing settlement of Creek country in western Alabama.

By 1788 the Spanish authorities, fearful of inciting an American military advance toward the Mississippi, began urging McGillivray to seek an accommodation with the United States. McGillivray had doubts: "These Americans are a sett of crafty, cunning republicans, who will endeavor to avail themselves of every circumstance in which I cannot speak or act with decission." Circumstance soon moved him to a different view, however, and led to his greatest triumph.

George Washington, horrified by Georgia's first sale of the Yazoo Strip and fearful of being forced to fight Indians both north and south, secretly sent Colonel Marinus Willett to Georgia to request McGillivray's presence at a meeting in New York. The envoy and the Indian instantly took to each other. Willett found his host "open and generous" when they met at McGillivray's Alabama plantation, Apple Grove. The Creek leader thought his guest "Candid and Benevolent." McGillivray, moreover, had reason to contemplate new friendships: the possibility (due to Spanish confiscation of British ships at Nootka Sound in the Pacific Northwest) of a war, which would cut off his trade with Panton. He presented Willett to the Creek leaders, nodded as the American invited them to "our beloved town that we may form a treaty strong as the hills" and made sure all agreed. He precipitated what might be described as the first traveling Wild West show in American history.

Willett had hoped to take his charges north by ship, but McGillivray pleaded a "mortal aversion" to water. The officer thus found himself guiding a procession along the roads of the Carolinas, Virginia and Pennsylvania such as none had ever witnessed: McGillivray rode with Willett at the head, followed by a military escort, followed by a sulky (to which the famous Creek retired when afflicted by hangovers or bouts of

tracted republick" of the United States. The Spanish governor made him Spain's agent among the Southern Indians and gave him $600 a year. But for all this McGillivray soon showed that he was his own man. William Panton, a Scottish contemporary of his father, had gone to Spanish Florida, after being ordered out of the United States, and had opened the trading firm of Panton, Leslie & Co. Through the good offices of Miró, McGillivray contrived to secure a Spanish trading monopoly for the company. McGillivray sent Panton thousands of deer hides, and Panton, who had direct access to London markets, responded with a flow of arms that gave the Creeks a growing independence.

Miró reacted to this development with a mixture of nervousness and irascibility. He wanted to have friends

French soldiers fire in salute as Old Glory replaces the Tricolor over New Orleans on December 20, 1803, the day Louisiana became American territory. The purchase doubled the size of the United States.

ill health), followed by wagons containing 26 lesser chieftains, baggage, eight warriors and McGillivray's servants. The Indians were applauded at Guilford Courthouse, North Carolina, dined by Governor Beverley Randolph at Richmond, forced to endure a theater performance at Fredericksburg and ogled at a series of public dinners in Philadelphia.

They were saluted on arrival in New York with the greatest public ceremonial since Washington's inauguration. Cannons were fired, and crowds were moved to vociferous applause as they were paraded up Wall Street with Secretary of War Henry Knox. McGillivray was lionized by official society, toasted at receptions, made an honorary member of the St. Andrews Society ("an organization of true Scotsmen"), and described as "grave and solid, intelligent and much of a gentleman," by Abigail Adams, wife of the Vice President. He was approved, if grudgingly, even by Massachusetts' archconservative Congressman Fisher Ames: "He is decent and not very black."

But McGillivray, though flattered — particularly at rubbing shoulders with Washington — dominated the haggling that produced the Treaty of New York. He resisted the President's attempt to undermine his relations with Spain. He did agree to surrender an eastern strip of Creek country to the United States but won the promise of federal protection against further encroachments by the Yazoo companies, plus a commission as a brigadier general and $1,200 a year.

The Senate quickly approved the agreement, and on August 11, 1790, at Federal Hall, Washington and McGillivray signed the document — stepping back to let the other chiefs mark it with Xs. The President then presented McGillivray with a string of beads and a "paper of tobacco" to smoke in remembrance of their meeting. The Creeks built a bonfire on returning to open air and danced around it, "hopping," as Mrs. Adams noted, "in true savage style."

Triumph in New York brought McGillivray to a peak of influence among the Southern Indians, produced a fleeting peace on the frontier — and increased his bargaining power in New Orleans. Miró suspected that the chief had conceded more to Washington than was publicly admitted. But the Spaniard felt bound, while fuming, to increase McGillivray's pension to a lordly $3,500 as a matter of insurance for the future.

The treaty proved short-lived — like most Indian treaties — and the Yazoo Strip eventually was overrun as if it had never been protected.

By then the Creeks no longer had their champion. McGillivray had died of "gout in the stomach" at 34 while visiting Pensacola in 1793. Panton, striving for some final salute, arranged for "full Masonic orders" before burying him in his garden there.

Time and the 1803 Louisiana Purchase solved the Spanish problem — which McGillivray had so cunningly represented — brought an increasing stability to the Southwest and made the Mississippi an American river at last. But time, likewise, moved pioneers both north and south of the Ohio River to fresh exasperation: a conviction that England — half forgotten after the Battle of Fallen Timbers — was again regarding them with hostility and greed.

Hard times fell on all the Western country after 1808. Westerners blamed the British — and with some reason. British blockading of Napoleonic France, the concurrent harassment of American shipping and Jefferson's retaliatory closing of American ports by the Embargo Act in December 1807 had stifled Mississippi River commerce by denying it an outlet to the world. And the settlers of Ohio, Kentucky and Tennessee became convinced that the British — not content with sending traders deep into the American wilds and draining furs into Canada — were inciting the Northern Indians to border war.

True or not, Westerners believed, by 1810, that the way back to honor and prosperity lay in invading Canada and seizing Montreal as a prize to be bartered for good behavior by the Royal Navy. The West, as a result, exerted real political force for the first time: Henry Clay of Kentucky led the Congressional war hawks, and Western pressure (augmented by support from Southerners who wanted to grab Florida) had a great deal to do with James Madison's decision to risk armed conflict in 1812. And if the resultant reaction by England proved hideously embarrassing in many ways, the Westerners' blind insistence on prompting it — like their remorseless march to the Mississippi — seemed to have reflected a kind of unreasoning visceral wisdom. European interference with expansion ceased forever at the war's close, and the West's first national leader rose into view at the Battle of New Orleans.

The modest birth of great cities

With the rush of immigrants to the country west of the Appalachians came the birth of towns, inspired by a need for protection, companionship and the services that a lone homesteader could not provide for himself. Some communities like Pittsburgh *(left)* grew up naturally around forts and trading posts that had been established earlier. Other settlements were the creation of land speculators, many of whom worked only from maps and never saw the land they dealt in.

The speculators bought up promising sites on waterways or in the midst of fertile farmland; they laid out lots and advertised for buyers with highly exaggerated broadsides and newspaper ads ("Perhaps the most desirable spot in the known world"). Not all were successful: such "paper towns" as New Athens, New Lisbon and Town of America never got past the planning stage. And more than one village nearly died a-borning. Cleveland was so vulnerable to disease from the malarial Cuyahoga River that by 1800, a few years after it was founded, the town's population was reduced to seven.

But those settlements favored by location and the drive of their citizens prospered mightily. George Washington saw the potential of Pittsburgh in 1753, when it was only a camp where the Monongahela met the Allegheny. A Pittsburgher could boast 33 years later that his was a town of "smoking chimnies, halls lighted with splendor, ladies and gentlemen assembled."

Pittsburgh in 1796 was a hamlet at the headwaters of the Ohio, already thriving as a jumping-off place for westbound settlers. A generation later it would be a town of factories, mills—and soot-filled air.

Cleveland was merely a dream of Connecticut speculator Moses Cleaveland when its first cabins arose in 1796 beside the Cuya-

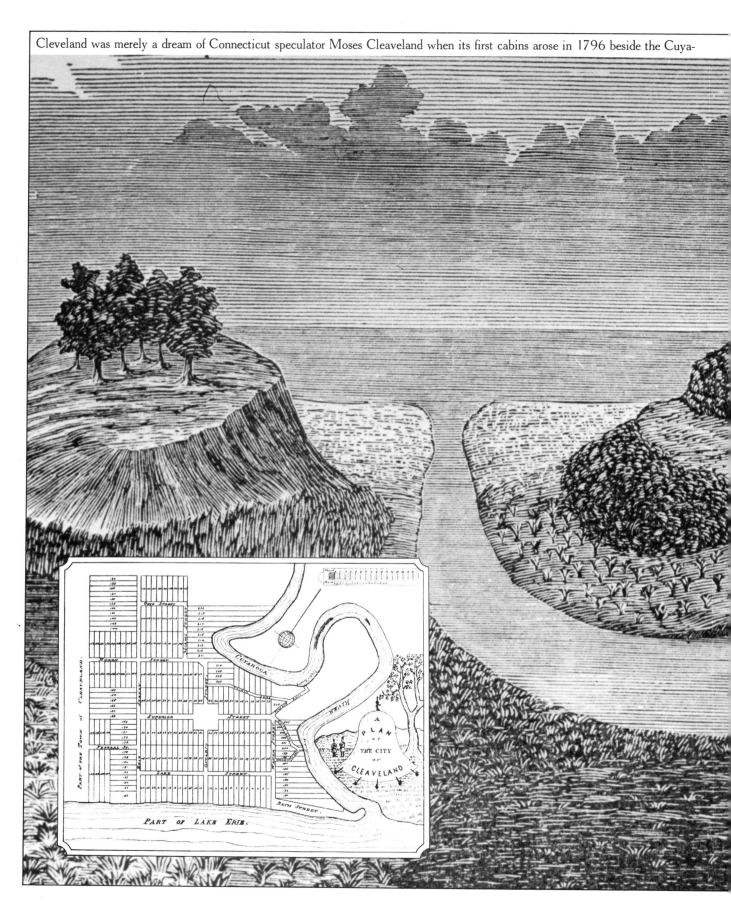

PART OF LAKE ERIE.

hoga River, on Lake Erie. But Cleaveland's surveyor soon made a plan of development *(inset),* and the city grew up following it.

Muskn. river

Marietta, the Northwest Territory's original capital, was settled in 1788 on a flood-prone point of land where the Muskingum River joined the Ohio. By 1792, as this drawing shows, the village was protected by a palisade and four blockhouses, one of which doubled as a schoolhouse.

ohio river

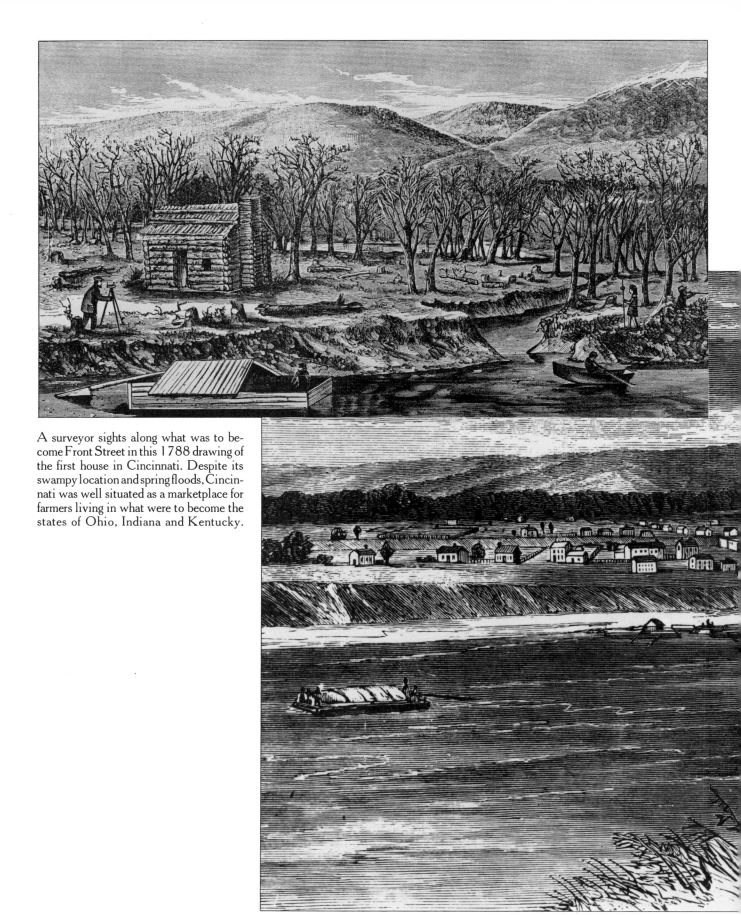

A surveyor sights along what was to become Front Street in this 1788 drawing of the first house in Cincinnati. Despite its swampy location and spring floods, Cincinnati was well situated as a marketplace for farmers living in what were to become the states of Ohio, Indiana and Kentucky.

Pioneer families wait their turn to be ferried across the broad Ohio to Cincinnati in 1802. In 14 years the town had grown from a primitive encampment to a busy commercial center whose citizens found time, as one surprised traveler noted, to enjoy "the harmonies of Gluck and Haydn and the reports of champagne bottles."

6 | The frontier forms a leader

When Andrew Jackson took office as the first American President from the West, with him came a new kind of muddy-boots democracy that owed more to backwoods pragmatism than to the classic philosophies that had influenced his predecessors. The champion of this new politics—some called it mob rule—had been shaped from childhood by the rough, direct ways of the frontier. Growing up in the Carolina hill country, Jackson knew enough of weapons and wounds by age 13 to make himself useful to the Revolutionary cause, whether by shooting redcoats or tending casualties *(left)*.

Orphaned at the end of the war, he headed across the Smokies to seek his fortune. He became a backwoods lawyer, then a landowner, legislator and judge. Jackson's judicial methods were unorthodox but effective; his legal opinions, wrote a contemporary, were "untechnical, unlearned, sometimes ungrammatical, and generally right."

At 35, with scarcely any military background, Jackson was elected a general of the Tennessee militia, and his extraordinary abilities then carried him to national celebrity and the Presidency. Many Easterners considered him even less qualified to lead the nation than he had been to lead an army. But he proved in the White House, as he had on the battlefield (and in the courtroom), that a frontiersman's presence of mind and strength of will were as valuable to a statesman as they were to the hunters and farmers who elected him.

Young Andrew Jackson looks down at victims of the 1780 Waxhaw "massacre" near his home in the Carolina hills. British dragoons had surprised a regiment of Americans and killed 113 of them; Jackson helped care for wounded survivors.

Assigned to a detachment guarding the house of a prominent Revolutionary, trooper Jackson, aged 14, fires at marauding Tories from the fork of a tree. Jackson's shot aroused his companions, one of whom fell wounded *(foreground)*. Together they held off the enemy until help arrived.

190

With the sheriff cowering behind him, Judge Jackson arrests the hulking fugitive Russell Bean in Jonesboro, Tennessee, in 1802. Bean had driven off two posses before Jackson approached him with a cocked pistol and an ultimatum. Realizing that the judge was not bluffing, Bean surrendered.

193

The citizen soldier who never shied from a fight

The parties met just after dawn in a poplar forest near Kentucky's Red River—each having ridden north with his seconds on the previous day to outdistance a Tennessee statute that forbade dueling within the boundaries of the state. The law was unenforceable, but both were lawyers and one, at least, had a future to be safeguarded by obeying it. Tall, gaunt Andrew Jackson, 39, was the challenger. However, 27-year-old Charles Dickinson, a dandy but a deadly snap shot, had prompted their meeting with insulting references to Jackson's wife, and a newspaper article ("I declare him to be a worthless scoundrel, a poltroon and a coward") after Jackson's horse, Truxton, had beaten Dickinson's father-in-law's, Ploughboy, for $3,000. The seconds had agreed to stated conditions: "Distance, 24 feet; the parties to stand facing each other with their pistols down perpendicularly. The single word, 'FIRE,' to be given. Should either fire before the word, we pledge ourselves to shoot him down instantly."

Jackson—aware that he was a mediocre shot despite a lifelong penchant for issuing challenges—had decided to let his opponent fire at will before acting. He had nevertheless eaten a dinner of chicken, waffles and sweet potatoes at Miller's Tavern the night before, had engaged in small talk on its porch until 10 o'clock, and had slept so soundly that some effort was needed to arouse him at sunup. The pistols—nine-inch barrels charged with one-ounce balls of .70-caliber—were Jackson's. Dickinson chose first. The two men walked into the open and faced each other, and Jackson's second, a former Revolutionary officer named Tho-

mas Overton, called: "Gentlemen, are you ready?"

"Ready," said Dickinson.

"Ready," said Jackson.

"Fire!" cried Overton.

Dickinson's pistol came up like magic and its heavy report broke the silence. A puff of dust flew from Jackson's coat—which hung so awkwardly upon his cadaverous frame that Dickinson was deceived by two inches in taking aim at his opponent's heart. Jackson's left hand started convulsively toward his chest, but returned to his side. "Great God," said Dickinson, stepping back in horror. "Have I missed him?"

Overton gestured with his weapon and said, coldly, "Back to the mark, sir."

Dickinson then stepped forward, folded his arms, and stared fixedly ahead. Jackson straightened, raised his pistol, cocked it—the click of the mechanism distinct to all—and aimed. He drew it back and carefully sighted again, and finally fired—sending its heavy ball plowing through Dickinson's intestines, knocking him to the ground, and inflicting a wound from which Dickinson died later in the day.

Jackson walked steadily back to his horse. It was not until he began to mount that Jackson's surgeon saw that his man's left shoe was red with blood. "Oh, I believe he pinked me," said Jackson—though Dickinson's ball was lodged near his heart, caused him suffering, and remained in his body for the rest of his life—"but say nothing about it." Then he added: "I should have hit him if he had shot me through the brain."

Few events in Jackson's life so accurately reflected those aspects of character that shaped his concepts of honor and that kept him striving so violently—as defiant backwoods boy and as westbound adventurer, as frontier lawyer, planter, speculator and politician, and as border captain, Indian fighter and England's fierce nemesis at New Orleans—for personal expres-

The hard eyes that faced down many a foe gaze from this portrait of a remarkably youthful Andrew Jackson, made after the Battle of New Orleans, when he was 48.

sion and the hot satisfactions of success and fame.

Jackson ushered in the era of the common man in the United States after having become its first Western President. His inauguration set the tone of the new era when thousands swarmed through the White House, grabbing for food, breaking dishes, and standing on chairs with mud dripping from their boots to the damask covers. The crowd, as one man said, was made up of "all sorts of people, from the highest and most polished, down to the most vulgar and gross in the nation." The people came to see the man whose campaign had appealed directly to them through rallies, parades, buttons and the distribution of hats with hickory leaves stuck in them.

Jackson is best remembered for founding the modern Democratic Party, for wrenching the nomination process away from Congress through the party convention, for advocating the principle of rotation in office, which unscrupulous bosses turned into the spoils system, and for opposing the South Carolina nullifiers who placed states' rights above the national interest ("Our federal Union, it must be preserved").

Jackson replaced the elitist attitudes of the East by those of the frontier in running the government, and instituted concepts that were to endure through a century of Democratic Party politics. But he was no theorist. He believed himself born to dominate rather than instruct men. His enduring reputation for political innovation seems, in a curious way, to have been almost accidental. He forged much of it as he had forged his earlier reputation in the West: by reacting to problems set before him as much as by any process of philosophic reasoning — and by then exercising an implacable willfulness against all odds.

Jackson's fits of bellicosity trembled, at times, on the brink of paranoia. His capacity for pain and his disregard of his own flesh sometimes seemed all but suicidal. He had great personal charm, was capable of deep loyalties and of a winning courtliness, and could demonstrate a gravity of mind, a shrewdness and a capacity for judgment that were at odds with the more violent aspects of his nature. But it was his driving will and his feverish refusal to be denied that made him unique. Jackson was a creature of the frontier. It was, very probably, the only theater in which his fortitude, pugnacity and ambitions could have found full expression

Long after Jackson's death this pistol was found secreted in the eaves of The Hermitage, his mansion near Nashville. An early 1800s Kentucky flintlock with silver trim, it was a weapon that a gentleman gun fancier like Jackson might carry in his pocket.

Replete with misspellings, this note launched Jackson's eventful career as a duelist at age 21. He sent it to Waightstill Avery, a distinguished North Carolina attorney, who had ignored Jackson's first challenge — written in fury on a page torn from a lawbook after Avery had joshed Jackson mildly in a back-country courtroom. The two men met on the field of honor, but cooler friends had prevailed upon them in the interim and both fired into the air.

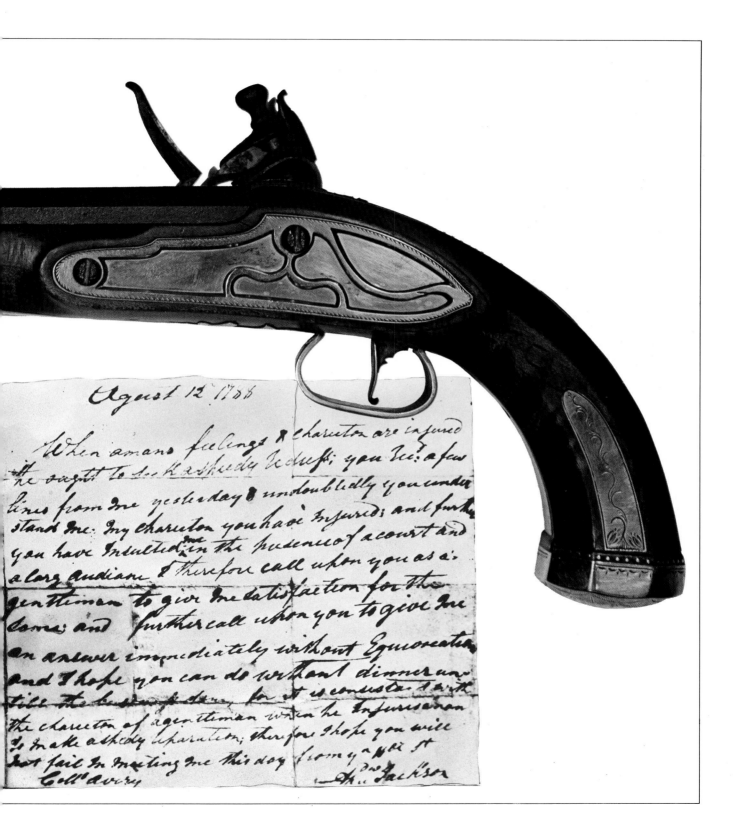

August 12 1788

When a mans feelings & chareter are injured he ought to seek a speedy redress; you rec: a few lines from me yesterday & undoubledly you understand me. My chareter you have injured; and further you have insulted me in the presence of a court and a large audiance. I therefore call upon you as a gentleman to give me satisfaction for the same; and I further call upon you to give me an answer immediately without Equivocation and I hope you can do without dinner until the business is done, for it is consistant with the chareter of a gentleman when he injures a man to make a speedy reparation; therefore I hope you will not fail in meeting me this day from yr Hbl St

Coll Avery   And[w]. Jackson

197

Captured at the home of a neighbor, the young rebel Andrew Jackson prepares to fend off a saber blow from a British officer as his brother Robert and the women of the house look on, horrified. The officer had ordered Jackson to clean his boots and became enraged when the lad responded: "Sir, I am a prisoner of war and claim to be treated as such."

in the years after the Revolution. But he did not fit the mold of the frontiersman, for all that. He strove to shape rather than to reflect the attitudes of the border country, and he reached heights of leadership when he rushed to rescue the Mississippi and the West from the designs of England at the Battle of New Orleans.

This feat of arms—in which backwoods sharpshooters made their greatest stand as fighting men—was the key, of course, to Jackson's place in the pantheon of national heroes. One has the eerie feeling that he spent his boyhood and youth creating the man who presided over the awesome struggle for New Orleans. Jackson's parents—Ulster Scots like so many other pilgrims drawn to the American backwoods—came to the United States in 1765 and settled in a hill district of South Carolina known as the Waxhaws. His father died, however, just before his birth in 1767. His mother, Elizabeth, was taken in 1781 by "prison fever," as cholera was called, while nursing American soldiers held captive on a British hulk in Charles Town harbor. So, when he was only 14 years old, he was left on his own—his parents having bequeathed him some land in the Waxhaws and the north-of-Ireland brogue that crept into his speech in moments of excitement or stress until the end of his days.

The boy was not without recourse to numerous kinfolk. Four of his mother's sisters were married to Waxhaws men and one of them, James Crawford, owned slaves, a gristmill and a great deal of land.

But young Andy led a wildly independent life even before his mother's death. He was wise to the ways of cockfighting at age 12, fought with a local militia company—and was captured by British Dragoons and imprisoned in a British jail at Camden, South Carolina—when he was 14. When the skinny prisoner refused to serve as a bootboy, the officer commanding his captors hacked at him with a sword, cutting his left hand to the bone and leaving an enduring white scar on his forehead. This act of careless sadism cost the British Empire dearly in the end. Jackson never forgot, and for years nursed a hatred of England and Englishmen.

If war shaped his character, a little fortune—£400 left him when he was 16 by a relative back in Carrickfergus, Ireland—shaped the manners and attitudes by which he was to reveal it to the world. A good many

Charles Town dandies had retreated to the Waxhaws after the British overran the coastal Carolinas during the Revolution. Jackson, having observed them with interest, now headed for the city (renamed Charleston in 1783 to diminish the royal flavor of its original spelling) and set out to emulate the life of a cavalier rake and to make himself a gentleman. The money was soon spent on brandy, horses and cards. But he was a hill boy no longer. He bet his horse against $200 at cards, won, returned briefly to the Waxhaws and then in December 1784 went to Salisbury, North Carolina, and persuaded an attorney named Spruce Macay to let him join the young bloods who were reading law in his office.

Jackson was a less than assiduous student. "The most roaring, rollicking, game-cocking, horse-racing, card-playing, mischievous fellow that ever lived in Salisbury," and, "the head of the rowdies hereabouts," was how a town resident remembered him. But he was intelligent. He learned to speak well. He was sensitive to the nuances of life among the propertied people with whom he ingratiated himself. He was admitted to practice at 20, attached himself to one John McNairy who

had just been made judge of North Carolina's western district (Tennessee) and rode "up West" with him—a pair of pistols slung from his saddle—as public prosecutor of the district. He set the tone for his practice of the law almost instantly: he challenged an old attorney named Waightstill Avery to a duel for twitting him over his inexperience and launched himself at debtors like a thunderbolt. The quarrel with Avery was settled amicably, but he carried out 70 writs of execution in 30 days against citizens of Nashville who had been refusing, en masse, to pay their bills—thus enforcing a new cognizance of the law and placing himself firmly on the side of people who counted in Tennessee.

He was himself soon a man who counted in Tennessee, and remained so for the rest of his life. The self-made gentleman speculated in land: in the mid-1790s he held title, personally or with others, to almost 80,000 acres, much of it recently taken by treaty from the Cherokees. He raised cotton on tracts near Nashville. And at one of them, the Hermitage, he raised a large house that would become his lifetime home.

He imported broadcloth, coffee, calico, rifles and skillets from Philadelphia, and traded them for cotton,

The original Hermitage, Jackson's home from 1804 to 1819, was a rough-hewn cabin (*foreground*). James Monroe, Aaron Burr and other famous visitors entertained here slept in the guesthouses in the rear.

tobacco, furs and slaves. He was often strapped for money, nevertheless. He was a shrewd businessman who would not be imposed upon, but he was also a man who would, a friend said, "beggar himself to pay a debt, and did so." He was sometimes seduced by the risk implicit in speculative ventures—being forced to divest himself in 1796 of tens of thousands of acres, including some of his cotton country, as well as relinquishing in 1804 a pre-Hermitage plantation he had called Hunter's Hill.

There were other reasons for the financial peril in which he often found himself. He liked to live well: he spent $1,668.05 on one occasion to have some parlor chairs and a settee brought from Philadelphia, the cost including 20 gallons of whiskey needed to sustain the 14 boatmen he hired to get the furniture along the Cumberland River. He was grimly determined to make himself one of the leading figures of the Western turf and spent thousands of dollars on blooded horses and risked thousands more in bets. And he was a public man. Business, no matter how vigorously he pursued it, became secondary, in the long run, to his political interests and the political associations by which he became Tennessee's first Congressman and one of its early Senators, a judge and—dearer to his heart by far—an officer and eventually a major general of the Tennessee militia.

His life was complicated, furthermore, by a ferocious preoccupation with personal honor. It was an idiosyncrasy that was exaggerated by his marriage to Rachel Donelson Robards, the dark-eyed daughter of an old Southern family that had been driven west by ill fortune in Virginia.

Rachel had married and then separated from a Captain Lewis Robards by the time Jackson—newly arrived in 1788 in Nashville—met and admired her while he was a boarder at the home of her widowed mother. After one of several failed attempts at reconciliation Robards insulted Jackson, who responded by threatening to cut off his ears. In 1791—on hearing that Robards had accused her of adultery and had filed for a divorce—Jackson followed her to the home of friends with whom she had sought shelter near Natchez and married her himself. He sentenced her to a lifetime of innuendo—and himself to an outraged defense of her good name. For the vindictive Robards let his divorce suit lapse for two years after the Jacksons' marriage and advertised the fact of her bigamy with cruel satisfaction until the divorce was finally granted.

The gossip was a sad burden to Jackson. He watched Rachel become a kind of recluse over the years, and when a Dickinson or—as was the case in 1803—a John Sevier abused her name he was moved to an explosive need for revenge.

The resultant proceedings, if deadly, sometimes lapsed into the ludicrous for all that. Jackson and Sevier were natural political rivals, if only because each believed himself the worthiest citizen of Tennessee. Their relations reached the breaking point when Jackson—having wrested the major-generalship of the militia from the other man—went on to expose Sevier's part in a vast land fraud in an unsuccessful attempt to deny him another term as Tennessee governor. Sevier was not pleased, thus, when General Jackson found him haranguing a crowd of legislators on the courthouse steps in Knoxville and broke in to suggest that he, Jackson, had been of more service to the people of Tennessee than a man who had used public office to grab a fifth of the state.

"Services?" yelled Sevier, yanking forth a cavalry saber he wore at his belt, "I know of no great service you have rendered except taking a trip to Natchez with another man's wife."

"Great God!" cried Jackson, "Do you mention *her* sacred name?" and ran for the governor swinging his walking stick. The combatants were dragged apart, but Jackson wasted no time in issuing a challenge. The governor temporized, having concluded, as his temper cooled, that he was too proven in battle and too old to risk his neck at so late a stage of his career. He announced that he would be pleased to meet his foe but failed to say where. Friends of both men importuned them to bury the hatchet. But Jackson wanted blood. "In the publick streets of Knoxville you appeared to pant for combat," he wrote Sevier. "You took the sacred name of a lady in your polluted lips. . . ." Jackson bought newspaper space to tell the world that "John Sevier is a coward and poltroon. He will basely insult, but has not the courage to repair."

This accomplished, he set out with an Army physician, Dr. Thomas J. Van Dyke, for Southwest

Rachel Jackson's dark-eyed beauty enthralled her husband, who kept this portrait over his bedroom mantel until he died in 1845.

Point — a corner of Cherokee territory — in the belief that Sevier, who refused to break the law in Tennessee, would be forced by public opinion to follow. The governor did so, but not before obliging Jackson to wait in the woods for five days. The two men engaged in an outlandish burlesque of the dueling process when Jackson finally spotted Sevier riding toward him with a group of armed men.

Both adversaries dismounted, cursing each other roundly, and advanced with a pistol in each hand. But they stopped, apparently in some confusion, when they were 20 steps apart, and put up their weapons. They did not cease to abuse each other, however, and Jackson came on, freshly infuriated, with his cane. Sevier yanked out his sword, frightening his horse, which galloped off with his pistols. He took refuge behind a tree. Jackson found a pistol and dodged forward looking for a clear shot while Sevier, still cursing, protested Jackson's attacking an unarmed man. Sevier's 17-year-old son yanked out his pistol and covered Jackson — only to find that the doctor, also armed, was threatening to kill him if he touched the trigger. Sevier's friends broke up this odd tableau — leaving Jackson to claim a kind of moral victory — and led their man to a nearby military post where the garrison soothed him and restored his ego with a 16-gun salute.

Jackson was all but killed, 10 years later, in another confused and violent confrontation. This one took place in the hallway of a Nashville hotel with Thomas Hart Benton (later a U.S. Senator from Missouri) and Benton's brother Jesse. A man less intent than Jackson on the rigid niceties of the code duello, and one less given to finding insult in the conversation of tale bearers, would never have become involved in such an episode. But it led to the beginnings of a heroic legend, for Jackson ignored the hideous pain he suffered as an aftermath of the brawl, and achieved the first of the military victories that were to make him an American hero and that were to open the way to the White House.

The incident had its genesis in Jackson's intense desire to conquer Canada for the United States when the nation went to war with England in June of 1812. He offered President James Madison 2,500 Tennessee militiamen and promised to have them in Quebec in 90 days. "He can most certainly do so," wrote his friend Willie Blount, who had superseded Sevier as

governor. "He feels a holy zeal for the welfare of the United States." Madison brushed Jackson off: people in Washington had not forgotten an incautious episode in which he had involved himself six years before — offering his friend Aaron Burr the hospitality of the Hermitage and procuring supplies for him, unaware that Burr was plotting the disunion of the West.

That fall Jackson led 2,000 Tennessee volunteers to Natchez; Blount put him in command when the government finally requested the troops. But he saw no action — except with the government, which suddenly and for no apparent reason ordered him to disband his force, 400 miles from home, without provisions for pay or rations. He refused with indignation, spent his own money to get his men home and earned the enduring sobriquet "Old Hickory" by marching on foot with them, while ailing privates rode his three horses on the long trip back to Tennessee.

Tom Benton, an admirer and protegé, served as a colonel on this expedition. After it was concluded, he went to Washington and acted there as a kind of unofficial envoy for Jackson in an effort to get him reimbursed for the expenses he had incurred. But this friendship ended abruptly and violently in June 1813. Two other officers of the volunteers quarreled and one of them, Littleton Johnston, challenged the other, William Carroll, to a duel. Carroll refused — Johnston, he announced, was not a gentleman. Benton's brother, Jesse, became embroiled in the dispute and challenged Carroll. Carroll reluctantly agreed to meet him and asked Jackson to act as his second. Jackson, to give him credit, did everything in his power to settle the matter by peaceful means. This failing, however, he felt duty bound to accept. Jesse Benton alas, suffered a fate worse, in many eyes, than death. He fired first and barely grazed Carroll on the thumb. In panic, he turned and was struck in the buttocks by Carroll's bullet, thus making himself the victim of a thousand coarse and demeaning jokes.

Thomas Benton returned home to Franklin, Tennessee, to offer his brother moral support and inspired a babble of excited speculation in so doing. Jackson soon heard rumors that the younger man proposed to challenge him and wrote, gravely, to ask if the story were true. Benton denied it, but did not mask his annoyance with his mentor. He replied that it was "very poor business of a man of your age and standing to be conducting a duel about nothing between young men who had no harm against each other."

Jackson was not one who listened readily to lectures on his own failings, particularly since he felt himself innocent of blame. Nor was he a man who received tales of continued criticism with equanimity. He announced hotly that he would horsewhip Tom Benton on sight. When he heard, on September 4, 1813, that the Benton boys were in town and staying at the City Hotel, he headed for the place, whip in hand, accompanied by his friend John Coffee.

He discovered Tom Benton in a hallway that led to a veranda at the rear of the inn and advanced upon him, yelling, "Now, you damned rascal I am going to punish you. Defend youself." Benton reached for one of a pair of pistols with which he was armed but Jackson raised a pistol of his own at the same instant, pressed it against his quarry's chest, and backed him down the passageway to the porch. He did not reckon, however, with Jesse Benton—who emerged from a doorway behind him and shot him through the left shoulder at point-blank range. The impact knocked Jackson down. His weapon, which went off as he fell, burned Tom Benton's coat sleeve—very probably at the split second Benton fired at him in turn, missing with both pistols as he tumbled to the floor.

A noisy new brawl ensued, with the contestants struggling and cursing above Jackson as he lay, stunned, on the floor of the hallway. John Coffee, a huge man, materialized amid the smoke, fired, missed and came on swinging his empty weapon at Tom Benton—who lurched back, tripped and tumbled down a flight of stairs. Another Jackson friend, Stockley Hays, rushed up and thrust at Jesse Benton with a sword cane, which snapped in two on hitting a button on Benton's jacket. Jesse pulled the trigger of his second pistol. It failed to fire and bystanders pulled the combatants apart, leaving Coffee and Hays to bend over the gory and ashen figure on the floor.

Jesse Benton had double-shotted his pistol. One slug smashed bones in Jackson's left shoulder; the other tore the flesh of his upper arm before lodging against the bone. He bled prodigiously, the blood soaking through two mattresses at the Nashville Inn. Jackson stood six feet one but he was lean to the point of emaciation and had lately been afflicted with arthritis. He seemed close to death when he was put to bed at the inn. He clung to consciousness, nevertheless, as a covey of physicians agreed, while toiling to staunch the flow of blood, that the arm had to be removed. Jackson interrupted. They were forbidden to amputate. He would recover, intact, on his own.

Messengers from Alabama tremendously hastened this process by bringing word, a few days later, that Creek Red Sticks, a hot-blooded warrior faction among the Creek nation, had stormed a backwoods bastion known as Fort Mims. Finding the gates open, the Red Sticks had swarmed inside and had massacred over 500 militiamen and settlers. From his sickbed Jackson issued a call to the militia: "Fellow Soldiers, The horrid butcheries perpetrating on our defenseless fellow citizens cannot fail to excite in every bosom a spirit of revenge." In a note to John Coffee, who commanded the state's mounted militia, Jackson declared: "the health of your general is restored. He will command in person." Willie Blount ordered an expedition of 2,000 men, and Jackson—having decided, in bed, to capture Florida as well as demolish the Indians—rose on October 7, suspended his arm in a sling, and led his forces off into the wilderness.

A formidable foe awaited him. The recalcitrant Creeks were led by one William Weatherford (a nephew of Alexander McGillivray's) who had decided, like his illustrious uncle, to live among the Indians although precious little of their blood tinctured that of his French, Spanish and Scottish ancestors. But Jackson was more worried about supplies than about his enemy. No roads existed in the country he invaded, and although he cut a rude track to the Coosa River "over mountains more tremendous than the Alps" as one soldier put it, Jackson wrote: "There *is* an enemy I dread much more than the hostile Creek, the meager monster, "FAMINE." But this concern did not lessen his determination "to push forward if I have to live upon acorns." He did both—although he fell so ill with dysentery that he could get relief only while hanging with an arm thrown over a crossbar suspended between two trees.

He reached the Coosa by November 1, built a fort there in the next week and meantime sent Coffee with

Thomas Hart Benton had become a distinguished Senator from Missouri when the lithograph at right was made in 1837 — a far cry from the young firebrand *(below, at left)* who confronted his former friend Jackson in a Nashville hotel brawl in 1813.

DREADFUL FRACAS ATWEEN THE GINERAL AND THE BENTONS AT NASHVIL

The Jackson legend fostered stories like the one illustrated here: a hungry soldier during the Creek campaign asks the seated general to share his meal with him — and finds that it is only a handful of acorns.

1,000 men to a Creek village called Tallushatchee. They marched 13 miles, killed 186 Red Sticks, and marched 13 miles back. "We shot them like dogs," recalled frontiersman Davy Crockett. A few days later, a member of a peaceable Creek. faction known as the White Sticks brought Jackson word that Weatherford — now losing followers — was marching on the informant's town, Talladega, to make examples of its inhabitants.

Jackson roused his army at one o'clock in the morning, drove it through 30 miles of forest in 28 hours, formed it in a crescent outside Talladega and sent a mounted detachment riding toward the town. A thousand Red Stick warriors rose, howling, from the brush. The horsemen retreated. The Indians pursued. The crescent became a circular trap of volleying militia — but after a few minutes of murderous, smoke-clouded chaos, the trap broke, and 700 warriors burst through a gap and vanished into the mountains beyond.

They left Jackson with 15 dead and 87 wounded men. He had no slightest rations for his hungry troops and his fortress on the Coosa stood unguarded. He fell back on it — though he had killed 300 Indians, was sure he had Weatherford in his grasp, and was burning to pursue. He thereupon found himself enduring one of the most difficult and frustrating periods of a difficult life. As days passed without arrival of new supplies, commanders of his starving volunteer and militia companies importuned him to turn back before it was too late. He gave in on November 17, but changed his mind and ordered all back to the stockade when the retreating army came upon a contractor with 150 head of cattle and nine wagons of flour a few miles down the road. One body of militia refused and set out for home. He spurred his horse across their path, balanced a borrowed rifle across his horse's neck with one good arm and threatened to shoot the first man who moved farther. The dissidents turned sullenly about.

Jackson's troubles, however, had only begun. A brigade of one-year volunteers insisted on being mustered out as of December 10 — the day he proposed to march after Weatherford again. A body of East Tennesseans — "1,450 of as fine looking troops as you ever saw," said Jackson — came in to replace them, and announced that their enlistments ran out in 10 days as well. This left him with only 500 men, of whom all

but 130, mostly cavalry under Coffee, were to depart in the immediate future. Ill, angry, and having managed but two hours sleep in 48, he now received the heaviest blow of all: a letter from Governor Blount — on whom he was depending for fresh soldiery — advising evacuation of the fortress and a retreat to Tennessee.

The general sat down at 12:30 a.m. on December 29 and composed a stinging reply: he and his few men were all that stood between civilization (expeditions from Georgia, Louisiana and Mississippi having had little success) and 5,000 Choctaws, Cherokees and once-friendly Creeks who would submit themselves, if unopposed, to Weatherford and his bloody designs.

And are you Dear friend sitting with yr. arms folded, . . . recommending me to retrograde to please the whims of the populace. . . . Let me tell you it imperiously lies upon both you and me to do our duty regardless of consequences or the opinion of these fireside patriots, those fawning sycophants who after their boasted ardor would let thousands fall victim. . . . Arouse from yr. lethargy — despite fawning smiles or snarling frowns — with energy exercise yr. functions — the campaign must rapidly progress or . . . yr. country ruined. Call out the full quota — execute the orders of the Secy. of War, arrest the officer who omits his duty and . . . let popularity perish for the present. . . . Save Mobile — save the Territory — save yr. frontier from becoming drenched in blood. What, retrograde under these circumstances? I will perish first.

"The trade of governing does not suit my genius," admitted Willie Blount, a land speculator who, nevertheless, served three terms as governor of Tennessee and wisely named his friend Jackson to lead its militia.

207

With his one good arm Jackson slings a
borrowed musket over his horse's neck and
trains it on a group of starving militiamen
threatening to desert him during the Creek
campaign. The men returned to duty.

S.F. BAKER SC.   W. CROOME DEL.

Jackson launched himself toward fame with this letter. Willie Blount scraped up 800 green militiamen for
him almost as soon as it arrived. Jackson forthwith
marched them south, got within three miles of Weatherford's stronghold in the Horseshoe Bend of the Tallapoosa River and fought two noisy little battles before
withdrawing again to his stockade on the Coosa. The
Indians initiated both of these actions, and neither was
conclusive; Jackson barely extricated his little army
from the second — after sections of it gave way in
"shame full retreat" at a stream called Enotochopco
Creek — by riding amid "showers of balls" and cursing
them into a semblance of order again. But with the war
going badly elsewhere, both encounters were featured
in newspapers all over the country and Blount and the
War Department hastened Jackson's plan of breaking
the Creeks forever.

The peninsula within the Horseshoe Bend contained 100 acres of land that was broken, haphazardly,
by gullies and covered, in many areas, with thick
brush. Nearly 1,000 diehard Red Sticks were assembled there on March 27, 1814, behind a heavy, loop-
holed log breastwork thrown up across the open end of
their natural fortress. But Jackson, at last, had men to
spare: 5,000 of them, plus Regulars of the 39th Regiment of the U.S. Infantry, as well as Coffee's dependable horsemen on hand to stiffen the militia. He proceeded with deliberation, sending Coffee's men across
the river to form up opposite the upper end of the
peninsula and ordering his Cherokee scouts to cut
loose a fleet of canoes moored along the inner shore.

The expedition's six-pounder began banging away
at the log barrier at 10:30 in the morning. But the
general still delayed the main assault. The reason is
unclear; according to some stories, Indian women and
children began attempting — and were allowed — to escape across the river. Finally, at 12:30 the drums of
the Regulars beat a roll, and 1,000 infantrymen
charged the smoke-cloaked barrier ahead. Major Lem-
uel P. Montgomery of the Regulars climbed it and fell

back dead, but Ensign Sam Houston leaped up after him, sword in hand; the yelling soldiers scrambled over in waves and into a murderous melee on the other side. The Indians, breaking into small bands, retreated to stand again amid the broken terrain toward the enclosing water of the river bend.

"The *carnage,*" Jackson wrote later to his wife, "was *dreadful.*" His forces lost 49 men before the battle ended at dusk; 157 were wounded. But 557 Indian corpses lay heaped within the Horseshoe Bend and another 300 were estimated to have floated away down the river. The Red Sticks were broken and the Creek nation — from which Jackson was shortly to exact 23 million acres of land — forced into an eclipse from which it would never recover. Weatherford, absent by fortuitous circumstance from the battle, presented himself — unarmed, on foot and naked to the waist — to his conqueror a few days later.

Jackson's aide, John Reid — who believed that the Creek leader must be "the greatest of the Barbarian world" — later wrote a description of the doleful little scene that followed.

"General Jackson?"

"Yes."

"I am Bill Weatherford. I am come to give myself up." Jackson asked him inside.

"I have done you much injury," said Weatherford. "I should have done you more but my warriors are killed. I am in your power. Dispose of me as you please."

"You are not in my power," said Jackson. "I had ordered you brought to me in chains. But you have come of your own accord. You see my camp — you see my army — you know my object. If you think you can contend against me in battle, go and head your warriors."

"Ah," said Weatherford. "There was a time when I could have answered you. I could animate my warriors to battle. But I can not animate the dead. I beg you to send for the women and children, who have been driven to the woods without an ear of corn. They never did any harm. But kill me, if the white people want it done." The general poured him a cup of brandy instead, shook his hand, and sent him on his way.

Back in Nashville, Jackson found himself being celebrated as the first genuine hero of the war, "standing," as his friend John Overton put it, "as high as any man in America." Applauding throngs lined the road as he rode into town. A ceremonial sword was tendered him at a state banquet and the administration in Washington — bowing, with reluctance, to public opinion — made him a major general of the Regular Army and commander of the 7th Military District (Tennessee, Louisiana and Mississippi Territory). The War Department did not hesitate, however, to caution him against new adventures: the fighting in the South, he was informed, was over and rumors of the Spanish attempting to stir up the Indians were "incredible." He was to dismiss all but 1,000 men and rest on his laurels. Yet Jackson still burned to take Pensacola and — after being measured for "one suit of full dress uniform with Gold Epaulettes" — he prepared, administration or no, to do so.

England, victorious at last over Napoleon and free of military commitment on the continent, spared him the need to justify these intentions. A great fleet under Vice-Admiral Sir Alexander Cochrane sailed northwest from the British base at Bermuda to blockade the United States coast. Landing parties struck at Eastport, Maine, and Stonington, Connecticut. The fleet entered Chesapeake Bay and punished Americans for their "perfidy and ingratitude" by shelling Baltimore, raiding Alexandria and burning Washington itself. Along the Canadian border 11,000 British veterans of the Napoleonic Wars were stopped, on moving south from the St. Lawrence River, when American gunboats denied them access to the Hudson Valley with a naval victory on Lake Champlain. But Cochrane's Chesapeake force still had ambitious plans.

The fleet sailed for Jamaica and a rendezvous with still more naval vessels, after which Cochrane headed north once again to launch an attack upon the Gulf Coast, which was calculated to take New Orleans, seize control of the lower Mississippi, and open the subcontinent beyond it to agents of the British Crown.

It is popularly believed that American resistance to this invasion was wasted effort since representatives of England and the United States had signed a truce at Ghent, Belgium, some weeks before the Battle of New Orleans took place. The British hoped for a brilliant victory before the treaty was ratified so that their diplo-

A "war of honor" that the West demanded

The United States' declaration of war against England on June 17, 1812, elated the growing bloc of Westerners in Congress. These avid "warhawks" burned to punish the British for inciting Indian violence on the frontier; more important, they regarded Britain as the main obstacle to American growth. Their spokesman, Representative Henry Clay of Kentucky, argued successfully that the time had come for Americans to "manage our own affairs without fear of insulting his Britannic majesty."

The warhawks anticipated a quick conquest of British Canada. Clay promised a reluctant President James Madison that "the Kentucky militia alone are competent to place Montreal and Upper Canada at your feet."

Events proved otherwise. British defenders fought the invading Americans to a standstill in Ontario and Quebec, and in October the main U.S. army of 2,000 men surrendered to a smaller British force at Detroit. Only Commodore Oliver Hazard Perry's victory over an English fleet on Lake Erie in September 1813 kept the British from overrunning the Northwest Territory.

By 1814 the British, having defeated Napoleon in Europe, turned their full attention to the lesser war in America. They dispatched a fleet, carrying 5,000 soldiers and marines, that raided American coastal cities and sailed unopposed into Chesapeake Bay. In August the British marched into Washington, burned the White House and Capitol, and put Madison's government to flight.

The British turned next toward Baltimore. There, however, they encountered much firmer resistance. Twelve thousand Maryland militiamen, led by Major General Samuel Smith, had labored around the clock to shore up the city's battlements. The British fleet drew up just beyond range of the guns of Fort McHenry, guarding the approach to Baltimore harbor. For 25 hours the fleet lambasted the fort (below) with nearly 1,800 shells and rockets. The Americans in the battered fort held on, their shrapnel-shredded flag flying defiantly. Poet Francis Scott Key, watching the bombardment, jotted down the verses that became "The Star-Spangled Banner."

At length the British, not able to crack Baltimore's defenses, withdrew to Bermuda where they prepared a new assault — this time against the frontier's major port, New Orleans.

The rockets' red glare reveals an American flag still waving over Fort McHenry (center) at the height of the British bombardment.

matic position would be one of intimidation rather than submission. But it would be naïve to assume that the British — who were investing vast sums in the expedition, who were sending civil administrators with the fleet, and who were giving passage to officers' wives bent on dominating society in New Orleans — would have sailed peaceably away, treaty or no, if they had seized the city. Indeed, Lord Liverpool remarked to the Duke of Wellington that "it is very desirable that the American war should terminate with a brilliant success" at New Orleans.

Jackson began anticipating these designs even as the President and members of his administration were fleeing Washington to escape British troops being landed from Chesapeake Bay: his spies brought him news of British marines in Spanish Pensacola and revelations, by a British officer in Havana, of much larger events to come. "His B.M. ships *Hermes, Carron* and *Sophie* has arrived at Pensacola," he wrote Robert Butler, an associate in Tennessee. "The *Orpheus* is expected in a few days. It is further added that 14 sail of the line and Transports has arrived at Barmuda, with 25,000 of Lord Wellington's army &c. &c., and before one month the British and Spanish forces expect to be in Possession of Mobile and all the surrounding country."

Jackson ordered mobilization of militia in Mississippi, Tennessee and Kentucky, marched to Mobile with 500 troops of the 3rd U.S. Infantry, and prepared to make sure — as he had written to Butler — that "there will be bloody noses before this happens."

A long, east-west spit all but closed the mouth of Mobile Bay. Jackson sent Major William Lawrence with 160 men to an abandoned fort armed with 20 guns on the tip of this neck of land and Lawrence so damaged H.M.S. *Hermes* in a fight with four British men-of-war — which attempted to get through the pass toward Mobile on September 15 — that the vessel was scuttled and her three companion ships were forced back to Pensacola.

The general seldom rested thereafter. He sent fresh men, guns and supplies to strengthen the fort, reinforced Mobile itself, sent troops to Baton Rouge, and then marched into Spanish Florida with some 4,000 men and stormed Pensacola at sunrise on November 7. The town and its Forts St. Rose and St. Michael were his by afternoon; the English garrison withdrew

to ships offshore after blowing up a third fort, Barrancas, and sailed away.

These feverish exertions were prompted by a sense of strategy rare in civilians turned soldier during middle life. Jackson assumed that the British would not advance upon New Orleans directly from the coast: "A real military man, with full knowledge of the geography of this country, would possess himself of [Mobile], draw to his standard the Indians, march direct to the Walnut Hills [present site of Vicksburg some 200 miles above New Orleans] and being able to forage on the country, support himself, cut off all supplies from above and make this country an easy conquest." He believed that the British would still feel impelled to pursue this course though it meant enmeshing themselves in the impediments he had thrown up to discourage them. And he was in New Orleans on December 1 (still ignorant of the fact that Cochrane had sailed from Jamaica's Negril Bay five days before) to prepare the city for any eventuality.

This, it became obvious at once, was a problem of enormous complexity. To make things worse, Jackson committed a couple of political gaffes. First, having been taken in hand by Governor William Claiborne and an old friend, Edward Livingston, the general passed up an offer of hospitality from Bernard de Marigny de Mandeville, a rich and influential Creole and a member of the legislature. Marigny was not pleased. And the Creoles, who thought little of Claiborne in general and even less of him for having recently raided the headquarters of the pirate Jean Laffite, at Barataria Bay, soon had another cause to shrug their shoulders at the rude soldier come to command them. New Orleans considered Laffite a good fellow: he attacked only Spanish ships and offered his booty for sale at reasonable prices in the city. He had refused attempts by the captain of H.M.S. *Sophie* to woo him to the English cause, and had informed Claiborne that he wanted — despite Claiborne's enmity — to bring his seamen and cannoneers to the defense of the city. But now Jackson, following Claiborne's lead, indignantly refused to associate with such "banditti."

The general, it must be said, had larger concerns: chief among them was the bewildering maze of approaches open to an invader willing to enter the labyrinths of slough and cypress swamp that lay between

An American eagle trails a reassuring banner over an already prosperous New Orleans in a painting, done to celebrate the Louisiana

Purchase. Stately homes line the crowded Mississippi riverfront, protected by a French-built fort now flying the American flag.

families. But his furious energy and "fierce glare" astonished the Creoles — as did his contrasting calm when naval gunboats reported, 10 days after his arrival, that British ships were dropping anchor off Cat and Ship islands at the mouth of Lake Borgne. "I expect," he wrote Coffee at Baton Rouge, "this is a feint to draw my attention to that point when they mean to strike at another."

He then settled down to wait, confident in the knowledge that the lake was too shallow for big ships to anchor within 60 miles of New Orleans. As a result, he left the lake guarded by only five small gunboats. He was stunned five days later when a horseman galloped in to tell him that he had been blind to British designs. They did mean to attack by way of the lake and had captured his five gunboats; this action not only deprived Jackson of his "eyes" but gave the British five valuable shallow-draft vessels to employ in transporting their troops.

Jackson, ill with yet another bout of dysentery, spent 36 sleepless hours on a sofa at his headquarters on Royal Street and tried to sustain himself with sips of brandy while preparing the city for whatever might befall it.

He sent for Coffee ("You must not sleep until you reach me") and for militia from Mississippi and Kentucky. He sent word of his plight to Tennesseans floating toward him down the Mississippi. He deployed one of the black battalions to reinforce defenses. He finally received Jean Laffite when that sociable pirate asked for an audience — and agreed to accept the buccaneer and his sailors as allies. He imposed martial law: "No person, no vessels permitted to leave the city. Street lamps shall be extinguished at nine at night. Persons found in the streets, or not at their respective homes, without permission in writing shall be apprehended as spies."

He was rewarded on December 20. Coffee and 800 men clad in "woolen hunting-shirts" and home-

the city and the coast. Jackson was certain that the British would not attempt to ascend the Mississippi itself. New Orleans lay 105 miles above the stream's multiple mouths, and batteries at English Turn, 14 miles below the city, were, he believed, capable of destroying any flotilla appearing before the muzzles of their guns. The Bayou Lafourche, however, snaked inland from the coast, west of the river, and so did waterways extending north from Barataria Bay. The River Aux Chênes penetrated deeply from the Gulf of Mexico farther east, and Lake Borgne, a great island-dotted bay, linked the Gulf with Lake Pontchartrain — which lay immediately north of New Orleans — and also opened into many meandering creeks, or coulees, that approached the Mississippi on the very outskirts of the city.

The general found brigades of axmen to block these swamp-hemmed watercourses with fallen trees. New Orleans boasted but 2,500 muskets, 7,500 pistols and a motley soldiery made up of free blacks, Creole aristocracy, and merchants and lawyers.

Jackson, still suffering from dysentery, had looked sick, shallow and shabby on December 3 when he reviewed at the Place d'Armes the gorgeously beplumed Battalion of New Orleans Volunteers, whose ranks were filled primarily by men of leading Creole

The 1815 ditty at right celebrates Jackson's Kentucky sharpshooters, who learned to fight in the swamps outside New Orleans as if "every man was half a horse and half an alligator." The words were sung to a rollicking English theater tune, "The Golden Days of Good Queen Bess."

The Hunters of Kentucky;

OR THE

BATTLE OF NEW ORLEANS.

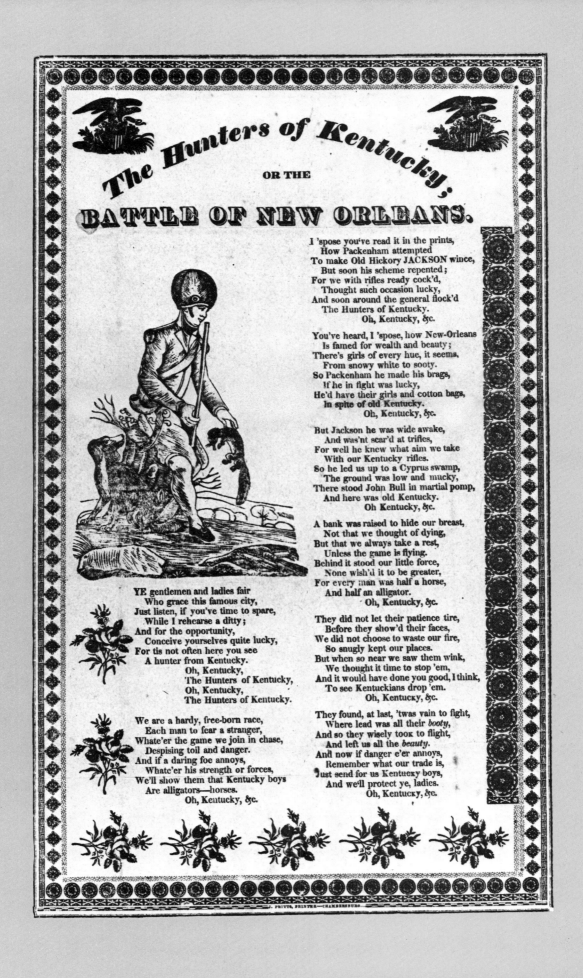

I 'spose you've read it in the prints,
  How Packenham attempted
To make Old Hickory JACKSON wince,
  But soon his scheme repented;
For we with rifles ready cock'd,
  Thought such occasion lucky,
And soon around the general flock'd
  The Hunters of Kentucky.
    Oh, Kentucky, &c.

You've heard, I 'spose, how New-Orleans
  Is famed for wealth and beauty;
There's girls of every hue, it seems,
  From snowy white to sooty.
So Packenham he made his brags,
  If he in fight was lucky,
He'd have their girls and cotton bags,
  In spite of old Kentucky.
    Oh, Kentucky, &c.

But Jackson he was wide awake,
  And was'nt scar'd at trifles,
For well he knew what aim we take
  With our Kentucky rifles.
So he led us up to a Cyprus swamp,
  The ground was low and mucky,
There stood John Bull in martial pomp,
  And here was old Kentucky.
    Oh Kentucky, &c.

A bank was raised to hide our breast,
  Not that we thought of dying,
But that we always take a rest,
  Unless the game is flying.
Behind it stood our little force,
  None wish'd it to be greater,
For every man was half a horse,
  And half an alligator.
    Oh, Kentucky, &c.

YE gentlemen and ladies fair
  Who grace this famous city,
Just listen, if you've time to spare,
  While I rehearse a ditty;
And for the opportunity,
  Conceive yourselves quite lucky,
For tis not often here you see
  A hunter from Kentucky.
    Oh, Kentucky,
    The Hunters of Kentucky,
    Oh, Kentucky,
    The Hunters of Kentucky.

They did not let their patience tire,
  Before they show'd their faces,
We did not choose to waste our fire,
  So snugly kept our places.
But when so near we saw them wink,
  We thought it time to stop 'em,
And it would have done you good, I think,
  To see Kentuckians drop 'em.
    Oh, Kentucky, &c.

We are a hardy, free-born race,
  Each man to fear a stranger,
Whate'er the game we join in chase,
  Despising toil and danger.
And if a daring foe annoys,
  Whate'er his strength or forces,
We'll show them that Kentucky boys
  Are alligators—horses.
    Oh, Kentucky, &c.

They found, at last, 'twas vain to fight,
  Where lead was all their *booty*,
And so they wisely took to flight,
  And left us all the *beauty*.
And now if danger e'er annoys,
  Remember what our trade is,
Just send for us Kentucky boys,
  And we'll protect ye, ladies.
    Oh, Kentucky, &c.

J. PRITTS, PRINTER—CHAMBERSBURG.

spun "pantaloons" arrived to join him, having come the 135 miles from Baton Rouge in three days and nights. Three thousand Tennesseans appeared a few hours later, having spent their time on the river making 50,000 cartridges, each containing a musket ball and three buckshot. Jackson now had something more than 5,000 men to face a British force of twice that number. But none involved knew how perilously their hopes lay balanced, at this moment, upon the knife edge of circumstance.

Admiral Cochrane, on finding Mobile fortified and defended, had wasted not a moment in committing himself to an advance upon New Orleans by the quickest means at hand. Evidence to support this decision lay all about him: more than 50 ships — one of the biggest fleets ever to sail from England to the New World — and 10,000 men prepared to surmount any difficulties that simple bear hunters and Creole dandies could conceive.

It was 30 miles from the fleet to Pea Island, which lay hard upon the inner shore of Lake Borgne, northeast of the city. After capturing the gunboats blocking the entrance to the lake, Cochrane quickly pressed them into service ferrying troops to Pea Island. To speed matters, sailors from the fleet were called upon to serve as oarsmen, and spent six days and nights rowing contingents of infantry to this "resort of wild ducks and alligators." They were splendid soldiers: four regiments fresh from victory on Chesapeake Bay, two from the West Indies, Royal Marines, sappers, engineers, artillerymen, rocketeers, the 93rd Highlanders all the way from the Cape of Good Hope, and a brigade of redcoats who had fought with the Duke of Wellington in Spain.

They suffered on Pea Island. "Than this spot," wrote a young subaltern, "it is scarcely possible to imagine any place more wretched. The army was assembled without any covering — exposed all day to a cold and pelting rain. As night closed, severe frosts set in, congealing our wet clothes upon our bodies. Salt meat and ship biscuit were our food." All, nevertheless, looked forward to "rich booty" and "bloodless conquest." And they soon had reason for these heady expectations. A Spanish fisherman named Gabriel Farerr, who had been paid to find a passage through the maze, discovered that Jackson's axmen had failed to block one of the canal-like coulees — Bayou Bienvenu on the far side of Lake Borgne. He reported that it lay open to small boats, and that it led to plantation houses and open fields just eight miles below New Orleans and to a road along the river that offered easy access to that shining prize. The fisherman confided, moreover, that the way was clear — that Jackson had but 5,000 troops and was holding them scattered around the city.

The British responded with alacrity: they had 1,600 men and two cannon under Major General John Keane on a field of cane stubble near the road at 10:30 a.m. on December 23. However, Keane then temporized. One Joseph Roldophe Ducros, a picket captured along the bayou, told him he faced not 5,000 but between 12,000 and 15,000 men in New Orleans — in addition to 4,000 of them at English Turn; Ducros refused, Jackson having intimated such strength to tale bearers in the city, to be shaken from his story. The British officer had reason to gamble on an immediate attack: a Creole soldier, Major René Phillipe Gabriel de Villeré had broken away after being seized on the porch of his father's plantation house, and had gone tearing off to New Orleans to warn Jackson. But Keane expected 800 more men by nightfall and further reinforcements the next day. He camped and waited.

Jackson seemed more infuriated than startled when he received the news. "By the Eternal, they shall not sleep on our soil. We must fight them tonight." He was in the saddle by three, having eaten a little boiled rice and napped on his sofa in the interim, and was within two miles of the British bivouac by nightfall. Messengers sent galloping off during the afternoon had delivered him 2,100 men: Coffee and 500 of his horsemen, some Mississippi Dragoons, some Regulars of the 7th Infantry, 18 Choctaw Indians, battalions of gaudy New Orleans militiamen who had run most of the way, and in reserve he had 1,000 Tennesseans under William Carroll, who was now a major general and whom Jackson had seconded during the duel with Jesse Benton.

He had yet another weapon to use in surprising those who had so rudely surprised him: the armed schooner *Carolina*, which drifted silently downriver to a mist-cloaked anchorage opposite the enemy as the general deployed his troops within sight of their camp-

PRIVATE

In contrast to the American defenders of New Orleans in their woolen homespun, the British were splendidly turned out. The uniforms of the Royal Regiment of Fusiliers, below, were lace trimmed. The officer and his standard-bearing color sergeant wear white gloves, and even the backpacking private sports a cocked hat.

SERGEANT

FIELD OFFICER

With a burst of cannon fire, Major General William Carroll announces the arrival of his overdue flotilla of riverboats, carrying 3,000 Tennessee militiamen to reinforce Andrew Jackson's army at New Orleans. During the weeks-long journey from Nashville, Carroll's troops had drilled on deck while the blacksmiths aboard cast 50,000 lead cartridges.

On the outskirts of New Orleans, General Jackson directs a subordinate in last-minute efforts to throw up an earthen barrier against the British. Black laborers were enlisted from nearby plantations to help build the breastwork and gun emplacements.

fires. The *Carolina* opened fire at exactly 7:30 p.m., the sudden flame from her guns glaring eerily in the fog as the noise of their discharge boomed over the water.

Jackson waited a half hour, still undetected, while the British labored to bring their own guns to bear upon the ship, and then sent his men off across the dark field. The Regulars were in front, followed by Coffee's Tennesseans, dismounted and operating as infantry. For almost two hours, the forces struggled in the gloom; the scene was a vast, confused melee with the Americans fighting hand-to-hand and shooting at shadowy clumps of equally disorganized Englishmen. The odd battle ended, almost as if by mutual agreement, after 9:30. Silence fell. At first light the next day

Jackson withdrew behind a long, dry millrace, the Rodriguez Canal, leaving the open fields to the enemy. But there they stayed — for good.

The British by now had 4,700 men — having received mud-spattered reinforcements brought up the bayou during the night — and the added advantage of fog. But they awaited the arrival on Christmas Day of Major General Sir Edward Pakenham, brother-in-law of the Duke of Wellington, who had command of English efforts on land and had been appointed overall commander of the expedition.

Pakenham, a boyish-looking man of 36, had been told he would become governor of Louisiana and an earl as well if he took New Orleans. After acquainting himself with the exposed position of his troops, he had begun thinking his chances of earning these honors would be improved if he were to withdraw and strike somewhere else.

Pakenham decided that no new attack should be contemplated until Cochrane's weary boat crews brought up guns capable of dispensing with the *Carolina* and a sister ship, the *Louisiana,* now at anchor nearby. He was heartened to discover that his redcoats were as contemptuous of Jackson's backwoodsmen — whom they had taken to calling the "Dirty Shirts" — as was Cochrane, who had boasted that his sailors alone could take the city.

The Rodriguez Canal, a 10-foot-wide ditch no more than four feet deep, ran at a right angle from the Mississippi levee to cypress woods bordering a gelatinous swamp farther inland. It lay, thus, between the distant city and the wide, flat stubble fields to the east on which the British were encamped. At first light on December 24, Jackson set his men to digging out the canal, using the mud to crown the bank with a rampart, while foragers set off to bring him every pick and shovel to be found in the city and country around. The troops dug furiously, in shifts, all day, all the next night, and all the following day while Jackson — sleepless and nourished only by boiled rice, often eaten as he sat his horse — moved restlessly along the line. An aide brought him a plea from Jean Laffite: the pirate wanted the rampart run through the woods to the swamp lest the British break through on the left. He ordered it extended at once.

"Uncle Jackson," wrote Rachel's nephew Captain John Donelson, "looks very badly and has broken very much." He slept at last — at a nearby plantation house known as the Macarty mansion — on the night of December 26. He was awakened by the banging of artillery: Pakenham's new guns were firing at the *Carolina* and she blew up, shortly, with an awful roar. Jackson, peering through a borrowed telescope, then watched an agonizing spectacle: the crew of the *Louisiana,* now so integral to his plans, were laboring at the oars of small boats — there being no wind — to tow her as the British trained their guns, in turn, on them. She moved, at last, to safety, and the general to fresh endeavor. New cannon — giving him five — were emplaced; a new rampart

begun two miles to the rear. He sent riflemen forth at dusk to snipe through the night. He was about to be attacked, and he wanted a tired enemy.

All the labors of the *Louisiana's* crew, all the labors of Jackson's soldiers turned ditchdiggers were repaid when the British tried to break the ramparts of mud on December 28 and New Year's Day. Two red-coated columns came forward — one along the river, one toward the woods — during the first attack, while enemy artillerymen hammered the trench with noisy Congreve rockets and a cannonade from 10 guns. The British artillery was withdrawn when fire from the *Louisiana* broke up the river column.

Pakenham had 24 guns on New Year's morning — 14 more having been hauled, by incredible labor, the 60 miles from the fleet — and had been provided naval gunners to serve them. They ruined the Macarty house and sent gouts of mud flying along the canal, but Coffee's riflemen responded with such fury when infantrymen advanced toward the woods that they, too, were recalled and the gunners were ordered to cease their noisy endeavors.

The British troops were discouraged — though more by frustration, mud, weather and a shortage of rations than by any awe of the oddly caparisoned foe. The Americans, many of whom had experienced war for the first time, were invigorated. The Creole elders of New Orleans were at once exasperated and enormously relieved. A good many of them had harbored grave doubts of Jackson's chances — and had been horrified by rumors that he proposed to burn the city, as the Russians had burned Moscow, if he was forced to fall back. Legislators, including Bernard de Marigny, had begun weighing the possibility of a separate peace with Cochrane to save their property. Jackson was informed of this by a volunteer aide, Abner Duncan, in the midst of the attack on December 28 and cried, in some distraction, "If they persist, blow them up!" Duncan interpreted this to mean that the legislature was to be dissolved and so told Governor Claiborne, who barred the doors of its chamber and triggered vast indignation — until the battle on New Year's Day.

Jackson sent Brigadier General David Morgan of Louisiana across the river to mount artillery on the plain overlooking the battlefield. Having kept the enemy awake with snipers he now dispatched "hunting parties" to stalk their sentries at night. He was stimulated — and exasperated — by the arrival of 2,300 Kentucky volunteers. Only 700 of them had weapons. "I have never seen a Kentuckian without a gun and a pack of cards and a bottle of whisky in my life," he said, and seized 400 fowling pieces from the auxiliaries policing New Orleans for distribution among the anomalous horde.

His energy, his decisiveness, his air of indomitability were contagious. "Although ready to sink under the weight of sickness, fatigue and continual watching," his chief of engineers wrote, "his mind never lost for a moment that energy which he knew so well how to communicate to all that surround him. The energy spread to the whole army, composed of heterogeneous elements, speaking different languages, and brought up in different habits. There was nothing it did not feel capable of performing, if he ordered it done."

Jackson's premonition of massive blows yet undelivered was correct. The British, too, labored mightily during the first week of January. Redcoats gathered vast heaps of cane and tied the stalks into bundles, or fascines, to be used in making quick, level causeways across the dry canal. They built ladders to be leaned against the dirt ramparts before the American line. Cochrane's sailors delivered not only endless loads of stores, rations and ammunition from the fleet but ship's boats as well. Pakenham, mulling the weaknesses revealed by his two earlier efforts, had evolved a plan that was to place his weight of well-tested infantry within bayonet length of the Dirty Shirts and open the way to New Orleans.

It was a complicated plan and one that demanded precise coordination — particularly since it was to be utilized at night to deny Jackson's riflemen visible targets. Colonel William Thornton was to take 1,400 men across the Mississippi in the new fleet of ship's boats, capture the artillery on the far shore, and prepare to fire the batteries at the American defenders. Two columns of troops were to advance across the field in the predawn darkness: 1,200 men under Keane along the river, and 2,100 men under Major General Samuel Gibbs — headed by advance troops from the 44th Regiment with the fascines and ladders — along the edge of the woods with orders to breach the rampart. Just before reaching the American lines, Keane's force

would split. Its left arm under Lieutenant Colonel Robert Rennie was to attack a redoubt by the river while its other arm was prepared to support either Rennie or Gibbs. The 7th and 43rd Regiments, troops that Pakenham had claimed "would storm anything," were to be held in reserve in mid-field and thrown into the battle according to the dictates of circumstance after it had begun.

Disaster yawned from the moment — shortly after midnight on January 8 — that Pakenham's army began attempting to fit itself to this ornate design. Thornton was four hours late launching his boats on the Mississippi and when he finally pushed into the river, the craft were seized by currents that swept them far below the point from which they had hoped to assault the Americans' guns. Keane's and Gibbs's columns formed but the 44th Regiment did not at once materialize with the ladders and fascines; these vital implements had been placed 300 yards from where the 44th Regiment expected them to be, and it took precious time to locate them.

Night began fading into dawn, diluting the opportunity for surprise with every passing minute. Pakenham, now a creature of ponderous events, could not force himself to postpone the enterprise for which so many had labored for so long. He ordered up a rocket to set his troops in motion.

Jackson's conglomerate army was awake and waiting. The 7th Infantry and New Orleans militia companies were nearest the river, Regulars of the 44th Infantry, Carroll's Tennesseans and General John Adair's Kentuckians in the middle of the line, and Coffee's hard-bitten sharpshooters behind the ramparts within the trees and swamp. The breastwork was jammed: a line of musketeers and riflemen stood ready on a firing step with two or three lines of men waiting to take their place after they had discharged their weapons. It was cold — freezing — and a ground fog obscured the dim prospect beyond the sunken redoubt. Pakenham's rocket was visible, however, to all as it rose, fizzing, and burst into silvery fragments. "That," said Jackson, standing on the parapet with his telescope, "is their signal for advance, I believe." All was silent. The day brightened.

A little breeze moved the mist: the stubble field was white with frost and on it, 650 yards away, moved a

British Admiral Sir Alexander Cochrane sailed confidently against New Orleans late in 1814 with a fleet of 50 ships carrying 10,000 men. But they were repelled in January 1815 by Jackson's "dirty shirts."

This miniature of the youthful Sir Edward Pakenham was left unfinished when he sailed from England in 1814 to take command of the British forces at New Orleans.

great body of British soldiers, crossbelts bone white against their scarlet tunics, bayonets gleaming in rows. They were tramping directly toward the Tennesseans. Thirteen cannons were emplaced along the American line — manned by Laffite's superb artillerists and seamen from the *Carolina* as well as by gunners from the Regular Army. They began firing at the advancing infantry, the guns emitting drifting clouds of smoke that obscured the view, while Pakenham's batteries began firing in return. Adair protested that the cannon smoke was impairing the aim of the sharpshooters. The guns fell silent in the middle of the line. The redcoats were 300 yards away, filling up gaps made by the cannon balls, and coming on the dead run.

"Aim above the crossbelts," said Jackson.

The riflemen from Tennessee and Kentucky aimed, fired a crashing volley at the command, and then stepped down.

The second rank leaped to the firing step while the first pushed to the back of the line and began, feverishly, to reload.

"Fire!"

Crash.

A third line was up and aiming.

"Fire!"

Crash.

The effects were stunning. Red-jacketed men began tumbling by the hundreds. Those coming up behind them tripped over their bodies or jumped awkwardly as they ran and began tumbling in new hundreds after doing so. Some of them halted and fired back. The lines lost coherence as the troops panicked and broke rank. "Never before," said a lieutenant who survived, "had British veterans quailed. But it would be silly to deny that they did so now. I had seen battlefields in Spain and in the East but nowhere such a scene."

Gibbs rode up, shouting, but the foremost soldiers were running to the rear, elbowing past those who still advanced. Pakenham arrived at a gallop just as Gibbs took a mortal wound. Pakenham tried to rally the column but a rifle ball shattered his knee and another broke his right arm; his horse went down. He mounted an aide's pony but a third bullet crashed into his spine. By now the whole column was in flight. All halted, however, once out of range of the rifles. They were joined by men from Keane's column, which had been turned to their rescue after a futile few of its men had reached the American line on the right.

The mass of redcoats took form again out on the field. The soldiers threw off their knapsacks, shuffled into ranks and moved stolidly forward once more, with the Highlanders massed in front. They, too, were slaughtered as Jackson's riflemen resumed volleying "with a briskness," as the general said, "of which there have been but few instances, perhaps, in any country." Captain Thomas Wilkinson of the 21st North Britain Fusiliers kept advancing as the disintegrating ranks began to falter. A hundred redcoats followed him as their comrades gave up. A score of them reached the canal. The captain climbed the parapet and fell, mortally wounded, into the American line. Keane was down with a ball through his neck, Pakenham and Gibbs both down and dying. It was only 8:30 a.m.

Jackson did not pursue. The British, with 2,000 dead or dying, were left to find the bivouacs they had vacated the night before. Jackson had seven dead, six wounded. It was a slaughter rare in the history of war.

There was one more flurry of action. Thornton attacked the batteries across the river in the forenoon — to Jackson's intense anxiety — but recrossed the river that night after being recalled by the new commander, Major General John Lambert.

Ten days passed before the English army moved back to the bayou in the night, leaving its campfires burning, and was transported to the fleet. It took with it a somber memento of its ordeal: Pakenham's body, preserved in a barrel of rum. Eighteen more days elapsed before Cochrane raised sail and finally vanished over the horizon. But the last serious foreign threat to American soil had been stifled the moment the Dirty Shirts' rifles had ceased firing from the rampart.

"I never," said Jackson, "had so grand and awful an idea of the resurrection as on that day. After the smoke of the battle had cleared, I saw more than five hundred Britons emerging from the heaps of their dead comrades, all over the plain, rising up, and coming forward and surrendering as prisoners of war."

For the West, it was a judgment day of a different sort as well: the Mississippi was an American stream forever after, and the way was now open to those who would follow Lewis and Clark into the vast plains and awesome mountains beyond the river's western bank.

Soggy battleground of American interests

When a large British war fleet appeared off the coast of Louisiana on the evening of December 10, 1814, a rich prize awaited them. During that year alone more than 8,000 bales of cotton, 15,000 tons of sugar, and large quantities of grain, flour and whiskey had passed through the port of New Orleans.

The presence of the British armada disturbed the New Orleaneans but did not panic them. They understood, after all, that governments came and went: three different flags—Spanish, French and American—had flown over the city in the past 15 years. And they believed that their city, as the primary port for all commerce in the Mississippi valley, was destined to flourish, whoever governed it.

William Claiborne, the American governor of Louisiana, had a different reaction. The loss of New Orleans would put control of frontier exports into the hands of a foreign power once again. Claiborne sent urgent appeals for troops and arms throughout the West. In Nashville, Brigadier General William Carroll read a proclamation requesting volunteers for an "immediate march to the lower country to protect that section of our Union which is so important to the people westward of the Allegheny mountains."

Frontiersmen answered the call; brigades from Tennessee and Kentucky started down the Mississippi to join Andy Jackson and "fight the bloody British" for control of New Orleans in a soggy neck of the river *(right)*.

The watery approaches to New Orleans are delineated in this contemporary map of "the seat of the war in Louisiana." Jackson's line of defense is colored blue, the headquarters of the opposing armies red.

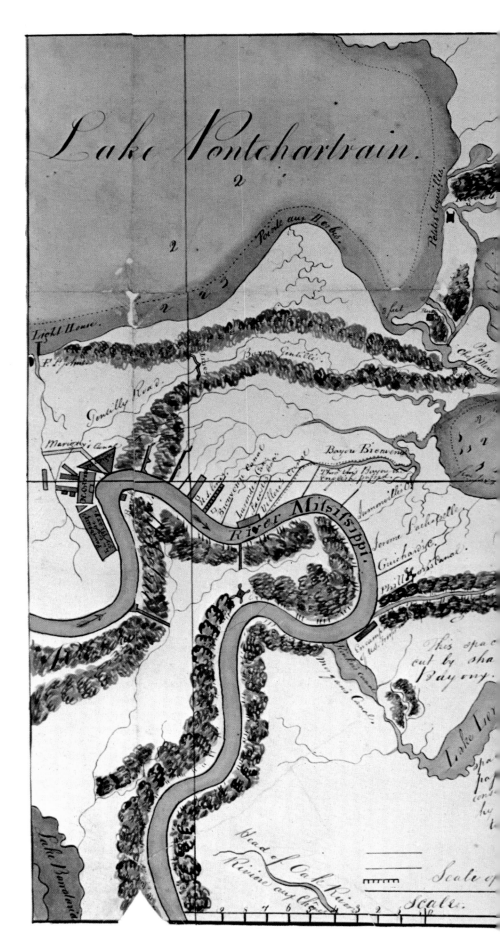

Paul River.

Many Riv.

Lake.

Pass aux Bois.

Point Three Bayous.

Bayou Canal.

Morass and ponds.

Bay of St. Louis

Pass Christian

Maryann Islands

Oyster Bar

Pass Maryann

Cat Island

South pass.

St. Joseph Islands.
Here the U.S. gun boats
were taken 14. Aug.st 1814.

Malheureux Islands.

Lake Borgne.

Grande Isle.

Longue Isle.

Bayou Point au Chicot.

This space has never been accurately surveyed, but is considered a Morass, checkered by Ponds and small Bayous the surface of the soil not more than six inches above the common tide. Bayou Point au Chicot has been penetrated by Hunters, who report, that it branches out into a variety channels, and is finally lost in the swamps. This latter Bayou is the only water course, which has wood upon its banks, near Chandeleur Bay.

Part of Chandeleur Bay.

Map
of the seat of the
War in Louisiana
in the years 1814 & 1815.

Swarms of oar-powered barges manned by 1,200 British soldiers exchange fire with five becalmed American gunboats on Lake Borgne in the opening skirmish of the Battle of New Orleans. Closing in, the British clambered aboard and captured the gunboats, then used them to ferry the army across the lake, which was too shallow for their fleet.

229

Formations of redcoats march resolutely across the cane fields of the Macarty plantation on January 8, 1815, in the main British assault on New Orleans. American rifle and cannon fire from behind the mile-long earthwork took a terrible toll, and within two hours 2,000 redcoats lay dead.

230

Comforted by his aides, Major General Sir Edward Pakenham *(center)*, the British commander at New Orleans, dies
of bullet wounds sustained in the battle. At left another
British general, Samuel Gibbs, is lifted mortally wounded
from his horse. Pakenham's successor appealed for a cease-
fire and the British withdrew, ending the last serious challenge to American control of the Louisiana Territory.

ACKNOWLEDGMENTS

The index for this book was prepared by Gale Partoyan. The editors wish to give special thanks to Robert A. Rutland, Editor of the James Madison Papers, Univ. of Virginia, who read and commented on portions of the text. The editors also thank the following: Beth Allen, Asst. Ref. Librarian, Marylin Bell, Manuscript Division, Fran Eads, Asst. Ref. Librarian, Tennessee State Library and Archives, Nashville; Jairus B. Barnes, Dir., History Museum, Virginia Hawley, General Ref. Supervisor, Kermit J. Pike, Dir., History Library, Western Reserve Historical Society, Cleveland; C. Frederick Beck, Springfield, Ohio; Silvio A. Bedini, Deputy Dir., Warren J. Danzenbaker, Research Asst., Dr. V. Clain-Stefanelli, Curator, Div. of Numismatics, Craddock Goins, Curator, Div. of Military History, Anne Golovin, Curator, Div. of Pre-Industrial Cultural History, Michael Harris, Museum Specialist, Div. of Medical Sciences, Dr. G. Terry Sharrer, Asst. Curator, Div. of Manufacturing, National Museum of History and Technology, Smithsonian Institution, Washington, D.C.; Natalie Belting, Dept. of History, Univ. of Illinois, Urbana; James R. Bentley, Manuscript Curator, Martin F. Schmidt, Librarian, Martha Vogelsang, Dir. of Museum Planning, The Filson Club, Louisville; William Bond and Deborah Kelly, Manuscript Collection, Houghton Library, Harvard Univ.; Margaret Brown, Fort De Chartres, Prairie du Rocher, Ill.; Col. George M. Chinn, Deputy Dir., Kentucky Historical Society, Frankfort; John J. Cooney, Dir., Ladies' Hermitage Association, Hermitage, Tenn.; Jerry Cotten, The North Carolina Collection, Wilson Library, Univ. of North Carolina, Chapel Hill; Alice C. Dalligan, Chief, Joseph Oldenburg, Burton Historical Collection, Detroit Public Library; Dr. Richard Doty, Asst. Curator of Modern Coins, American Numismatic Society, N.Y.C.; Arthur M. Fitts III, Acting Curator, American Numismatic Assoc., Colorado Springs; Paula Richardson Fleming, National Anthropological Archives, Smithsonian Institution, Washington, D.C.; John J. Ford Jr., Rockville Centre, N.Y.; Charles E. Gillette, Senior Scientist of Archeology, Kenneth M. Hay, Senior Museum Exhibit Specialist, New York State Museum and Science Service, Albany; Madison Grant, Glen Mills, Pa.; Neal O. Hammon, Louisville, Ky.; Ellen Hassig, West Virginia Archives and History Museum, Charleston; Howard Hazelcorn and Joseph H. Rose, Scott Publishing Co., N.Y.C.; Mrs. West T. Hill, Manager, McDowell House, Danville, Ky.; Don Hutsler, Dr. Charles A. Isetts, Arlene Peterson, Ohio Historical Society, Columbus; Prof. Richard C. Knopf, Kent State Univ.; Diane Lazarus and Miriam V. Lovel, Indianapolis Museum of Art; Bill Marshall, Special Collections, Margaret I. King Library, Univ. of Kentucky, Lexington; Douglas W. Marshall, Head of Map and Print Division, William L. Clements Library, Univ. of Michigan, Ann Arbor; John Francis McDermott, St. Louis, Mo.; Mary Jane Meeker, Indiana State Museum, Indianapolis; Andrew Modelski and Richard Stevenson, Library of Congress, Map Division, Alexandria, Va.; James Mooney, Dir., Peter Parker, Prints, Linda Stanley, Manuscripts, The Historical Society of Pennsylvania, Philadelphia; Charles E. Morrison Jr., Cartographer, U.S. Geological Survey, Reston, Va.; Dr. Patrick J. Mullin, Special Collections Librarian, Dawes Memorial Library, Marietta College; Eric P. Newman, St. Louis, Mo.; Prof. James M. O'Donnell III, Marietta College; Harriet C. Owsley, Dr. Robert Remini, Dr. Sam Smith, Editors of The Papers of Andrew Jackson, Hermitage, Tenn.; Hershel Payne, Nashville Room, The Public Library of Nashville and Davidson County, Nashville; Dr. William Phenix, Curator of Military History, Fort Wayne Military Museum, Detroit; Margaret Roberts, Archives of American Art, Smithsonian Institution, Washington, D.C.; Charles H. Ross, Morganton, N.C.; Tom Rumer, Ref. Librarian, Indiana Historical Society Library, Indianapolis; T. W. Samuels Jr., Star Hill Distilling Co., Louisville; Ruth Selig, Public Information Specialist of the Dept. of Anthropology, National Museum of Natural History, Smithsonian Institution, Washington, D.C.; Richard E. Slavin III, Curator, New York State Historical Association, Cooperstown; Dwight Smith, Dept. of History, Miami Univ.

TEXT CREDITS

For full reference on specific page credits see bibliography.

Chapter 1: Particularly useful sources for information and quotes in this chapter: Ray Allen Billington, *Westward Expansion,* Macmillan Co., 1967; Capt. John Dillin, *The Kentucky Rifle,* George Shumway, 1967; Joseph Doddridge, *Notes on the Settlement and Indian Wars of the Western Parts of Virginia and Pennsylvania from 1763-1783,* Burt Franklin, 1972; John P. Hale, *Trans-Allegheny Pioneers 1748 and After,* Derreth Printing Co., 1971; J. Evetts Haley, *Charles Goodnight,* Univ. of Oklahoma Press, 1949; Richard J. Hooker, ed., *The Carolina Backcountry on the Eve of the Revolution: The Journal and Other Writings of Charles Woodmason,* published for the Institute of Early American History and Culture by the Univ. of North Carolina Press, 1953; Theodore Roosevelt, *The Winning of the West,* Vol. I, G. P. Putnam's Sons, 1917. Chapter 2: Particularly useful sources: John Bakeless, *Daniel Boone,* Stackpole Co., 1965; Thomas Boyd, *Simon Girty,* Minton, 1928; Lawrence Elliott, *The Long Hunter,* Reader's Digest Press, 1976; John Filson, *The Discovery, Settlement, and Present State of Kentucky,* Corinth Books, 1962; Richard Slotkin, *Regeneration Through Violence,* Wesleyan Univ. Press, 1973; 58—Simon Girty quote, Guthman, p. 129. Chapter 3: Particularly useful sources: Billington, *Westward Expansion;* William Brandon, *The American Heritage Book of Indians,* Dell, 1971; Frederick Webb Hodge, ed., *Handbook of American Indians North of Mexico,* Vols. I and II, Rowman and Littlefield, 1971; Milo Quaife, ed., *The Western Country in the 17th Century,* Lakeside Press, 1947; Theodore Roosevelt, *The Winning of the West,* Vol. I; Col. James Smith, *A Treatise on the Mode and Manner of Indian War, Their Tactics, Discipline and Encampment,* Joel R. Lyle, 1812; Virgil J. Vogel, *This Country Was Ours,* Harper & Row, 1972; Wilcomb E. Washburn, ed., *The Indian and the White Man,* Doubleday and Co., 1964; 83—Black Jack Schwartz, Dillin, pp. 21, 25. Chapter 4: Particularly useful sources: John D. Barnhart, *Henry Hamilton and George Rogers Clark in the American Revolution,* R. E. Banta, 1951; H. W. Beckwith, ed., *General George Rogers Clark's Conquest of the Illinois,* Collection of Ill. State Hist. Library, Vol. 1, 1903; Thomas Boyd, *Mad Anthony Wayne,* Charles Scribner's Sons, 1929; James A. James, *The Life of George Rogers Clark,* AMS Press, 1970; Richard C. Knopf, ed., *Anthony Wayne: A Name in Arms, The Wayne-Knox, Pickering-McHenry Correspondence,* Univ. of Pittsburgh Press, copr. 1959; Francis Paul Prucha, *The Sword of the Republic,* Macmillan Co., 1969; Milo Quaife, ed., *The Capture of*

Old Vincennes, Bobbs-Merrill Co., Inc., copr. 1927; Theodore Roosevelt, *The Winning of the West,* Vol. IV; Robert A. Rutland, ed., *The Papers of George Mason, 1752-1792,* Vol. 2, Univ. of North Carolina Press, 1970; Harry Emerson Wildes, *Anthony Wayne,* Greenwood Press, 1970; 139—William Clark journal, McGrane, pp. 420, 424. Chapter 5: Particularly useful sources: Thomas Perkins Abernethy, *The South in the New Nation,* Louisiana State Univ. Press, 1961; Billington, *Westward Expansion;* Carl S. Driver, *John Sevier,* Univ. of North Carolina Press, 1932; James Ripley Jacobs, *Tarnished Warrior,* Macmillan Co., 1938; C. Peter Magrath, *Yazoo,* Brown Univ. Press, 1966; Gary L. Roberts, "The Chief of State and the Chief," *American Heritage,* October 1975; Bernard A. Weis-

berger, *They Gathered at the River,* Little, Brown and Co., 1958; Samuel Cole Williams, *History of the Lost State of Franklin,* Press of the Pioneers, 1933; 147—Austin on pilgrims, Eaton, p. 128; 152—Finley quote, Bucke, pp. 513-514; hymns, Federal Writers' Project, *Tennessee,* p. 113. Chapter 6: Particularly useful sources: John S. Bassett, *The Life of Andrew Jackson,* Archon Books, 1967; H. L. Coles, *The War of 1812,* The Univ. of Chicago Press, 1965; Marquis James, *The Life of Andrew Jackson,* Bobbs-Merrill Co., Inc., 1938, copr. 1933 by Marquis James; Robin Reilly, *The British at the Gates,* Cassell, 1974; Robert V. Remini, *Andrew Jackson,* Harper & Row, 1969; 222—description of Jackson, Latour, Preface, pp. xvii and xviii.

PICTURE CREDITS

The sources for the illustrations in this book are shown below. Credits from left to right are separated by semicolons, from top to bottom by dashes.

Cover—From *A Fight for Life* by Otto Sommer, copied by Hugo Poisson, courtesy Frank Sellers, Alpine Galleries, Denver, Colorado. 2—Courtesy West Virginia Department of Archives and History. 6 through 9—From *Events In Indian History* by James Wimer, published by G. Hills & Co., Lancaster, 1841, courtesy Library of Congress. 10,11—From *The Great West* by Henry Howe, published by Henry Howe, Cincinnati, 1851, courtesy Library of Congress. 12,13—Charles Phillips, courtesy Lancaster County Historical Society, Lancaster, Pennsylvania. 14—Culver Pictures. 16—Map by Nick Fasciano. 18,19—Charles Phillips, courtesy Charleston Museum, Charleston, South Carolina; courtesy Colonial Williamsburg Foundation—Charles Phillips, courtesy Charleston Museum, Charleston, South Carolina—courtesy Colonial Williamsburg Foundation; Charles Phillips, courtesy Charleston Museum, Charleston, South Carolina. 22—Culver Pictures except inset, top left, courtesy Mrs. Allen R. Potts. 24—Courtesy Library of Congress. 26,27—Henry Beville, courtesy C. Frederick Beck Collection—Henry Beville, courtesy Ohio Historical Society; Henry Beville, courtesy Collection of Anne and Madison Grant, Glen Mills, Pennsylvania; Charles Phillips, courtesy National Museum of History and Technology, Smithsonian Institution. 28—From *A Journey In North America* by Victor Collot, published by Arthur Bertrand, Paris, 1826, courtesy Library of Congress. 31—Courtesy American History Division, The New York Public Library, Astor, Lenox and Tilden Foundations. 32—Courtesy Tennessee Historical Society (2). 36,37—Culver Pictures. 38 through 44—Henry Beville, courtesy The Filson Club, Inc., Louisville, Kentucky. 47—Morris Burchette, courtesy The Inn at Wise, Wise, Virginia—courtesy Library of Congress. 48,49—Courtesy Library of Congress. 51—Ellis Herwig, courtesy Miss Amelia Peabody. 53—Courtesy Guthman Collection. 54,55—Courtesy Library of Congress. 58—Mark Mong, courtesy Ohio Historical Society. 61—Courtesy The Filson Club, Inc., Louisville, Kentucky. 63—Culver Pictures. 64 through 69—Henry Beville, courtesy The Filson Club, Inc., Louisville, Kentucky. 71—Courtesy Missouri Historical Society Pictorial Library. 72,73—James Boroff, courtesy Board of Trustees, Seneca County Museum, Tiffin, Ohio. 74—Courtesy New-York Historical Society, New York City. 76—Map by Edward Frank. 78,79—Hudson's Bay Company, courtesy The Honorable John Petre, Essex, England. 80,81—The Bettmann Archive—courtesy Library of Congress

(2). 82—Courtesy Ohio Historical Society. 84—Courtesy Library of Congress. 85—Thaddeus S. Beblowski, courtesy New York State Museum (4). 89,91—Courtesy Library of Congress. 92—Courtesy Historical Society of Pennsylvania. 93—Courtesy Rare Book Division, The New York Public Library, Astor, Lenox and Tilden Foundations. 94—Courtesy Library of Congress except inset, top left, courtesy U.S. Signal Corps, Photo No. 111-SC-92541, National Archives. 95—Henry Beville, courtesy Library of Congress. 99—Courtesy The Thomas Gilcrease Institute of American History and Art, Tulsa, Oklahoma. 101—Courtesy The New-York Historical Society, New York City. 102,103—Courtesy Clements Library, University of Michigan, Ann Arbor. 104,105—Nemo Warr, courtesy Burton Historical Collection, Detroit Public Library. 106—Courtesy British Library Board (21782/5). 107—Courtesy Clements Library, University of Michigan, Ann Arbor. 108,109—Nemo Warr, courtesy Burton Historical Collection, Detroit Public Library. 110—Henry Beville, courtesy The Filson Club, Inc., Louisville, Kentucky. 112—Courtesy Edward E. Ayer Collection, The Newberry Library, Chicago. 115—Culver Pictures. 117—From *Our Western Border* by Charles McKnight, published by J. C. McCurdy & Co., Philadelphia, 1886, courtesy Library of Congress. 118,119—Culver Pictures. 121,122,123—Courtesy Houghton Library, Harvard University. 124—Robert Wallace for The Indianapolis Museum of Art, lent by Houghton Library, Harvard University—courtesy Houghton Library, Harvard University. 126—State Historical Society of Wisconsin, courtesy American Heritage. 127—Charles Phillips, courtesy Library of Congress. 129—Courtesy National Portrait Gallery, Smithsonian Institution. 130—Courtesy National Anthropological Archives, Smithsonian Institution—courtesy Clements Library, University of Michigan, Ann Arbor; courtesy Library of Congress. 132—Courtesy Guthman Collection. 134,135—Courtesy The Henry Francis du Pont Winterthur Museum. 136—Courtesy Ohio Historical Society. 138—Courtesy The New-York Historical Society, New York City. 142,143—Courtesy Chicago Historical Society. 144,145—Henry Beville, courtesy Collection of Anne and Madison Grant, Glen Mills, Pennsylvania. 146—Elroy Sanford, courtesy Western Reserve Historical Society. 148—Courtesy American Antiquarian Society. 149,150,151—Courtesy Library of Congress. 152—Courtesy Disciples of Christ Historical Society. 153—The Bettmann Archive. 154,155—Courtesy General Research and Humanities Division, The New York Public Library, Astor, Lenox and Tilden Foundations except inset, bottom right, courtesy Atwater Kent Museum of Philadelphia. 156—Courtesy University of Kentucky Libraries. 159—Courtesy West Virginia Department of Archives and History. 160—Leslie Pritikin, courtesy Tennessee Historical Society, Miscellaneous Collection, State Library and Archives, Manuscripts Section, Nashville, Tennessee. 162—Jack Coleman, courtesy McDowell House & Apothecary Shop of Danville, Kentucky (owned by Kentucky Medical Association). 163—The Bettmann Archive. 164—Charles Phillips, courtesy McDowell House & Apothecary Shop of Danville, Kentucky (owned by Kentucky Medical Association). 166—Henry Beville, courtesy The Filson Club, Inc., Louisville, Kentucky. 167—Stephen Duplantier, courtesy Collection of the Louisiana State Museum (2). 168—Courtesy Eric Newman—Edward J. Fleischmann, courtesy Museum of The American Numismatic Association—Elroy Sanford, courtesy Western Reserve Historical Society. 169—Courtesy Collection of John J. Ford, Jr.—courtesy Eric Newman. 170—Courtesy Library of Congress. 173—Courtesy University of Georgia Libraries, Special Collections (2). 175—George M. Cushing, courtesy Massachusetts Historical Society. 176,177—Courtesy Library of Congress. 178—Jack Beech, courtesy Collection of the Louisiana State Museum. 180,181—Courtesy The I. N. Phelps Stokes Collection, Prints Division, The New York Public Library, Astor, Lenox and Tilden Foundations. 182,183—Courtesy Cleveland Picture Collection of The Cleveland Public Library (2). 184,185—Courtesy Samuel Prescott Hildreth Collection, Marietta College Library. 186,187—Charles Phillips, courtesy Ohio Historical Society—courtesy Cincinnati Historical Society. 188,189—Charlie Brown, courtesy Library of Congress. 190 through 194—Courtesy Library of Congress. 196,197—Dan Quest, courtesy The Ladies' Hermitage Association—courtesy Charles H. Ross. 198,199—Courtesy Chicago Historical Society. 200—Courtesy Library of Congress, 202—Dan Quest, courtesy The Ladies' Hermitage Association. 205—Courtesy Library of Congress (2). 206—Charles Phillips, courtesy Library of Congress. 207—Courtesy Tennessee Historical Society. 208—Charles Phillips, courtesy Library of Congress. 210—Courtesy Library of Congress. 212,213—Walter Krutz, courtesy Chicago Historical Society. 214—Courtesy Collection of the Louisiana State Museum. 215—Courtesy Lilly Library, University of Indiana, Bloomington. 217—Derek Bayes, courtesy Royal Fusiliers Regimental Museum, London. 218,219—Courtesy Library of Congress. 220—Charles Phillips, courtesy Library of Congress. 223—Derek Bayes/National Maritime Museum, London, courtesy The Honorable Mrs. Grisell Hastings. 224—Courtesy National Portrait Gallery, London. 226,227—Courtesy Manuscripts and Archives Division, The New York Public Library, Astor, Lenox and Tilden Foundations. 228,229—Derek Bayes, courtesy National Maritime Museum, London. 230,231—Roy Trahan, courtesy New Orleans Museum of Art, from the Collection of Edgar William and Bernice Chrysler Garbisch. 232,233—Courtesy Library of Congress.

BIBLIOGRAPHY

Abernethy, Thomas P.: *The Burr Conspiracy.* Peter Smith, 1968.
   From Frontier to Plantation in Tennessee. Univ. of North Carolina Press, 1932.
   The South in the New Nation 1789-1819. Louisiana State Univ. Press, 1961.
Alden, John Richard, *The South in the Revolution 1763-1789.* Louisiana State Univ. Press, 1957.
Armstrong, Virginia I., *I Have Spoken.* Swallow Press, Inc., 1971.
Bakeless, John, *Daniel Boone.* Stackpole Company, 1965.
Barnhart, John D., *Henry Hamilton and George Rogers Clark in the American Revolution.* R. E. Banta, 1951.
Bartlett, Richard A., *The New Country.* Oxford Univ. Press, 1974.
Bassett, John S., *The Life of Andrew Jackson.* Archon Books, 1967.
Beckwith, H. W., ed., *General George Rogers Clark's Conquest of the Illinois.* Collection of Ill. State Hist. Library, Vol. 1, 1903.
Billington, Ray Allen, *Westward Expansion.* Macmillan Co., 1967.
Boatner, Mark M., III, *Encyclopedia of the American Revolution.* David McKay, 1966.
Boles, John B., *The Great Revival 1787-1805.* The Univ. Press of Kentucky, 1972.
Bond, Richmond P., *Queen Anne's American Kings.* Clarendon Press, 1952.
Bowman, Joseph, "Journal of the Taking of Post Vincennes," *Louisville Literary Newsletter.* November 21, 1840.
Boyd, Thomas: *Mad Anthony Wayne.* Charles Scribner's Sons, 1929.
   Simon Girty. Minton, 1928.
Brandon, William, *The American Heritage Book of Indians.* Dell, 1971.
Bucke, Emory S., ed., *History of American Methodism,* Vol. 1. Abingdon Press, 1964.
Buley, R. C., *The Old Northwest,* Vol. 1. Indiana Univ. Press, 1951.
Carson, Gerald, *The Social History of Bourbon.* Dodd, Mead & Co., 1963.
Caughey, John W., *McGillivray of the Creeks.* Univ. of Oklahoma Press, 1938.
Chroust, Anton-Hermann, *The Rise of the Legal Profession in America.* Vol. 2. Univ. of Oklahoma Press, 1965.
Clark, Thomas D.: *Frontier America.* Charles Scribner's Sons, 1969.
   The Kentucky. Farrar & Rinehart, Inc., 1942.
Coles, H. L., *The War of 1812.* The Univ. of Chicago Press, 1965.
Dick, Everett, *The Dixie Frontier.* Knopf, 1948.
Dillin, Capt. John, *The Kentucky Rifle.* George Shumway, 1967.
Doddridge, Joseph, *Notes on the Settlement and Indian Wars of the Western Parts of Virginia and Pennsylvania from 1763-1783.* Burt Franklin, 1972.
Driver, Carl S., *John Sevier.* Univ. of North Carolina Press, 1932.
Eaton, Clement, *A History of the Old South.* Macmillan Co., 1949.
Elliott, Lawrence, *The Long Hunter.* Reader's Digest Press, 1976.
Farmer, Silas, *History of Detroit and Wayne County and Early Michigan.* Silas Farmer & Co., 1890.
Federal Writers' Project, *Tennessee.* Viking Press, 1945.
Filson, John, *The Discovery, Settlement, and Present State of Kentucke.* Corinth Books, 1962.
Flexner, James T., *Doctors on Horseback.* Dover Publications, 1969.
Frick, George F., and Raymond P. Stearns, *Mark Catesby.* Univ. of

Illinois Press, 1961.

Gillette, C. H., "Wampum Beads and Belts," *The Indian Historian,* Vol. 3, No. 4. Fall 1970.

Gray, Laman A., "After Office Hours," *Obstetrics and Gynecology,* Vol. 16, No. 4. October 1960.

Guthman, W. H., *March to Massacre.* McGraw-Hill Book Co., 1975.

Hale, John P., *Trans-Allegheny Pioneers 1748 and After.* Derreth Printing Co., 1971.

Haley, J. Evetts, *Charles Goodnight.* Univ. of Oklahoma Press, 1949.

Hay, Thomas Robson, and M. R. Werner, *The Admirable Trumpeter.* Doubleday, Doran & Co., 1941.

Heckewelder, Rev. John, *History, Manners and Customs of the Indian Nations.* Arno Press, 1971.

Henderson, Archibald, *The Conquest of the Old Southwest.* The Century Co., 1920.

Henshaw, Lesley, ed., "Burr-Blennerhassett Documents," *Quarterly Publication of the Historical and Philosophical Society of Ohio,* Vol. 9, No. 1. January 1914.

Hinchman, T. H., *Banks and Banking in Michigan.* Wm. Graham, 1887.

Hodge, Frederick Webb, ed., *Handbook of American Indians North of Mexico,* Vols. 1 and 2. Rowman and Littlefield, 1971.

Holland, James W., *Andrew Jackson and the Creek War.* Univ. of Alabama Press, 1968.

Hooker, Richard J., ed., *The Carolina Backcountry on the Eve of the Revolution.* Univ. of North Carolina Press, 1953.

Horsman, Reginald, *The Frontier in the Formative Years 1783-1850.* Holt, Rinehart and Winston, 1970.

Howe, Henry, *Historical Collections of Ohio.* Derby, Bradley & Co., 1847.

Jacobs, James Ripley, *Tarnished Warrior.* Macmillan Co., 1938.

James, James A., *The Life of George Rogers Clark.* AMS Press, 1970.

James, Marquis, *The Life of Andrew Jackson.* Bobbs-Merrill Co., Inc., 1938.

Josephy, Alvin M., Jr., *The Patriot Chiefs.* Penguin, 1976.

Knopf, Richard C., ed., *Anthony Wayne.* Univ. of Pittsburgh Press, 1959.

Latour, A. Lacarrière, *Historical Memoir of the War in West Florida and Louisiana in 1814-15.* John Conrad and Co., 1816.

Lessem, Harold I., and George C. Mackenzie, *Fort McHenry.* Natl. Park Service Hist. Handbook No. 5, 1954.

Lord, Walter, *The Dawn's Early Light.* W. W. Norton & Co., Inc., 1972.

McGrane, R. C., ed., "William Clark's Journal of General Wayne's Campaign," *Mississippi Valley Historical Review,* Vol. I, No. 3. 1914-1915.

Magrath, C. Peter, *Yazoo.* Brown Univ. Press, 1966.

Morgan, Henry L., *League of the Iroquois.* The Citadel Press, 1975.

Morison, Samuel E., and Henry S. Commager, *The Growth of the American Republic.* Oxford Univ. Press, 1962.

Newman, Eric P., *The Early Paper Money of America.* Western Publishing Co., Inc., 1976.

Norelli, Martina R., *American Wildlife Painting.* Watson-Guptill Publications, Inc., 1975.

Parton, James, *Life of Andrew Jackson,* Vols. 1 and 2. Ticknor and Fields, 1866.

Paxson, Frederic L., *History of the American Frontier: 1763-1893.* Houghton Mifflin Co., 1924.

Peckham, Howard H., *Pontiac and the Indian Uprising.* Princeton Univ. Press, 1947.

Philbrick, Francis S., *The Rise of the West 1754-1830.* Harper & Row, 1965.

Priddy, O. W., "Wayne's Strategic Advance From Fort Greenville to Grand Glaize," *Ohio Archeological and Historical Quarterly,* Vol. 39. January 1930.

Prucha, Francis Paul: *American Indian Policy in the Formative Years.* Harvard Univ. Press, 1962.
  The Sword of the Republic. Macmillan Co., 1969.

Quaife, Milo, ed.: *The Capture of Old Vincennes.* Bobbs-Merrill Co., Inc., 1927.
  The Western Country in the 17th Century. Lakeside Press, 1947.

Reilly, Robin, *The British at the Gates.* Cassell, 1974.

Remini, Robert V., *Andrew Jackson.* Harper & Row, 1969.

Richmond, Robert W., and Robert W. Mardock, eds., *A Nation Moving West.* Univ. of Nebraska Press, 1966.

Ridge, Martin, and Ray Allen Billington, *America's Frontier Story.* Holt, Rinehart and Winston, 1969.

Riegel, Robert E., *America Moves West.* Henry Holt and Co., 1956.

Roberts, Gary L., "The Chief of State and the Chief," *American Heritage,* Vol. 26, No. 6. October 1975.

Roosevelt, Theodore, *The Winning of the West,* Vols. 1 to 4. G. P. Putnam's Sons, 1917.

Rosenthal, S. Fred, "An Ohio Numismatic Rarity," *Western Reserve Historical Society News,* Vol. 16, No. 9. September 1962.

Rutland, Robert A., ed., *The Papers of George Mason, 1752-1792,* Vol. 2. Univ. of North Carolina Press, 1970.

Safford, William H., *The Blennerhassett Papers.* Moore, Wilstach & Baldwin, 1864.

Slotkin, Richard, *Regeneration Through Violence.* Wesleyan Univ. Press, 1973.

Smith, Col. James, *A Treatise On the Mode and Manner of Indian War, Their Tactics, Discipline and Encampments.* Joel R. Lyle, 1812.

Sosin, Jack M., *The Revolutionary Frontier, 1763-1783.* Holt, Rinehart and Winston, 1967.

Swanton, John R., *The Indian Tribes of North America.* U.S. Government Printing Office, 1952.

Taxay, Don, *The Comprehensive Catalogue and Encyclopedia of U.S. Coins.* Scott Publishing Co., 1975.

Tebbel, John, and Keith Jennison, *The American Indian Wars.* Harper and Bros., 1960.

Vogel, Virgil J., *This Country Was Ours.* Harper & Row, 1972.

Wade, R. C., *The Urban Frontier.* Univ. of Chicago Press, 1959.

Washburn, Wilcomb E., ed.: *The Indian and the White Man.* Doubleday and Co., 1964.
  The Indian in America. Harper & Row, 1975.

Weisberger, Bernard A., *They Gathered at the River.* Little, Brown and Co., 1958.

Wellesley, Arthur, Duke of Wellington, K. G., *Supplementary Despatches, Correspondence and Memoranda,* Vol. IX. John Murray, 1862.

Wildes, Harry Emerson, *Anthony Wayne.* Greenwood Press, 1970.

Williams, Samuel Cole, *History of the Lost State of Franklin.* Press of the Pioneers, 1933.

Printed in U.S.A.